To John,

As you go through, you will see how lucky I was!

With best wishes

Yours.

# THE LUCK OF THE DEVIL

## AIR VICE-MARSHAL
## A.G. DUDGEON CBE DFC
### AN AUTOBIOGRAPHY 1934-41

*[signature]* Dudgeon

*14th May, 1987*

**Airlife**
England

ISBN 0 906393 54 X

First published 1985
by Airlife Publishing Ltd.

Printed in England by Livesey Ltd., Shrewsbury.

# Airlife Publishing Ltd.

7 St. John's Hill, Shrewsbury, England.

# Contents

# Acknowledgements

I would like to express my sincere thanks to four people who have encouraged and helped me to achieve this book. First, to Mr Richard Riding, Editor of *The Aeroplane Monthly* who, having published some articles and photographs of mine, enthusiastically persuaded me to put my nose to the grindstone and keep on writing. Next, to Mr Edward Bishop who gave me invaluable help with political and background information concerning the 1941 Rebellion in Iraq. Third, to Mr Mike Scott-MacKirdy who was at Cranwell with me and who lent me some of his photographs. Fourth, to his daughter Jane Scott-MacKirdy who typed most of it.

# Prologue

To anyone who cares to listen, and for that matter to many who do not, I will claim to be one of the luckiest people in the world. Obviously, not everything has gone well for me, but by far the greater proportion has.

I had a vastly interesting, varied and exciting career but, far more important, it was above all fun. It began with flying well-built but somewhat elementary aeroplanes — with no radio, no oxygen, usually no specialist aircrew and no outside assistance to help you in the air. It ended with flying highly sophisticated single- and multi-engined jets under close radio and radar control from the ground. Above that, I was lucky because from my pilot colleagues who started and flew as I did, including war flying, six out of seven were killed along the way. I was one of the survivors.

My work, though I hardly realised it then, began as being a small cog in the machine which guarded our far-flung Empire of the time. My luck in serving four monarchs and my country required me to fly around and over most of the countries between Singapore and San Francisco — taking the long way round to do it.

I did not reach the very highest pinnacles of rank in my service of 34 years. This was totally just because I am not the diplomat that a really top brass-hat must be. In the RAF one is never permitted to see one's own personnel reports — but I am reliably assured that mine are bespattered, like spots on a measly schoolboy, with the words 'Lacks Tact'. Moreover, I committed the unpardonable crime, frequently, of fighting tooth and nail against the opinions of my superiors and then, occasionally, turning out to be the one who was right. It can only have been luck which allowed me to reach at least two promotions higher than I ever aspired to in my wildest dreams — and about three to five promotions higher than that forecast by the most sanguine of friends in my early days.

I paid suit to and was accepted by a most lovely lady. When she was my fiancée, before she finally committed herself, one of her friends said to her 'Good God! If you marry Tony Dudgeon your life may be many things — but it certainly won't be dull!' I think that on her side she would probably endorse her friend's remark. Assuredly it has applied most accurately to mine. And, after more than 40 years, despite some crass stupidities on my part, she still bears with me.

How lucky can you be?

# Chapter 1
# Introduction

My father was a doctor. I wanted to be a doctor too, leading to becoming a top surgeon or gynaecologist. A medical degree would have taken three years after leaving school and cost my father another £1,000 — a very substantial sum in those days. As he was nearing 60 and had nearly bankrupted himself sending my brother and me to Eton, I decided to get off his back, financially, as soon as possible. Becoming a crack surgeon or obstetrician went out of the window.

At Eton no one got any careers advice. It was somehow assumed you would take over the family estates, the family business or go to the colonies. My career planning was therefore quite straightforward. There were four points. First, my brother had joined the Air Force, and had no complaints. Second, a friend when I was 12 had given me a couple of flips in a Moth biplane, which I had enjoyed. Third, you could be accepted for training in the Air Force at 17½. Fourth, if you got a scholarship to Cranwell the training was free. On this in-depth analysis my career decision was made. I could, and therefore would, begin my training to be a Royal Air Force pilot before my eighteenth birthday — for nothing. My big brother was scornful; the kid wasn't up to it.

The first hurdle was to get a good 'School Certificate', forerunner of O- and A-levels. The masters were scornful; the boy wasn't up to it. I had always been in trouble over work at school. I was idle. Luckily, however, I had an examination brain; facts which apparently had no right to be there, after an apparently lazy and happy-go-lucky term, would pop out of my head to go down on the exam paper.

For example, one master who had me as a *bête noire* was Mr H. K. Marsden, known to one and all as 'Bloody Bill' or, in public, 'Sweet William'. He was tall with iron grey hair, beetling eyebrows, piercing eyes and a big, grey, bushy moustache. Bloody

Bill was a wonderful enthusiast, a fine rowing-coach and a superb mathematician. He went everywhere on a bicycle with his heels on the pedals and his toes turned out. One day, coaching his House rowing-four on the Thames, riding along the towpath and shouting at them through a megaphone, he got so carried away that he, the bicycle and the megaphone rode headlong into the river. In World War I his job, as he was unfit for the trenches, was to plan and control the trains coming into and going out of Paddington Station. Wartime chaos had defeated all the experienced railwaymen. Computers had not been invented. Bloody Bill, with his toes turned out, rode his bicycle sedately up and down the platforms, giving precise instructions to the staff as he rode by, doing all the timings and calculations in his head.

Idle schoolboys like me got short shrift. I was up to Sweet William for Advanced Maths; good maths results were essential for the RAF, even then. I had no academic successes at school, save just this one time. After a simply horrible experience for both of us he wrote on my end-of-term report these unkind words: 'This boy may, if he is lucky, scrape up a 'Pass' in Elementary Maths.' Bloody Bill did not realise his own strengths. He was not only a remarkable man but also a great teacher. He got maths into my head without realising it. I did better than 'Pass'. I achieved 'Credits', not only in the Elementary Maths but also in his beloved Advanced Maths.

Having got my 'good' School Certificate I was allowed to sit the entrance exam for Cranwell. There were 384 candidates for 32 places. Of these, the first six got a 'prize' which paid the tuition fees normally exacted from the parents. Just by a whisker I got the sixth place and therefore my first objective was gained; I was paddling my own financial canoe at 17. Unknown to me my luck was continuing to work overtime. A year into the Cranwell course, just when I might have been relying on my father to ante up the second year's fees (and long before I could ever have seen a doctor's degree) he died. But, my fortunate Prize Cadetship allowed me to complete the course.

My Royal Air Force indoctrination began very early. New boys were required to report to Cranwell College in Lincolnshire at about 5 pm on an early January evening. We arrived at the imposing building, by bus, from Sleaford railway station. We were shown to our rooms.

I met Herriot; he, rather, met me and introduced himself. He was about 5 ft tall, was a World War I veteran and had thinning red hair over a rather pinched face, for he had been gassed. He was to be my batman for the next two years. He would brush and press my uniforms, clean my rifle and make the brasses gleam on my equipment. He would put a magical shine on those parade boots. He would bring me an early morning cup of tea when he woke me. That first evening we were encouraged to wander around the place, discovering, as far as possible, where things were. As nothing official was scheduled until parade next morning, at 8 o'clock, I went to bed early. The old hands did not have to be back before midnight. The bed was hard and it was a long time before I slept.

Next morning it was still pitch dark when Herriot turned on the light and put a great 'Service Issue' cup of tea beside me. 'Good morning, Sir. Seven o'clock. Your early morning cup of tea. Unfortunate news I am afraid. Mr. Southby, a third-term cadet, coming back last night in his Aero-Morgan three-wheeler misjudged the corner at Brancaster. He was killed in the crash. A very nice young gentleman. Most regrettable. Breakfast is at 7.30. Thank you, Sir.' He went out to awaken his other 'young gentlemen'.

I, green, young and soft from school was very upset. Death, soon to become my familiar, still shocked me. I dressed and went down to breakfast. I did not realise that my new environment was tough and unforgiving. My first lesson came with the cornflakes. Two senior cadets who had arrived by midnight were talking beside me. 'Did you hear about that fool Southby? No? Stupid clot was coming round the Brancaster corner and didn't make it. Went into the ditch and wrote off his Morgan. And himself too. Must have been spectacular. He should have known better.' They both laughed light-heartedly. I stood there with my eyes popping out of their sockets; were all so callous and unfeeling? What on earth had I come into? A two-year *pot-pourri,* from elements of Hell to pure delight had just begun.

The Hell was the square bashing, marching hither and yon, endless inspections, come here and go there. The Oxometer (a mythical device for measuring the amount of 'bull') was set very high at Cranwell. That very morning I was on parade for the first time. RAF uniforms were made, by Messrs Gieves of Bond Street, after you reported to Cranwell. Thus it was that in January young Dudgeon could be seen marching awkwardly up and down the parade ground in clumping great shiny, black, issue boots, shouldering an 11½ lb Lee-Enfield rifle, wearing his restrained brown civilian suit. On the top of this astonishing get-up was poised, according to the rules laid down, a black bowler-hat. The sole officer cadet who did not sport a bowler was a South African, Tommy Rivett-Carnac, straight off the boat, who wore a voortrekker's stetson.

Our mentor in the art of making unnatural movements in unison was Flight Sergeant Digby. He had a masterly way of handling young cadets and in doing so he had his own particular language which took a little time and effort to learn. 'Aaa . . . tee — waitforit — SHAH!!' was, of course, 'Attention'. A crisp 'Hup — hi — hup — hi' translated as 'left, right' and so on. One picked it up immediately because if you didn't it was a brisk run, at the double, with rifle, boots, bowler and all to the end of the parade ground and back, smartly of course. He was not, one might say, a very erudite scholar but he had the gift of making himself crystal clear. At one point he deigned to give us a short 'stand easy' after a particularly energetic bout of turns, movements, marches and runs. He turned from us to survey the vista and be sure that nothing unsmart was to be seen. A voice from the rank behind me said wearily, 'No death is more sharp than this!' Digby spun round and barked 'WHOSAIDTHAT?' No one moved a muscle but the same voice muttered, quietly, 'Shakespeare.'

Digby's eyes drilled into us like gimlets but the speaker, sensibly, did not identify himself. The ensuing comment was lucid, although probably not attributable to some bygone university professor of the English Language. 'Now, Gentlemen,' he said in a voice to be heard comfortably at 50 yards, 'if I want any of you clever sparrows to chirp, I'll rattle the chain under your perch! Till then, PIPE DOWN!'

The middle part of the *pot-pourri* was the interesting chore of learning the basics of twelve skilled trades or professions. From carpentry (some aeroplanes were still made of wood) and blacksmithing to meteorology and law.

The magical and exciting part was the flying. It was magic then and, for me, it never changed. It gave a sense of individuality and power, maybe needed to sate my burgeoning and chauvinistic manhood. The machine could, at my sole behest, go up, down, right, left — and roll round and round. It would travel in any direction, quite unconstrained by roads, buildings, hedges or waterways. A wonderful mixture of dodgem-cars, roller-coasters, motors, bicycles, boats, skis, skates, horses, swings and roundabouts all rolled into one. A veritable magic carpet.

I suppose that the remarkable lack of outside aids to the early pilot was, if anything, the factor that built up an independence of spirit with moral and physical courage, initiative and oomph that enabled us to win World War II — well, if not the whole war, great chunks of it like the Battle of Britain. Once you were airborne in an early aircraft you were on your own. No one could guide you, help you or advise you — or tell you not to do something dangerous. Perhaps this explains why so many of us killed ourselves through 'pilot error'. The excitement of flying, backed by a devil-may-care personality, is a great mixture for war — if you survive to reach it. Slowly, all too slowly, I was to learn that my machine was a simply superb servant — and a staggeringly dangerous toy.

Those stick-and-string contraptions were simple to fly, but needed a delicacy of touch and judgement largely absent in the modern jets. Roughly, a joystick in your right hand for up and down and round and round, with a throttle in your left hand for fast and slow. Your feet on the rudder-bar for left and right, which I found, to my horror during my first trip, works the opposite way to handlebars or a steering wheel. That used up both hands and both feet. (I thought. Using wrists, thumbs, different fingers, ankle movements and even head movements to operate flying-controls on modern aircraft was still to come.) On the dashboard were a few, elementary, instruments. The task of the long-suffering instructor was teaching you to co-ordinate hands, eyes, brain and feet so that you could get where you wanted, when you wanted, in the right attitude. That spread over two years. Gunnery, photography, bombing and those kinds of skills were taught in the front-line squadrons, later.

On the second day after I arrived I was commanded to report to 'the flights'. I had imagined weeks if not months of tedious 'bull' and ground instruction before I was even allowed to smell an aircraft. They had a special smell — burnt castor oil and dope — which will still bring nostalgic sparkles to the eyes of an old pilot. There, I was issued with flying gear. A brown soft helmet lined with yellow chamois leather; fur-lined flying suit which was thick, heavy and did not bend easily; leather gloves with flannel inners and gauntlet cuffs; goggles which I would find did not fit my face snugly and the wind coming in round the edges made my eyes water; bulging earpieces to fit into the helmet and which had tubes joined together at the bottom, to plug into the instructor's speaking tube. The parachute, to be my seat for many years to come, was added to the rest for good measure. Accoutred, and carrying the parachute, I could barely walk across the broad hangar to the tarmac on which were parked the silver aeroplanes standing waiting. But, who cared? The almighty Wallace had said we were going to be airborne.

Flight Lieutenant Wallace was my instructor. Sir. I never got to his Christian name. Sir. To me he was a god-like being who, by virtue of being an instructor, knew everything about aviation and in his hands any aircraft must always do precisely what he desired. I saw him as a middle-aged man (middle-aged? Say, twenty-five) with bushy black eyebrows, a face disfigured by rugby scrums and with a surprisingly soft voice. He was a god, rather than a kindly and extremely competent young man who, like others, was human.

I remember that first trip well. I dare say Wallace's memory is equally vivid. The two open cockpits were one behind the other. I was levered up to the back one, wedged and strapped in. Ahead, through my little windscreen on the turtle back of the fuselage I could see the smooth-fitting, black helmet of my mentor. To earn a smooth, black leather helmet suddenly became infinitely desirable. An airman fitted the starting handle at the side, and wound it energetically; the engine fired, caught and the prop went into a spinning blur. We taxied out across the bumpy grass and took off.

My first shock was to discover that I couldn't hear a word being said. This was not surprising because my issue helmet fitted my head about as well as a wellington boot fits a turnip. The exhilarating roar of the engine and the rush of the wind stopped any useful transfer of information from the speaking tube. Wallace must have gone nearly insane when I did not take the controls when he besought me to do so, and then clung on with a grip of iron when he wanted to save our joint lives. I later heard that some instructors carried a large spanner in the knee-pocket of their flying suits. This was so that, having loosened their straps, they could turn and strike a pupil insensible if he 'froze' on to the controls.

I was having the time of my life. I was in the air, in a mighty mechanical bird. In front was a superman, all knowing, all capable. He, poor fellow, must have thought that seated behind him was a deaf congenital idiot, bent on murder and suicide in one sudden go. Finally he wrested the controls from my reluctant grasp and took us home to land. I suppose I should have been crestfallen and apologetic. Far from it. I was beside myself with excitement. It had been pure delight all the way, even when I was lumbering through the hangar with the parachute banging against my thighs and the metal buckles chinking against my calf muscles.

Wallace was very restrained. He would have made me a better pilot sooner if he had kicked my backside till my throat was sore, and then continued till the following breakfast time. It took me many years and many close shaves to accept that flying was a serious business, and not a game.

# Chapter 2
# Poor Wallace

Most old, and therefore experienced, pilots will agree over a drink that sometimes it seems an evil-intentioned devil, demon or bad spirit lies in wait for them — and nowadays for other aircrew or air traffic controllers as well. If in the aviation business you relax, or make a slip, you will be savaged. I visualise a creature in my mind and I call him my Black Dog. I was to make his acquaintance early on. My dog wears a bland and beatific smile like a young bull-terrier, smugly offering to lick my hand and wag his tail approvingly when all goes well. However, when I took liberties, or was careless, or idle-minded, or over-confident, then the black beast leaped out. If I was fortunate he only growled fiercely and gave me a nasty fright. In worse circumstances he could cause me or my aircraft severe injury. In extreme cases Black Dog can kill you stone dead.

My mentor, Flight Lieutenant Wallace must have had nerves of steel. After only 4 hours 20 minutes dual we came in to land just before lunch when the airfield was fairly deserted. Instead of taxi-ing into the hangars, we stopped. 'OK,' he said, 'take her round for a circuit and landing on your own.' He climbed out of the cockpit and I watched him standing in the footholds on the side of the fuselage, fastening straps and making sure the dual controls remained unrestricted in the front cockpit. He climbed down, gave me a 'thumbs up' and walked clear. There was no black helmet between me and the propeller and it looked a hundred miles away. The adrenalin was streaming through my veins and my stomach was taut with excitement.

I took off and climbed gently to 1000 ft. The exhilaration was intense. The first of my term to go solo! It was terrific. I had become an ace aviator! My Black Puppy must have raised his eyebrows in astonishment — so soon? — and licked his chops in expectation. Surely the first of his several intrusions into my career would not be too long in coming? I came round and in to land. I was so steamed up that the landing itself was lousy. I bounced the machine all over the place. I was so cross with myself that instead of taxi-ing back to pick Wallace up, I took off again to do another, better one. Poor man. Sending a student solo for the first time takes a lot of moral courage. You are, quite literally, staking his life on your judgement. I wonder how he found the restraint not to run after me the second time screaming 'Don't!' Even more, when I eventually taxied back to him he found the self control to say, flatly, 'Why did you do two circuits when I said one?' He should have hammered me into the ground till only my scared eyes were showing.

One of the advantages of Service aircraft in those days was that most of them were slow enough to be landed nearly anywhere, with a bit of luck, when your engine failed. This could and did, occur at any time. The engine-failure drill was carefully laid down and taught exhaustively. The bits of useful advice were legion. 'Upon engine failure turn off the petrol; this will reduce the risk of fire, both in the air and upon landing. Then switch off the ignition for, if the propeller is still turning there might be a sudden burst of power which would ruin what would otherwise have been an excellent glide approach. Then pick a suitable field . . . ' At this point the advice became almost hysterical and, in those brief remaining moments of real fear, almost incapable of implementation.

Landings should always be made into wind if possible; sage advice. Therefore always keep the wind direction in mind; not so simple for a novice with so much else to think about. Watch for smoke from chimneys and bonfires; splendid — in autumn and winter. See the washing hung out to dry; Mondays are but one day in seven. Failing those, cows and sheep graze with their backsides to the wind; I never found it so. Then see the way the trees are bending; a pious hope from over 1000 ft!

Having determined the wind (?) you picked a field to give you a long landing run with clear approaches. Its surface was equally important. Recently reaped stubble was the prime choice; hard, smooth and not such as would catch the wheels and tip you on your nose. Also, if you landed in hay or crops — and even if you didn't tip up — farmers were very unco-operative with the rescue vehicles. Further, they followed up with monumental and avaricious claims for crop damage. So, try and land close to a road. Marshy ground and ploughed fields were to be eschewed but, if the latter, landing along the furrows was better than across them. You would have to report in and you might need victuals whilst you slept under your never-to-be-left-unguarded aircraft — an inn, for example, could meet this requirement. And you might need fuel later, so a garage with petrol pump. . .

From a couple of thousand feet you would have about two minutes available before you were on the ground. And the longer you took to choose, the smaller became the circle you could choose from. The instructors really made it sound so perfectly simple. In the few panic-stricken moments left to you, all you needed to find within gliding range would be a pub, with a garage, backing on to a stubble field, which gave a long landing run, into the wind, with a low hedge to land over on the near side, and beside a good road, alongside which were telephone poles to prove it had communications to the outside world. And so on . . . and on . . . and on . . . .

The flow of essential advice seemed about as stoppable and usable as a runaway horse. Practice forced-landings took up a lot of the training hours.

Naturally, it was impractical to have trainers landing next to pubs all over Lincolnshire. The College therefore leased two fields nearby which were kept in mown grass for this purpose. One was about 400 yards square known as Ermine Street and the other was near Digby airfield. I can still hear Wallace's smooth patter echoing in my ears. 'Now, here we are, cruising along at 1000 ft.' He closes the throttle. 'The engine has failed! We would now, but will not as this is a practice, close the throttle, turn off the petrol and switch off the ignition. Pick a suitable field. There! I see a field.' What he really could see — surprise surprise — was the landing ground with about half-a-dozen silver Arno Tutor biplanes approaching it, on it, or taking off. 'So now we set up our approach. Glide to the downwind side and begin our figure-of-eight pattern backwards and forwards along the downwind edge. Always turn towards the field and never away from it. Then, when we have lost sufficient height but are still quite sure of reaching the field, turn in to land. Aim for a point one-third into the field for, if you misjudge the approach, it is far better to run slowly into the far hedge than to hit the near hedge while you are still travelling fast. Now, when you are absolutely sure of getting in, sideslip off the surplus height . . . and land in the normal manner . . . Now, as the engine is still running, we can take off again for another practice.'

I suppose I must have done not much over 12 hours all-told when I was sent off for solo practice forced landings at the Digby field. A very grown-up moment. After about a couple of times, when I landed only *just* over the hedge (didn't I say somewhere I had graduated to ace aviator?) I decided to test myself further. I would grind my way up to *two* (not one) thousand feet and do my practice from there. 'Hah!' said my Black Dog, 'Lesson number one coming up. He must be taught not to inject new factors into his flying without getting mature information and advice first. Such as from his instructor.'

So it was that at 2000 ft I chopped the throttle and started the long glide. All went entirely according to plan till the last few seconds when I suddenly realised she was going to drop out of my hands this side of, and not beyond, the near hedge. I slammed the throttle wide open.

The Black Dog must have laughed so much he probably blew a gasket. Nothing happened. To be more precise quite a lot of things happened in very rapid succession. So fast, indeed, that I had trouble later in recalling the exact sequence. First, the hapless air-cooled engine, unwarmed by a brief spell of power half way down, was stone cold; the sudden application of full throttle produced one brief fart of black smoke and nothing else. Without the power, the doughnut wheels dropped neatly into a small ditch beneath the near hedge, and stayed there. With an almighty bang the undercarriage chose to part company with the fuselage and remain wedded to its wheels. The wings, well below stalling speed after the undercarriage dismemberment and lacking a deal of fabric which they had left on the hedge, failed totally to keep anything airborne. The fuselage, with me in it, dug the bottom cylinders of the Armstrong-Siddeley Lynx engine into the turf. This additional and severe braking brought the whole shebang to rest in about 25 feet.

I was very surprised. One moment the Red Baron was guiding his monster effortlessly and skilfully through the ether and four seconds later he was a bloody idiot on his backside in a field, with a busted prop, bent engine, torn wings and sans wheels. Every pilot in Lincolnshire chose then to land, taxi back and have a look. Each had a grin so wide beneath his goggles that it disappeared into the sides of his helmet. Slowly realisation dawned that the moment was not far off when the wrath of God, personified in the form of Flight Lieutenant Wallace, would appear from Cranwell in another aircraft — and he would have a great deal to say. Let us face facts; Flight Lieutenants were much more alarming than God. They were unequivocal and directly audible.

On the other hand I did not distinctly hear, but should have, the chuckling and wheezing of unbridled mirth from my Black Dog after his success. He had not had to wait long before getting his first bite. It was to be several more bites before I took him seriously, and even more before I realised that he *never* gave up.

After that episode my flying training proceeded normally. That is, it is no good telling a student that he is going wrong — you have to let him go wrong, so far wrong that even *he* can see his error. Then you save his neck, and your own. Poor Wallace. My faith in him was unrealistically touching and total. I didn't know enough to realise that he was fallible. Nothing like so fallible as I was, but perfection does not exist in aviation, ever.

I was now so nervous of letting the machine drop short that I was touching down further and further up the field and was in grave danger of running into the far hedge. One morning Wallace said to me: 'Look; it's not so difficult. We will go and do landings on Ermine Street. It's the smaller of the two fields. I'll do the approach; you have your hands and feet on the controls; you follow me through and then you can do one on your own.'

So it was. The air was clear. The sky was blue. The sun shone and the fields beneath were green and pretty. The figure-of-eight turns were near. The final turn in was gentle. The small sideslip was just right. We flattened out and, about six feet up, the prop stopped dead. We landed and came to a standstill in the field.

I saw Wallace's helmet turning from side to side as he checked everything till he said, quite calmly, 'Are your ignition switches 'off'?' Till then I had been, in effect, admiring the scenery and watching the cows in the adjoining field. However, as bidden, I looked at my switches. They were, indeed, off. 'Oh yes!' said I brightly, 'They're off.'

There was such a long pause I wondered what was up; after all, he had been in control, doing a demonstration forced-landing; what matter whether the engine worked or not? Wallace must have been fighting a desire to carve me up into little pieces, verbally or physically. And also, taking some time off to thank his Maker that he had happened to get it exactly right when a nincompoop in the back had, by mistake or on purpose, made a crash 100 per cent certain if he hadn't.

Finally, a very strangled voice said, 'Well, turn them on again.' He gave a twist to the hand-starter magneto and the engine re-started. Without another word we flew quietly home. To this day I have not the slightest idea how or why I managed to knock those switches off. I am sure he never believed I hadn't done it on purpose. But I would dearly love to know, now, what remarks he made to his instructor colleagues back in the office.

Another time we were just airborne over the far end of the airfield when the engine cut dead. This is the most perilous moment as, with no height and not much speed, options are almost zero. I heard him shout 'I've got her!' With consummate skill he nosed down, turned slightly, did a savage sideslip and swishtail to kill the remaining speed, and dropped the machine undamaged just over a stone wall and into a miniscule field. I climbed out and looked around. The field was indeed very small. Other aeroplanes were flying past overhead, the occupants' heads craned over the side in curiosity. It was rather fun to be the centre of attraction. Wallace, having turned everything off, slowly climbed out also. I grinned at him.

He looked at me incredulously for a few moments. I smiled back pleasantly. 'W-weren't you s-scared?' he stammered. 'What? Me? Scared?' I answered; 'Why should I be? You'd got her.' 'Good God,' he said, 'Look at me!' He held out his hand and it was shaking like a leaf.

At last, with a total of about 25 hours under my belt, and with my eighteenth birthday behind me, Wallace judged me competent to make my first cross-country flight. This was heady stuff. A flight of 55 miles; 45 minutes going all in one direction — well, nearly, for I was to go from Cranwell to Bircham Newton and that would entail a 60-degree turn to port at King's Lynn, to get round the Wash. Moreover, it entailed a landing at a strange aerodrome, never before seen and not a training airfield — a real live operational one. Once there, the novel experience of reporting one's arrival to the Duty Pilot in his hut. Not forgetting to get his signature on your log to prove you had been where you were supposed to go and had not gone beating up your girl-friend's house or some such. I did not realise that my mood would be like meaty bones to my Black Dog.

It was June, and on the appointed day the weather was gin-clear. Had I known how to look, I might well have seen Bircham Newton from a couple of thousand feet over Cranwell but I was put through all the ropes. Weather report. Wind speed and strength. Great calculations, tooth-sucking and furrowed brow over the C.S.C. (Course and Speech Calculator). Next, proper folding of the 'quarter-inch topo' map and completion of the details on the pilot's knee-pad. I went to the Duty Pilot in his hut to book out. I had my four pennies in my pocket.

I walked out to the aircraft, looking like a Christmas tree, bearing pads, maps and heaven knows what, all to be strapped on and stowed into my fur-lined flying suit so that they would not blow out of the open cockpit. One hand gripped the webbing of my parachute, slung over one shoulder and with its D-rings clinking behind my thighs. The airman beside the Tutor, as if he didn't know, asked 'Dual, Sir?' I shook my head and he climbed up to the front cockpit to fasten its straps clear of the controls.

Having duly craned my neck round to make sure no one was coming in to land I took off. As directed I climbed in the circuit to my allotted 2000 ft. I set course, carefully passing over the white circle painted in the centre of the grass airfield. I wrote the time on my knee-pad. I looked around. To my surprise and pleasure 20 or 30 miles in front, I could see the whole of the Wash. Its rectangular snout poked into Lincolnshire with Boston and its Stump at the left corner with the smudgy brown of King's Lynn to the right. Spread below on the flat ground of Lincolnshire and Norfolk were the large green fields starting to turn golden. They were intersected by straight line canals reflecting blue water if the sun was right. Matchbox-like cars followed the roads, easing to left or right when they wished to pass or overtake. Black spots in the fields indicated men working, sometimes with brown or grey blobs that were the horses. It was more magic; all magic.

Mentally I relaxed to enjoy the view and my feeling of superiority. Those poor earth-bound people like ants below. They could but move from side to side. I, rushing through the sky at 80 miles an hour could go up and down as well. I sat back and waited for King's Lynn to pass beneath me. The Black Dog half closed his eyes, and waited also.

At King's Lynn I made my turn to port. I had 13 miles to go. Idly I waited, assuming that Bircham Newton would appear before me, as if conjured up by some genie. It was such a perfect day. The beaches to my left looked white and inviting. The little villages had red and grey roofs. Trees and woods were a darker green. White, fluffy cumulus clouds floated above, casting patchy shadows on the fields. The blue sea of the Wash in the sunshine looked lovely. The Black Dog yawned, and then barked.

I looked at my watch, and frowned. It was some minutes past ETA and Bircham, thoughtlessly, had not appeared. I scanned the ground ahead. I flew on some minutes for it must appear soon. I almost reached the coast. Still no Bircham Newton. This was hardly surprising as, day-dreaming, I had gone almost clean overhead and it was already several miles behind me.

I felt panic creeping up. So very simple with experience; probably the easiest thing would have been to turn left and follow the coast 20 miles back to King's Lynn and do it again, carefully. In my ignorance I was scared, and lost. I was 2000 ft up and nobody, but nobody, could give me any help at all. Obviously, I must pin-point my position by map reading. No one had ever told me the easy and logical ways of doing it. I began to cast around in ever wilder and less reasonable circles and eights trying to find something — anything — underneath me that would match my map. The Black Dog snarled, and then he bit.

The engine made a graunching noise, spat out a few puffs of black smoke and with a thump the propeller stopped dead, diagonally rigid before my bulging eyes. My first reaction was of utter disbelief. I was sure I had fuel and this couldn't be happening to me. That was followed by stark fear — I was going down, right now and I wanted to stay up. A confused jumble followed, of what the blazes was I going to do about it?

Oh yes! First thing: the wind. After all my twists and turns I had not the slightest idea where the wind blew, or even which direction was which. Some earlier advice seeped through. Smoke from bonfires and chimneys: wild searchings of the countryside; it was June — no dice. Washing on lines: it wasn't Monday. Cattle and sheep with their backs to the wind; the only ones visible lay or stood in every direction. I was going down and down. The precious seconds were running out in a crazy headlong rush and no one else was going to do one single thing to help me avoid killing myself.

One thing became insistent, crucial and all-pervading. Look for the biggest stubble field, and do the best you can. All other wise words — land near a road, or a garage for help, or a pub for food, or a telephone box — never for one instant crossed my mind.

It must have been a hair-raising and ugly dart at a brownish field amongst the green ones. Suffice to say that I came over the near hedge too fast, in a screaming sideslip, flattened out, touched down, bounced, touched again and stayed down, heaved mightily on the brake lever and, with a desperate swing, just missed hitting some trees at the far end. The Black Dog must have gnashed his teeth with disappointment.

I sat very still, sweating and trembling. Then I turned off the petrol and the ignition, both of which I should have done at the start. Small children and farm hands were running towards me from every direction. I climbed out and took stock. I had landed almost directly down wind, but Allah had been kind for it had been up a steepish slope which fortunately had brought me to rest before the trees. I enlisted the help of two farm hands to guard the aeroplane while someone took me, clutching my four pennies for a public telephone, to a nearby box.

I soon had Cranwell on the line, and then my instructor. The conversation must have tried him sorely. The longer it went on, the more alarmed I became.

'Where are you speaking from?'

'A telephone box, Sir.'

Long pause; then carefully enunciated 'Where is the telephone box?'

'About three miles north of Fakenham, Sir.'

Another pause. 'But that is *beyond* Bircham Newton. How did you get there?'

'I overshot; I must have missed the aerodrome on the way by, Sir.'

Anguished voice 'In *this* weather! How *could* you? And why didn't you fly back?'

'I was lost, Sir, and while I was trying to find myself the engine stopped. So I landed in a field, Sir.'

Incredulously 'Engine *stopped*! Are you sure? Why?'

'I don't know; it went bang and the prop stopped, Sir.'

'How much fuel was left?'

'I don't know, Sir.'

'What were the oil pressure and temperature just before it stopped?'

'I don't know, Sir; I never looked.'

'I think you were playing the ass and ran out of fuel. Is the aircraft damaged?'

'Not as far as I know, Sir.'

'Thank God for small mercies. Can I land in the field?'

'I don't know, Sir. I suppose so,' (brightly, to help) '*I* did.'

Pregnant pause. 'What's the surface?'

I realised I had not the slightest idea. Total concentration on not killing myself had obliterated all other thoughts. Praying hard I said stoutly, 'Stubble, Sir.'

'Well done, choosing a stubble field. Keep the aircraft facing into wind, and I'll be with you in about an hour.'

I put down the receiver as though it had been a cobra.

Back at the aircraft, strong arms helped me lift the tail and turn it round, facing into wind as instructed — and, of course, pointing down the hill. Poor Wallace. When he appeared overhead he saw a Tutor, tucked in the shade of some fairly tall trees. He saw the unenviable choice of landing into wind but over a high obstruction and down a steepish hill — or down wind and up a hill of deep hay. He chose to come in over the trees, into the wind but down the hill. Only by the most massive sideslipping and frenzied swishtailing did he manage to get her down in time, and then missed by a hairsbreadth running into a dewpond at the bottom, hidden by the long grass.

I, by the time he taxied back, was fairly twittering with fright. Wordlessly he and a fitter with a box of tools, climbed out of the cockpits. The fitter, having checked that the ignition was off, heaved on the prop. It would move only a short distance but some very expensive crunching and grinding noises were produced. His verdict was 'Strewth — a piston must've gone!'

Shivering with fear and with my knees knocking together like castanets, I waited for the guillotine. Quite quietly Wallace said: 'Good show, getting it down OK. But two things puzzle me; how in hell did you manage to drag the machine back up this steep slope after the landing — and I *thought* I heard you say that the field was stubble?'

# Chapter 3
## 'The Generous Briton'

The excitements of increasing age were legion. For the present-day price of 25 pence you could get a driving licence. No tests, no 'L' plates and few questions asked, provided you had passed your seventeenth birthday. Car tax was low, and you could buy it quarterly if you were short of cash. Petrol was under two bob a gallon — about ten pence now. Only insurance, hardly surprisingly, was pricy and, sometimes, difficult to get at age seventeen. An increased insurance premium was demanded for being under 21; also a second increase was payable, reserved remarkably for those in three somewhat dissimilar categories — Jews, stockbrokers and Air Force pilots. We cadets, naturally, were liable for both the increases, one on top of the other.

The rules on cars for cadets were strict and simple. No sports cars, not over ten horsepower, and not to cost more than £100 — say £1500 in modern figures. This latter point was academic for what young cadet had £100 in those days? These three simple rules had the most valuable side-benefits for the Royal Air Force. Since no cadet had enough money to pay someone else to work, car owners soon taught themselves to be highly skilled in engineering and overhaul, developing an excellent 'feel' for things mechanical. Secondly, because no cadet's car ever went fast enough, the owners learned a vast amount about tuning engines, their finer workings and how to extract maximum efficiency from them. That remarkable youth Frank Whittle even invented the jet engine when he was a cadet at Cranwell — and the pundits for years all told him it would not work. Any evening in the cadets' garage — an old World War I hangar — you could see rows of cars with cadets' feet sticking out from underneath, or cadet bums sticking up in the air as the possessors buried their heads in the entrails.

It was on a Saturday, not long after pay day. Also, it was during one of the three quarters during which I could find the necessary money to have the car on the road. A lovely evening in late spring, cool but not cold. Scotty Lumsden strolled into my room, saying 'How about rounding up some bods and making a sortie to the Generous Brit?' It sounded a splendid idea to me so we went to search out some other co-operators.

Naturally there was no question of our going anywhere without a full car-load to share and reduce the costs of motoring, even though measured only in pennies. Cadet pay, roughly a pound a week, had to be stretched. Our objective was not far away. Three miles up the Leadenham Straight, over the crossroads, two miles more towards Newark and turn into Brant Broughton. There, on the right opposite the church, was the targeted pub.

It transpired that six other chums also had had supper and were sufficiently in funds to pay their whack. Scotty took his aged Riley-Nine four-seater tourer, and I took my 1925 Standard two-seater — two in the front, that is, under the canvas folding hood and with a dicky-seat behind for another two out in the open air. Luckily for them it did not look like rain. Scotty and I ran a continuing argument as to which of our machines went faster. So, the three-mile Leadenham Straight would be a convenient testing track.

We hurtled up the road, jeers flung from one car to the other. The race was, as always, inconclusive as we slowed up a fraction to cross the A607 in Leadenham village. Our delightful but lunatic Wally Rowbottom, as usual, complained bitterly at this needless danger on the crossroads. He held tenaciously to the logic that the faster you went over a crossing, the less time there was to hit anybody, and therefore it must be safer.

The public and the police were, on the whole, remarkably kind about our darting hither and yon. There was not much traffic about. The 30 mph speed limits had not arrived in towns and villages. We were, if feckless, pretty good at keeping out of physical trouble. At least, the car drivers were; the motor-cycle riders seemed to fare worse. Indeed, there was a corner on the way back to College from Grantham that we called 'Cadets Corner'. A deceptively sharp bend had, on its outside edge, a low wall round a garden. The owner kept, behind the wall, a large and well-dug flower bed with only a few flowers in it. Almost regularly on Saturday nights, after the pubs closed in Grantham, some cadet hurrying home would fail to make the bend. His front wheel would stop at the wall and he would sail gracefully over the top into the thoughtfully dug flower bed.

The Good Samaritan householder would solemnly come out in his dressing gown and hitch a small trailer to his car. Then, understandingly saying nothing, he would drive the cadet in the car, and the remains of the motor-bicycle in the trailer, back to the cadets' garage. Then he returned to his bed — and re-planted his flowers on Sunday. The police got no complaints, and chose not to know.

The landlord of The Generous Briton was his usual pleasant self. We were a raucous lot with a host of vulgar songs and even more reprehensible stories. Our language contained only a few, but unprintable, adjectives. We had not yet grown up enough to realise vulgarity was not the stamp of tough, adult he-men. Mine host, sensibly, accommodated us in a little room behind the bar, away from his more decorous local customers. They were served by his wife. He stayed with us and, when the songs were at their worst, leaned his backside hard against the door. This, he always said, was to stop his wife being shocked if she came in inadvertently. As our noise was flushing the roosting pigeons from the village church-tower across the road, this was hardly likely.

At ten o'clock, closing time, mine host said that Time was Upon Us, and we must leave; further, the village policeman was in the bar to see that the law was upheld, and so our departure was inescapable. This was the signal for a little charade. A couple of us, promptly, would go into the public bar and invite the bobby in 'for a last drink.' He, carefully, would leave his helmet outside, on the bar, so that he was not in uniform, and come with us to the back room. Then, as long as we could get him to sink free drinks with us, we and the landlord had the law on our side. He must once have been in the trade of something like a steelworker or a miner as his capacity for free beers was miraculous. This ten o'clock corralling of the local law made plain common sense; par for the course of six miles to Cranwell at that time of night would only be around eight minutes — and we did not have to book in till midnight. Why leave at ten o'clock?

It must have been around 11.30 when Dickie Longmore came up with a splendid proposition. Both cars had running boards along each side which you could stand on; so, how about going down the Leadenham Straight, flying in formation as it were, at about 45 mph. Then, during the four minutes it would take us to do the three miles at that speed, in the dark, both the drivers and all the passengers would change cars — if we did not meet someone coming the other way. The more we thought about it the better it seemed. We planned the details.

The link man would be the right-hand driver. He, sitting on the right, could follow a very precise line down the right-hand side of the road, at a constant 45 mph. The driver of the left-hand car, also sitting on its right, would be excellently placed to hold his position about 18 inches away, and to keep the same speed. As soon as the cars were running together the two front-seat passengers would stand up and go backwards over their seats to land on the knees of the man behind. This would allow each driver to slide across to his left, still driving but making space for a new driver who, at the same time, would be clambering out of the back of one car and into the back of the other. Then, with the help of the two chaps already there, he would go feet first, up and over the driving seat and slip down into the empty driving position — and take over from driver number one. We reckoned we could do this in two minutes. Easily.

Then, when the new drivers signalled 'in position' — and only then — it was every man for himself. Up, over the side on to the running board, step across, keeping a vice-like grip on one car or the other, and on to a vacant seat. Another two minutes? Equally simple.

Finally procedures were worked out for an emergency, such as approaching headlights observed in front. Either or both drivers would blow the horn. Instantly, everybody would freeze and cling like grim death to whichever car he happened to have in his hand at the time. The left-hand car would accelerate if possible; the right-hand car would brake hard and fall in behind, shedding no one from the outside — we hoped.

Filled with excitement and beer we said goodbye to our host and to the friendly policeman whose eyes were sticking out of his head like chapel hat-pegs. A last-minute check to establish beyond doubt who were the two starting drivers, and the two finishing drivers, before everyone piled into the vacant seats and we were away.

As soon as possible after the Leadenham crossroads we picked up the stipulated 45 mph and, considering the bumpy road, the dark, and the beer, things went surprisingly well. The new drivers were in position well before half-way and the shambolic switching of passengers began. People were on both running boards, trying to climb in or out of either car, laughing uncontrollably and offering gratuitous unheeded advice. Suddenly both drivers banged down on the horn buttons and held them down.

There, standing right in the middle of the road, his dark uniform barely illuminated by the miserable headlights, holding his hand up to signify 'Stop', stood a policeman. Instinctively each person grabbed the edge of the car he was standing on with a grip of iron and pulled himself in so as to become as thin as possible. The reaction of the drivers was just as prompt, considering the few seconds available. They parted in the nick of time, one going to each side of the road. We could see as we flashed past, horns blaring, only inches away, that the man in blue had his mouth wide open and his eyes tight shut.

Someone and I think it was Mike Scott-Mackirdy, peering over the back, reported that the figure disappeared behind us into the night, standing frozen to attention with his arms clasped rigidly to his sides, facing woodenly towards Leadenham and never turning to look after us. I have often wondered how long it was before he moved.

At least we could be sure he did not read our number plates.

# Chapter 4
# Getting Even

In any school, college or university there are always 'societies' for every persuasion and interest that you can think of. Personally, most of them leave me cold. However, the Cranwell Amateur Dramatic Society put on *Journey's End* — a World War I drama. I didn't care for it much, but there was a splendid spin-off.

Johnny Darwen, who was dripping with DSOs and DFCs by the time he was killed in the War, was kind enough to satisfy my curiosity on a technical point of stage management. He explained that the off-stage shell fire, bombs and mines which rattled the windows of the theatre were produced by fireworks. He showed me one. Obtained from a London theatrical supplier it was a cardboard tube, something like the tube from inside a roll of lavatory paper, but closed at each end. It had a couple of wires sticking out and, if you connected some electricity across the wires, it went off. No; I couldn't have one. They cost money and the Theatrical Society was short of dough. A mole in the Society discovered for us that they were not kept under lock and key, and I don't believe anyone noticed that the final performance of *Journey's End* was two bangs deficient.

Our next problem was how best to profit from our ill-gotten boomability. A committee meeting of the renegades was held. At that time Cranwell had recently had an influx of specially selected students from the universities. We felt rather strongly about this. Our training took two years and at the end of which we rose from the status of Gentleman Cadet to that of Pilot Officer. These university upstarts (we thought) came straight in as Acting Pilot Officers and did only six months' training. In short, and for all the future, they got an 18-month start on us. This, by itself, would have been a shoulder-shrugging matter but one or two were a bit high-handed. They would call us to attention and aver: 'I am an Officer. You are a cadet. You must salute me, or I will have you put on a charge.' Most of us were big-headed enough to consider an *Acting* Pilot Officer was not worthy of a salute, if you could get away with it; a sort of pouffe that anyone could sit on. One of the APOs was particularly stroppy about the matter. Let us call him Craven.

Having the advantage of being officers, they did not have to book in and out of camp. They frequently returned very late. Fortuitously, Craven was singularly chummy with a girl who, so an earlier cadet boy-friend assured us, was a very co-operative young lady indeed. We decided to profit from the present, as well as the earlier, friendship.

The ex-boy-friend had remained on good terms and he arranged that she would tell him when Craven next asked her for a date that she could keep. This would provide us with the requisite undisturbed time to doctor his room, undetected because all right-minded cadets and college staff could by then be presumed to be asleep.

Our chance came on a Sunday. The early-morning Monday parade ensured that by a few minutes past midnight only the sounds of snores were filtering down the passages. My prime task was to use the skeleton key I had made for this purpose. Next man in the team took the chair from in front of his table and stood on it to remove the bulb from the hanging ceiling-lamp. He then broke its glass into the waste-paper basket. Number 3 man, who had electrical knowledge, took the broken bulb and carefully connected the two wires protruding from its innards to the wires of the firework. Then, making particularly sure that the ceiling light was not switched on, he gave the contraption back to No.2 man who, still standing on the chair, plugged it in. Finally, when the chair had been carefully replaced, someone took the bulb out of the bedside lamp and left it on the bed. We withdrew, leaving the room in darkness behind the re-locked door.

I suppose it must have been around two in the morning when we saw Craven plodding, sleepily and contentedly, up from the officers' garage. He came through the door at the back of the college and, at peace with the world, ambled into his room. He fumbled for his key, found it and opened the door. Peeping through cracks and over fanlights we watched him enter. He must have tried the table-lamp first because we heard him swear when it wouldn't turn on. Then he went for the ceiling light switch, found it and flipped it down.

Those fireworks were made to impress the audience in a large

*Cranwell RAF College, seen from the air in 1934. Since that date the fourth, missing, wing has been built on the right, making it symmetrical. It was built largely upon a design produced by Sir Christopher Wren.*

*A formation of the aircraft used for training at Cranwell in 1934. Led by the trainer used for ab-initio instruction – the Avro Tutor, probably batting along at about 100 mph. On its left a single-seater Bristol Bulldog fighter, capable, if pressed, of about 150 mph. On its right a dual version of the same machine. On the far side a Hawker Hart Trainer – fitted with dual controls and an exhaust-pipe so that the instructor could make himself heard. On the near side, an Armstrong Whitworth Atlas, used mainly for Army-Co-operation duties but here fitted with dual controls for training.*

*Learning the basics of twelve skilled trades at RAF Cranwell. Flight Cadets being shown the inner structure of a Hawker Hart. (1934).*

*Some Flight Cadets receiving instruction on the innards of a Cirrus engine.*

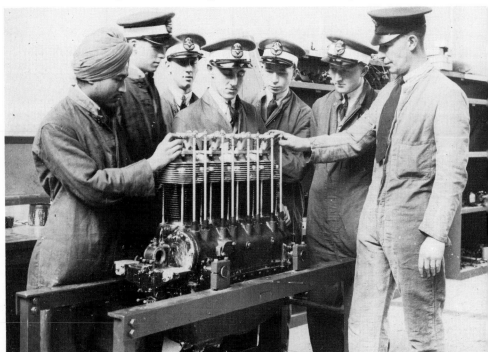

*The author, aged 17, about to go solo in an Avro Tutor aircraft.*

*When gliding in to land, if you get too low and too slow, the machine will 'drop out of your hands'. The pilot of this Atlas caught his wheels on the low dry-stone wall in the foreground, and flipped upside-down on to the airfield. The old adage that 'the Almighty looks after drunks, children and fools' operated in the second and third categories, and the pilot was all right.*

*Passing-out Parade – Flight Cadets at Cranwell being inspected by the Prince of Wales who became King Edward VIII not long afterwards. He is wearing the uniform of an Air Marshal. It will be noted that the senior officers are wearing nice shiny field-boots while the Flight Cadets have the detested breeches-and-puttees.*

*My first effort on aerial photography. A Bristol Bulldog above Cranwell. It is flown by Flight Cadet Johnny Darwen. He was killed in a Beaufighter over Sicily in World War II, as Group Captain Johnny Darwen, DSO, DFC, and several bars.*

One of our many stops between Karachi and the North West Frontier. I got a monster reproof, and the threat of arrest, for not wearing a solar topee between the hours of sunrise to sunset; as it was, a few moments after this picture was taken I was ordered into the train and forbidden to emerge except in darkness. I thought the Army Major concerned was somewhat bombastic. Note the two water-men on the train-roofs. Elsewhere the authorities provided us with seven water carriers with goat-skins holding about 15 gallons each – this was to fill 27 water-tanks of 500 gallons each!

The oil-refinery at Abadan.

*The author's bungalow, which he shared with Gerald Elsmie.*

*The Mali (Gardener) mowing the lawn with two assistants.*

*Risalpur cantonnment from the air. On the right is the 700 yard square grass airfield with its hangars. On the left is one of the two polo-grounds. My bungalow has been circled.*

*At the back of the bedroom the author takes his bath.*

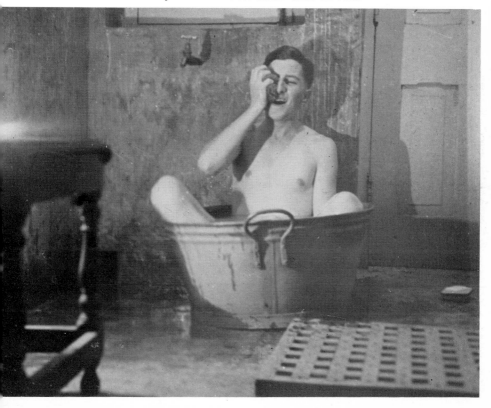

*My splendid car — a Model 'T' Ford which was one year older than I was – 1915. It never missed a beat in three and a half years. You had to have a chock to put in front of the wheel, otherwise it ran you over as you wound the starting-handle. Obtaining tyres posed problems, even as far as back as 1936.*

*The Station Commander, Wing Commander Bill Ankers, gets a birthday cake and some ribald speeches. Bill Ankers was later killed on the way to Singapore in a Blenheim.*

theatre when let off back-stage. The effect in a small bedroom was fantastic. A blinding flash was synchronous with a mighty roar. A dense cloud of smoke billowed out into the passage through the open door, producing a strong smell of cheap fireworks like Guy Fawkes night. In moments only, doors were thrown open all along the passage, including ours, as everyone less-or-more sleepy came out to see what on earth had happened. There was a long pause before he tottered out, his eyes staring and face grey with fright. His mouth opened and shut but for a while no words came. At last he stammered: 'I j-just turned on the l-light and the whole b-b-bloody place b-b-blew up.'

We suggested politely that perhaps a fuse had blown. What else? 'It's you bloody cadets!' he screamed. 'You've no respect for officers.' Someone, unidentified and unidentifiable at the back of the crowd, opined gently that we returned to the officers just as much respect as they showed to us.

My admiration for him exists even now. I thought at first he was going to have a heart attack, but he didn't. He clamped his mouth shut, swallowed a couple of times and thought hard. Then he said 'Sorry,' and went back to his room. Someone said helpfully, 'The good bulb's on the bed.' From that moment on, from being a self-important ass he became a most delightful colleague.

The second boomer took longer to arrange. After the miraculous success of the first one, we did not want to waste it on some minor effort. Finally, we decided that the victim this time should be a certain individual who was unbearably pompous. Let us call him Bateman. He was very sure of himself, lacking in humour and we thought he was thick.

Very early one Saturday morning we connected the second cracker by a longer wire to the starter terminals of his car, and then laid it on the top of the engine. When morning parade was over and Bateman was going to collect his suitcase for the weekend, Ted Thornewill artlessly offered to bring his car round to the front of the Mess for him. Ted was a past-master at keeping his face expressionless when necessary. To our joy Bateman did not smell a rat and was soft enough to be flattered by Ted's thoughtfulness. We hugged ourselves. Right in front of the Mess he would press the starter button and, doubtless, a good laugh would be had by one and all at the unfortunate's expense. Ted, suitably reminded to start up only by using the starting-handle, went off and was back in a few minutes.

Bateman had come back and, as the car pulled up, he said

'Many thanks, Ted. Don't stop the engine and I will push off right away . . . ' Our emissary didn't think fast enough; instead of switching off and saying 'Oh, I'm so sorry old boy' and getting out, he did as he was bid. He got out, leaving the motor running. Bateman got in and drove happily away. Each one of us could cheerfully have murdered Ted, messily and painfully.

It was not till much later that we learned our jest had ended far, far better than we had ever envisaged. Bateman was motoring placidly towards his destination when he passed through a country town. This Saturday they had a fair. A farming fair in the old style with animals being bought and sold. For some reason — maybe a cow in the way — he stalled his engine. Naturally, he pressed the starter button.

The result was magnificent and awe-inspiring. With a thunder-clap the bonnet flew open, smoke belched out, and then it fell back again. The fair turned into a pandemonium. Chickens and ducks became airborne. Any unpenned cattle and sheep took off for the wide open spaces, pursued by bucolic farmhands. Horses reared. Dogs barked. Panic reigned.

No one, and that included Bateman, dared touch the vehicle in case worse befell. At last a garage man was fetched who peeped very gingerly under the bonnet. There he found some blackened fragments of cardboard and a length of wire. Having pulled the wire clear and given Bateman a very dirty look, he pressed the starter and the engine started perfectly normally.

Bateman had the devil of a time persuading the local bobby, and the farmers, that he had not done it on purpose.

# Chapter 5
## 'The Groves'

Shades of its Army origins for the Royal Air Force! Flying horsemen, by Gad, Sir. Circling about, above the *real* troops. Just like the cavalry, except they could see a bit further. Thus it was that RAF Squadron Leaders wore black riding boots with their best uniform on parade, and carried black leather-covered canes. The *hoi polloi* meaning all those of lower status, wore upon their lower halves blue riding breeches, and puttees over black boots.

Who invented puttees, and why, I know not but I hated him with all my heart. A puttee (and you had two — one for each leg) was a form of long bandage made of blue woollen serge. You began by winding it over the top of your boot and then gradually layered it up your ankle, calf and ended at the bottom of your breeches. There, it was held in place by a length of tape. Simple, apparently, but . . .

To be smart it had to fit snugly so that there were no 'pockets' or folds as the turns wound evenly up your leg. Further, the end of the puttee had to finish in line with the outer seam of your breeches, precisely. Imagine the horrible complications for an ignorant seventeen-year-old! Too many turns around the ankle and you haven't enough puttee left to reach the top. Unwind it and begin again. The turns are not evenly spaced. Begin again. Too much round your fat calf and it is too short. Dammit! Parade is all too soon. Wind the turns tighter to stretch the end to the right place. Now you have made a tourniquet stopping all flow of blood to your foot. Getting late. Try the other one. At last you hobble on parade with needles-and-pins in one foot and a sloppy uneven winding-sheet above the other. Even now I can hear the Cadet Sergeant saying: 'Puttees, Mr. Dudgeon. Report after parade.'

The result was a foregone conclusion. punishment drills; appearing at frequent intervals on each day, except Sunday when we paraded only once — for church. Full uniform and rifle, with the puttees wound *correctly*. The last of the daily appearances, properly accoutred, was in the dark after dinner — having changed from dinner uniform back into parade uniform. They inspected you minutely, with a torch.

I was, on the whole, one of the renegades. I did endless punishment drills and by the end of my time at Cranwell could whizz my puttees up my legs like winding a cassette-tape; perfect layer spacing, no loose pockets, not too tight, and ending within a fraction of an inch of the right place. Indeed, I did more time 'on the square' — a euphemism for punishment drills — than any other cadet of my term. Correction; my friend Dickie Longmore got 28 days' 'jankers' (another euphemism) in one awful award for some heinous scallywaggery, right at the end of our time and he just beat me. Or, if you put it the nicer way, just permitted me to vaunt a better record than his, to the tune of one day spread over the two years.

I suppose the real reflection of the marvellous time I had during my training, and what a pest I was to my mentors, is highlighted by my overall results. I was a Prize Cadet on the way in; a scholarship boy, near the top. I passed out one from bottom. In between was a wildly enjoyable two years, learning assiduously all the subjects which appealed to me and driving the staff gaga when I was uninterested. To be really truthful, the only subject in which I was totally absorbed was flying.

I was born in Egypt and four years later a senior officer called Robert Marsden-Groves was killed in a flying accident in that same country. His family gave a beautiful silver trophy in his memory, to be competed for and awarded to the best cadet-pilot of the term leaving the College. One term-member got the Sword of Honour, recognition of outstanding overall performance. Others got prizes for science, English, engineering, and many other indications of excellence by the standards set. These hallmarks had the chances of a celluloid cat in hell of coming my irresponsible way. For me and for a few others like me there was one prize, and only one, to be desired passionately above all others — 'The Groves'.

The contest took place upon an appointed day when a team of ace instructors flew themselves in from the Central Flying School. These (from the cadets' starry-eyed point of view) astral beings were the teachers and testers of all our instructors — who, we thought, were themselves close to the angels. Only the six best cadet-pilots would fly with them, be checked by them, and later sent solo for a brief aerobatic display above them — which would be completed by a simulated forced landing on the airfield in front of them.

Being on the whole an *enfant terrible* who lived almost permanently under a black cloud, I had come, over two years, to accept a fact of life; the Powers That Be never selected me for anything good — even if I was skilful enough to merit it. Nevertheless, clean out of the blue as we walked across the tarmac, Flight Lieutenant Wallace said, flatly and with no encouraging overtones, 'I've decided to put you in for the The Groves.' I pulled up as though I had been shot and looked at him in total disbelief. 'You must be joking, Sir!' 'No,' he answered, looking carelessly into the middle distance, 'the Flight Commander says he doesn't mind if I let you have a go.'

Well, it was hardly an enthusiastic send-off but . . . The Groves! I went off to my room in a roseate daze. Merely to compete was a privilege far beyond my wildest dreams.

Two competitors were selected from each flight of the operational aircraft types. Scotty Lumsden and Robin Press were chosen from the Atlas flight. Gerald Elsmie and Mad Wally Rowbottom (he of the high speeds over crossroads) from the Bulldog flight; Dave Green and I from the Harts. Amongst knowledgeable cadets it was generally opined that Wally would win; he was a very precise pilot and the Bulldog was a lovely and accurate aeroplane to fly. For the rest, we were all classed as an indeterminate bunch. I hoped like mad that I would not come bottom in the final placings.

Almost to my surprise on the great day, my 'instructor of the instructors' did not have wings on his shoulders, nor did he have a halo like an archangel. Indeed, he looked quite ordinary and not unlike Wallace. He too had a black, leather, tailor-made helmet below which the two speaking tubes dangled, joining in front of his navel. He was a short, stocky man and had a kind voice. 'Taxi out, take off and climb straight ahead to 1000 ft.' In the Hawker Hart biplane the instructor sat behind the pupil and I felt as if gimlet eyes must be boring two holes in the back of my neck. Now, with the wisdom of hindsight, I would not be surprised to learn he was wondering if his girl-friend would be free next Saturday evening. I set about my business. Taxi out gently at 'a brisk walking pace'. Keep a 'good look-out for other aircraft' coming in to land or taking off. Stop cross-wind and check that all controls and switches (four of them) are properly set. Have a last good look around, turn into wind and off we go.

At 1000 ft my examiner began a steady flow of commands. Level turn to the left; climbing turn to the right; and so on for about half an hour. Then, suddenly, he pulled the throttle closed. 'Your engine has failed. Do me a forced-landing. Tell me exactly what you intend to do and in which field you would land. Do not in fact land but, at 50 ft open the throttle and fly me back to Cranwell.'

Dead silence except for the gentle popping in the exhaust pipe of the idling engine and the whistle of the wind past the struts and bracing wires. I began to talk. 'First, I would turn off the magneto switches and the fuel, but will not now do so as this is simulated. Then I do a complete circle to choose the best field within easy gliding range. There is a stubble field, down there, to our left, and which gives a good run into wind. I now set up a figure-of-eight pattern on its downwind side . . . ' I was absolutely sweating with concentration and effort to make it really good. At last, on the final turn I judged I had left it too late and was too low. I fairly heaved the machine round in what felt like an ugly swoop. In fact, I was too early and so I was too high. Even a wicked sideslip, held a bit too long, hardly saved it completely. I felt I could easily, if it had been for real, have run into the far hedge. My only consolation was that it was a lesser fault to do that than to hit the near end at speed. To add to my chagrin the 'stubble' turned out to be, on low-level inspection, long grass which might have caught the wheels and tipped us on our nose. It all seemed to me a total disaster for such a competition. Miserably, and furious with myself, I opened up the throttle and turned for home.

On the tarmac my tester climbed out of the rear cockpit, said 'Thank you' and walked away, deep in thought. 'That,' I muttered to myself, 'is that. Oh well — at least I was given a chance.'

The solo aerobatic programme was to be the same for everyone. Start at 3000 ft. First, a full loop; up, over the top and down again, finishing precisely at the same height that it began. Dive to get up speed. Pull up, up and over in the first half of another loop and then, on the top, roll out from the upside down back to straight and level, going back the way you went in. Then, turn back and execute a nice, leisurely slow-roll. Finally, close the throttle and do the simulated forced-landing.

Slap in the middle of the airfield was a white painted circle. Its near-side rim represented a fatal ditch on the edge of a field, over which the landing had to be made. The one who landed over and closest to the fatal ditch would get the highest marks — *provided* there were no little tweaks from his engine to help him succeed!

First to perform, poor fellows, were the Atlas competitors. An Armstrong-Whitworth Atlas was built like a brick loo. To make it aerobat you needed forearms like a blacksmith and the finesse of a stevedore. Next came the Hawker Harts. These day bombers were not so manoeuvrable as fighters built for fleeting aerial combat, but they were a deal better than the Atlas. Dave was before me and I was fourth in line. Last were Gerald and Wally in the Bristol Bulldog fighters.

My Achilles Heel, I knew, would be the slow-roll. It does not sound difficult to do. First select a point straight ahead and keep your machine pointing at it. Then bring one wing up, further still, past the vertical and keep rolling. Hold the nose always lined up with your chosen point ahead as the horizon goes round you the opposite way. Ignore the fact that the engine cuts out as you get upside down. Close the throttle. Carry on with the horizon rolling round the point ahead of you till you finish up straight and level once more, still aiming at the same spot you started with. Wait while the fuel in the carburettor sorts itself out and the engine comes on again. Open the throttle and fly happily away. Then, and ever afterwards, I became disoriented and confused in the second half, when straightening to the upright from the upside down. Result: lose the aiming point and come out crooked, without fail. However, as I felt I had blown it earlier, I was not too concerned. It went as I had expected. First manoeuvre quite passable; second, ditto; third, the roll. True to form it was as straight as a dog's hind leg, although the ensuing forced-landing, as I compared it with my earlier supposed disaster, was not too bad. Well — it was over, for better or worse. I taxied in.

By the time I had clambered out of my Hart, Gerald had almost finished his show and Wally was due to start. Typical of Mad Wally, who always knew better than anyone else, he made sure that no one would miss the finesse of his flying by being too far away — he began at 1500 ft. He was a joy to watch. His aerobatics were immaculate. His Bulldog fighter swept itself around the sky in lines and curves seemingly drawn by geometrical instruments. Finally, on his forced-landing his little aircraft dropped itself, delicately as a sparrow, slap in the middle of the white circle. The instructor-testers went off to add up marks.

The final placings were interesting. The poor Atlas pilots had, as feared, no luck. Mad Wally as expected had top marks for execution and to my amazement I had got second highest. Gerald came next and the three of us were only a mark apart. However, the axe fell on Mad Wally and me. He was docked marks for aerobatting lower than stipulated, and I for drawing a corkscrew in the sky instead of doing a slow-roll. So, in the end, Gerald got The Groves. We made Gerald help us drown our sorrows in beer at The Generous Briton the following Saturday evening.

The friendly rivalry between Gerald, Wally and me did not last long. A year later all three of us, posted to the same station, were flying operational Harts. Wally thought he had devised a splendid madcap joke. An aeroplane seen from above always looks much lower than it really is; so Mad Wally proposed to fly in formation with some unsuspecting colleague and, with a wave of his hand, would pull up, stall and go down in a spin. The unfortunate individual would then watch Mad Wally spinning down and become hysterically convinced he was going to fly into the ground and be killed. Then at the last moment Wally would recover, pull out at low level and fly home. There, a good belly-laugh would be had by everybody, according to Mad Wally. Gerald and I, his most irresponsible friends, told him he was being even crazier than usual. Wally was unconvinced.

One day, Wally saw a cruising Hart at about 6000 ft and, picking up close-formation, recognised Stew Saunders from the rival squadron. While Stew was watching, he pulled up his Hart, stalled and went into a deliberate spin. Stew watched him curiously at first, wondering what was up. He became alarmed as the machine got lower and lower. At last, precisely as Wally had forecast, Stew became almost hysterical, screaming 'Come out, Wally! For Christ's sake come out!' Wally did come out of the spin as Stew besought him — but not high enough to flatten out and fly away. No one laughed at Mad Wally's joke when Stew came racing home to tell us about the crumpled remains of steel, aluminium, silver-painted fabric and blood lying ten miles north of the airfield.

Only weeks later, Gerald was doing his very first night flying practice. Contrary to instructions, he had picked up with a friend and was flying in close formation. After passing over the airfield he broke formation in a lovely sweeping turn, up, over, away and down. Friend said there was a wonderful beauty in the ghostly shape of the Hart against the night sky, picked out by coloured navigation lights, the blue flames from the exhausts and the gleam of moonlight on polished aluminium. Unfortunately, not being very experienced at night, Gerald lost his bearings as was only too easy with our elementary instrumentation. His machine met the ground while he was still diving down, fast.

I took no pleasure from becoming, in such a manner, the No. 1 of our Groves competition. Flying was, and is, an unforgiving trade.

# Chapter 6
# To The Raj

Shortly before leaving Cranwell we had been asked to state a choice of posting. In common with most of my term, I naturally opted for fighters. Defence of the Realm. Dog-fights. And, above all, the glamour of hand-to-hand combat. To my surprise and joy I got my choice. I was sent to No. 111 Fighter Squadron at Northolt. Bristol Bulldog biplanes to fly. Although I had never flown one (and they were not as fast as even our Hart bombers) they would be joyous machines with which to draw patterns in the sky. A straight slow-roll might even become possible.

Junior Air Force pilots were alleged to have three main interests — aeroplanes, sports cars, and girls — in that order. With biplane fighters to fly, and a couple of years near London with its theatres, movies and nightclubs to visit . . . It only needed an exciting car to complete my paradise. Postings staff had done a wonderful job for me, or so I thought.

My flight commander on 111 Squadron was a bit of a martinet. When I duly reported in on Monday morning and gave him a polite salute with a courteous 'Good morning', he answered: 'Let's get this straight right away. I am a Flight Lieutenant and therefore not *entitled* to the courtesies of a Field Officer. Nevertheless, I am your immediate CO and when you come in to my office you come smartly to attention, give me a cracking salute, and say "Good morning, SIR!" Also, here, in the Flights you will always call me "Sir". You do not have to call me "Sir" in the Mess or elsewhere. Now, get out of my office and I will send for you when I want you.' This, to me, sounded ominous.

Sometime during the afternoon he sent for me to see my flying log-book with my Bulldog flying hours. When he discovered they were zero, he was not pleased. His demeanour became even sourer after an incident a few nights later. He was doing a night exercise, cruising around at several thousand feet, in his single-seater, over the (then) open fields in the Watford area. Life was peaceful. The weather was good. The lights of London away to the south looked like coloured jewels spilled on a black velvet cloth. He would shortly be turning for home, a late supper in the Mess, and a welcome beer in the ante-room.

Suddenly, with a couple of jerks and an expensive thumping noise the engine ceased to turn the propeller and, inevitably, from that instant his only way was down.

In considerable alarm he scanned the dimly glowing instruments to see if he could identify and then rectify the trouble. Everything was very dead and ominously quiet. The night air whistled through the struts and bracing wires. He took the immediate safety actions such as turning off the petrol and the ignition. Then he prepared to go over the side and float down safely in his parachute. He craned over the edge of the cockpit to have a look below. It was black. Inky black nothingness. Down there were trees, water, houses, electricity pylons, ponds or whatever. He shuddered at the thought and muttered to himself, 'Not for me. I'd better land the brute.'

To make a dead-stick landing at night he had the dubious assistance of a couple of magnesium filled fireworks in holders below each wingtip, called Holt Flares. He could light one or both by pressing a button in the cockpit. They would burn with a brilliant light for a couple of minutes, allegedly illuminating the countryside beneath. Could he . . . should he . . . then make a glide approach and land? He had never tried before. It was difficult enough in daylight. Land it, or take silk? He hesitated. The alternatives, each more unpleasant than the last, unwound before him. If the flare was still alight after a safe touchdown he needed to taxi about briskly or the heat would probably set the doped-fabric wing on fire — and he had no engine to taxi about with. Worse, if he crashed (and became trapped?) with the flare alight, conflagration and burn-out were a certainty. If he pressed the button too early, the flare would extinguish before he got down, leaving him far too low to bale out and in no position to light the other one; he would be in total ignorance of what he was going to hit, how, how hard, and when.

These were all unpleasant facts which he could in no way change or circumvent. He checked the altimeter. His detailed analysis had cost him dear. He was now too low to scramble up and over the cockpit edge against the slipstream and fall safely clear before pulling the rip-cord, even though he now wanted to.

A night landing on-the-glide was inevitable and, judgement of the instant to press the flare button, above a terrain he could not see, was to put it mildly a delicate matter of life and death. A poor decision could kill him very dead.

He glided down in the black void until, he hoped fervently, he was just two minutes from touch-down. He pushed the button. He could hear the crack as the flare lit, the glare of its light was immense and a long disquieting trail of sparks and smoke streamed back from under the wing. He peered down, first this side and then that. He could distinguish practically nothing — underneath him were only different shades of dark grey and black.

After about a minute of increasing concern, he thought he could pick out an area of uniform blackness. Its shape led him to hope it was a field, and not a lake or a wood. For better or for worse, he set up his approach. When he was about 200 ft up, the flare went out. With little beads of sweat on his forehead and prickles up his spine he glided straight ahead, seeing nothing at seventy miles an hour and feeling as if he had his head in a black velvet bag. After an eternity there was a frightening bang as the wheels hit, followed by silence for a bounce; more bangs as the machine bounced again and again. Then, wonder of wonders, miracle of miracles, a rumbling as the wheels ran along the ground. 'My God!' he thought, 'I've got away with it!' He put on the wheel brakes as hard as he dared.

Just before he came to a standstill there was an even bigger bang, a tearing of fabric, rending of metal, snapping of branches and a gigantic lurch as the machine slipped forwards and over on to its back. Total quiet reigned except for the trickle and strong smell of petrol coming from the inverted fuel tanks. He, totally unhurt, was hanging upside down from his straps. There was no room for him to get out, he discovered by feeling around in the dark, because the cockpit had acquired a tarmac lid. He deduced, correctly, that he had gone through a tall hedge and been flipped upside down, across a road at the end of the field in which he had most skilfully landed. There was nothing to do but hang there in his straps, listening to the petrol, hoping that the first person to find him would not be smoking.

The first thing was headlights approaching on the road and the second was an alarming squeal of tyres as a very startled driver managed to stop before hitting the obstruction. After a few moments while the driver tracked down the disembodied voice coming from a small space beside his feet, he agreed to go off and get help to lift up the tail, so allowing the unfortunate pilot to get out. And, no smoking please! Help arrived in force remarkably quickly, being the total content of a local pub which was getting perilously near closing time.

The pilot's instructions were explicit. The message he conveyed was, 'Everybody, get round the tail. Then, lift it as high as possible and hold it there at all costs. I will lower myself gently to the ground and wriggle out. This will take some time for I have, strapped to my inverted backside, a parachute weighing eighteen pounds. You should know that several similarly placed pilots, undoing their straps too quickly, have had their leather-helmeted heads driven into the ground, and been concussed. Releasing the safety lock of the shoulder-straps needs considerable care, and time.'

All the beery customers gathered round the tail, offering and receiving much valueless advice. All the customers, that is, save one. He got down on all fours and managed to edge his face about three inches from that of the victim. 'I,' he said, 'am the local reporter for the Watford Whizzbang,' . . . or some such . . . 'and I wondered if you could be kind enough to give our readers your immediate impressions?' The reporter certainly received the pilot's immediate impressions but it is almost certain that the readers never got them even though, suitably expurgated, the message merely said, 'Do not waste my time you silly fellow. Move your being to the tail, and LIFT!'

When the tail was raised as high as could be, our unfortunate pulled the safety pin and lowered himself gently towards the ground. Unluckily he had forgotten to undo his radio-telephone connection which, under his chin, came within an ace of hanging him. As the R/T had never worked anyway, this was an unkind cut. However, having circumvented this final predicament he scrambled clear and, with the delighted customers, repaired to the pub which the publican most thoughtfully kept open to accommodate them all. A telephone call was made to Northolt, summoning help.

A forced-landed aeroplane in the early '30s was quite an event and, with the landlord being willing and the local bobby in attendance, the rescuers settled in to drink to his lucky escape. And also to hear the story of his miraculous skill time after time. The details improved with every round and the reporter sat there goggle-eyed, crossing out and amending his copy until he could barely hold his pencil.

It was well over an hour before a lorry containing guards for the machine, the Orderly Officer and another flight commander arrived. Our hero greeted them all with unrestrained bonhomie. 'Shmarvelous ol' boy. Lemme tell you too wha' hap-happened.'

We did not see him next day till after he had had a very sticky interview with the Squadron Leader. His contention that he was stone-cold sober before the mishap, and fell amongst dubious company only afterwards in the pub, had fallen on deaf ears. He gave us all hell. So much so that a change of scene was eminently called for. It seemed as if my guardian angel was looking over my shoulder: a perfect and Heaven-sent opportunity came my way — an exchange posting.

Another Cranwellian colleague was at Northolt. Eddie Miller had been a term or two senior to me and he now found himself posted to a torpedo-bomber squadron in Singapore. Singapore sounded wonderful, and my present flight commander sounded awful. So with Eddie's happy agreement and no constraints from the flight commander, I applied to change places with Eddie. This was normally permitted — Eddie would get my job, while I got his. The answer from Air Ministry Postings took only a few days to return. It was curt and tart. 'It is not the policy of the Ministry to send officers from Cranwell overseas during the first two years of their service.' Full stop, end of message.

Every cloud has a silver lining. The flight commander was still a pain, but Postings had settled on two assured years near the fleshpots. I got rid of my old banger and, slavering with anticipation, invested in a scarlet Singer-Nine Le Mans-Special sports car. Well, to be more accurate, a hire-purchase company did the investing. Admittedly it produced three lifts on my insurance premium; one for under 21, another for being an Air Force officer and a third whopper for a sports model. Nevertheless it opened an avenue to girls who hopefully could also be classified as 'Sports Models'. These, now that I was 19, seemed eminently desirable. They would have to suffer some economies, with three insurance lifts and hire-purchase, all on a Pilot Officer's pay — but, who could be luckier? Biplane fighters to fly, a scarlet sports car to drive, and opportunities unlimited. It was worth enduring a savage flight commander.

Two weeks later on a Friday night, I was 'Flare Path Officer'. On the grass airfield, big ironwork baskets held asbestos wool. Called Money Flares after their designer, they were lined up to make a 'T' facing into the wind. These, flooded with paraffin and lit, literally made a 'flare-path' for take-off and landings. The FPO, dressed in his fur-lined flying suit, stood beside the first flare and controlled aircraft in the circuit with a battery-operated signalling lamp, because the radios never worked reliably. It was by no means dull if you had several aircraft in the circuit, each jockeying to be in the best position to get your OK for the next landing. Also, the pilots could choose to make their landing on whichever side of the T took their fancy. This meant, without radio, that you needed four eyes; two to follow the aircraft up in the circuit and two more to watch the one already making his approach. Even though it took only seconds to get self, battery and lamp over to the other side of the first Money Flare, an FPO on a busy night could have given a ballet dancer points and a beating, fur-lined flying suit notwithstanding. On the other hand, you stamped your feet, became bored and felt as cold as charity when pilots were away doing navigation exercises, or landing for dinner elsewhere.

It was during one of these lulls that a morse signalling-lamp began laboriously to flash me a message from the Duty Pilot's hut, forebear of Air Traffic Control. Word by word the message came across. 'Signal from Air Ministry Postings for Pilot Officer Dudgeon. You are posted to 11 Bomber Squadron, Risalpur, India, for flying duties. Report to RAF. Manston for one week's parachute-packing course next Monday. To be followed by one week privilege leave before embarking on HMT *Dorsetshire*, Southampton.' My jaw dropped. Bombers, India, and only two weeks hence? But indeed it was.

Service travel pre-war, on the ocean, left something to be desired. His Majesty's Troopship *Dorsetshire* was four weeks on its way to the Far East, dropping off soldiers and airmen to help guard the Empire for periods between two and five years. Only two years in Iraq where no women were allowed — save only four nursing sisters at the RAF hospital in Habbaniya; three years in Hongkong, Singapore and Egypt; five long years in India. It was damnably hot on board and if there was any wind it was behind us. We had none of the luxuries of fans or ducted air — just canvas scoops and metal ventilators which carried the breeze below, if there was a breeze. Conditions for the 2000 troops aboard were reminiscent of a mid-eighteenth century prison-ship. Six levels of wooden planks had been fitted in the holds to make decks. These had beams roughly six feet apart. From these beams the soldiers and airmen slung navy-type hammocks each night and took them down again each morning. They were so close together that you could not walk between them — you had to crawl underneath. Part of the Orderly Officer's duties was to make his rounds every two hours, followed by the Orderly Sergeant and Orderly Corporal, crouching and crawling behind him, to make notes of anything wrong. Not that any change was possible or contemplated.

The officers were luckier and shared a normally two-berth cabin among four. Also, being amongst pilots, my colleagues were not sea-sick. During the two days and three nights of storms in the Bay of Biscay, the OC Troops had delegated all Orderly Officer's duties to the Air Force. Only they had stomachs so toughened by aerobatics that they could get round the troops' decks without being sick. Even then it was touch and go as troops' vomit with its nauseous stench dribbled through the gaps between the boards on to the hammocks of the decks below. For the men themselves, confined there by the storm and with no effective ventilation, it was horrendous.

In good weather, when all troops came on deck, such as for the daily 8 o'clock 'parade' and roll-call, none could sit down for lack of room; all had to stand. For the rest of the day, fresh air was taken in shifts. Officers were allowed enough deck space to get fresh air at any time.

The consequences of an emergency, such as a collision at night, were awful to contemplate. The lifeboats were stacked in two rows, one on top of another, on the upper decks. Having lowered and successfully launched the upper lifeboat, it would have been necessary to send up the ropes and re-attach them to the under boat before it too could be got away. Simple arithmetic showed that, to accommodate the number of men, every lifeboat from both levels and both sides of the ship, would have to be safely launched, with its full complement. Some pundits announced that even then there would be a couple of dozen left over for lack of space.

# Chapter 7
# Kali

I leaned over the side, watching the white foam as the bows cut through the calm metallic blue of the Indian Ocean, somewhere between Aden and Karachi. Every few moments green and silver flying-fish would pop out of the water and scoot away from the ship, inches above the surface. Its aviation techniques were all absorbing. Each few feet it would let the lower half of its tail fin dip into the water, wiggling and working like an outboard motor; this could prolong the flight for 50 yards or more. Then 'plop', it was gone into the sea again leaving nothing but a row of spreading ripple-rings as though a boy had been playing ducks-and-drakes with skilfully flung pebble. These fishes that became airborne directly from underwater, and which then kept flying by water-propulsion, were an unending source of admiration and discussion for the pilots.

I mused over the lead-in to my departure for India. Only two weeks earlier the Postings staff had refused my request for Singapore. More, they had assured me of a couple of years near London. To pile Ossa upon Pelion I got only one week's leave before a five-year spell abroad; that hurt a bit. Losing the prospect of fighter aircraft and sporting girls hurt some more. The devastating cash loss on the forced sale of my sports car, the unforeseen winding up of the hire-purchase agreement, the insurance to be surrendered and the lost car tax — that was a financial beating of disastrous proportions on a Pilot Officer's pay.

Little did I know that the real kick in the teeth would come after reaching my new squadron in Risalpur. Air Ministry Postings had told them many months earlier that I was coming to fly their Hart bombers. Not merely some time before I was erroneously and fatuously informed that such a posting contravened their policy but, when with forked tongues they asked me at Cranwell what field I desired, it was already on their books that I wasn't going to get it. I thought a little 'leak' that their decision had already been made would have been kindly, and money-saving! I was very young, and had much to learn about the exigencies of the Service. Over the years I would suffer many similar little surprises. Nonetheless, they did not stop me experiencing a fabulous mixture of fun and fascination, in the air and on the ground. Leaning over the rail, watching colourful fish flying above the Indian Ocean, was an early step along that path.

One morning in the velvety darkness before dawn, *Dorsetshire* tied up at Karachi. When the first patches of pink and orange light in the sky began to vie with the electric bulbs on tall poles, we could pick out more clearly the troop train sitting on the quayside. Its massive steam locomotive hissed gently as the vapour curled upwards. Our travelling home for the last six weeks looked very tall beside the quay, painted white with a blue band round its middle, for all the world like a gigantic RAF kitbag. Endless lines of airmen, permitted to take for five years only what they could carry, shuffled down the gangplanks and across to the train. British supplied khaki drill seemed to fit only where it touched. Faces and knees were pink and unseasoned by the sun. The pith helmets — solar topees — sat either right back or pitched down on noses. No one looked happy or comfortable. I was not a little lost myself.

A tall Indian in immaculate white uniform appeared, apparently from nowhere. He stood straight as a ramrod, his features were aquiline and his skin a clear, light brown. He looked a proud and self-assured individual. His fine looking white puggaree (turban had on its side a flash in RAF colours. To my alarm he placed his hands together in a praying attitude and bowed to me. With deep respect he said, quietly, 'Salaam, Sahib.' I took a nervous half-pace backwards as he added, 'You Dudgeon-Sahib?' I nodded. He beamed and said 'I Kali. I am your bearer sent from Risalpur to look after your journey. If you like I can look after you at Risalpur. If you not like you can get new bearer. I get coolies and take your luggage. You tell me which pieces.' Before I could recover from my astonishment he had discovered which was my remarkable collection of baggage, deemed necessary by the RAF, and disappeared.

In moments only he was back, accompanied by two exceedingly scruffy bare-footed porters. Their only badge of office appeared to be a dirty red puggaree. They also first prayed and then bowed to me. I supposed, in my ignorance, that these individuals would be making several trips to convey my (black japanned) insect-proof cabin trunk, my similar (black japanned) topee case, my canvas bedroll with folded camp-bed and travelling wash-basin, my two suitcases and a motley assortment of smaller items. Kali, flailing them with a stream of words, insisted that everything was moved in one go, so that all would remain under his eagle eye. Even I, with no word of Urdu at my command, could recognise their pleading for more porters from those hanging around nearby. He made a single comment only: 'Karachi-coolies all lazy wallahs.' He dragooned them, festooned with my belongings like Christmas trees and with the trunk between them, down the gangplank towards the train. 'You come, Sahib' said Kali and, somewhat bemused, I followed.

My first-class compartment was to be shared with another junior officer. I took stock. Along one wall was a brown leather-covered bench as a seat, which would become a bed at night. Above it another was folded up, to be let down as the second bunk. There were some cupboards. On both sides of the train were pull-up glass windows with pull-down blinds, and slatted pull-up shutters. It had a little lobby in which was a hand-basin, an electric fan, a tin hip-bath, a shower and a loo. The entire decor, except for another electric fan and a mirror, was in brown stain, varnished. There was no corridor to the carriage. This I learned with some alarm, was to protect its occupants from dacoits and assassins who could otherwise enter the compartment during the night.

Kali produced from somewhere a feather duster and a cloth. With these he bustled about stirring up but generally removing acres of dust and sand from the seats and ledges. Having got it all on the floor he wetted it with water from the shower. A sweeper with a bundle of twigs as his broom was conjured up from somewhere and, for a small coin, the dust-and-water paste was swept out on to the track. It was my first glimpse of the caste system. Kali, a bearer, could not sweep. He suggested politely that I went on to the platform — to get out of his light, in fact. I did as I was bid.

Sometime later Kali approached and, having waited politely till I noticed him, asked me to come back to the carriage. There, the two porters were waiting patiently. Kali said 'You pay coolies, Sahib. One anna, each piece, normal price; you, Officer-Sahib, pay two. They ask four annas you no pay. You give me two rupees. I arrange.' I had acquired Indian money and so I gave him the two rupees. Then followed the most monumental verbal war that had ever come my way. To me, it seemed but a hairsbreadth as to who first would strike, or stab, whom. Either the porters together would join forces to strike Kali down or he, rising in wrath would annihilate the pair of them. Finally, the two porters shuffled off, muttering imprecations for the first few yards and then gradually easing up and finally laughing together as they got out of range. Kali solemnly handed me five annas change — I had paid out exactly two annas per piece, plus one anna for the sweeper.

I did not then recognise that one of the basic ground rules of our future relationship had been demonstrated. No one, but nobody, could be seen to overcharge me. Except Kali himself, if he could get away with it. Which he did courteously, charmingly and frequently — but not seriously. Indeed, he had probably extracted a small commission for himself from the porters.

Inside the compartment Kali had unpacked and hung up my clothes for the journey. He had selected a towel, two sheets and a blanket from the bedroll. He had found my wash-bag and had laid out brushes, comb, toothbrush, toothpaste and razor in the bathroom. He had found a book to put on the seat. Everything else that I possessed, save only my immediate needs, had vanished into some guard's van somewhere.

At last, perfectionist that he was, he stood back and checked his handiwork carefully before pronouncing judgement. 'Now Sahib will be all right. You give me twenty rupees. I get maund of ice when I bring lunch basket.' Meekly I handed over the money. I was learning fast. He beamed, bowed, and disappeared.

At last, all aboard, the great engine hissed and puffed as we pulled away from the quayside and the *Dorsetshire*. It was about eleven o'clock and I had visions of streaking across the Indian countryside which would look like . . . what? It was all exciting and stimulated the imagination.

The countryside was in no hurry to appear. We must have reached all of 10 mph during the ten minutes it took us to reach Karachi station from Karachi docks. We stopped. We were drawn up at a minor platform. For how long? No one seemed to know, or care. Troop-trains took priority below any other form of railway traffic. It was the first of many, many stops and waits in sidings while expresses, local puffers and even slow moving goods-trains went by. The normal eleven-hour journey stretched to over

60 hours. The sun beating down on the carriage roof was practically lifting the paint. The water came from a tank in the roof and was too hot for one's hand. That is, when there was any water, for it ran out frequently and at most halts we were not parked in the type of siding where it could be refilled. If we moved, it was at a snail's pace. Our splendid engine broke down once and another had to be fetched. Finally, days afterwards, we worked out that *Dorsetshire* and its magnificent nine knots had been significantly faster than the troop-train.

It was only much later, when I came to know the country better, that I appreciated just how many minor miracles Kali had worked. The 'maund of ice' turned out to be a block weighing 80 lbs, which he obtained somehow each morning. This he placed in the tin hip-bath and turned the electric fan on to it. The cool air was blissful. To prevent the air escaping he got an old newspaper which was pushed into every available crack around the window-frames and the door. It wasn't pretty but it certainly kept out both dust and the hot outside air. At midday and in the evenings, he achieved picnic baskets from the stations en route. The empties were handed in at the next station up the line. The fare was simple (nearly always scrawny chicken, freshly killed and very tough) and the bread was stale, but it was edible. Some officers said there were not enough baskets and they had to go hungry. Not so for me, for Kali always got me one. At night-time he courteously hoofed me out on to the platform, during one of the interminable stops, while he made my bed. In the morning he did the same thing in reverse. I shall never know how he did all this for three days and two nights, remaining clean, attentive and polite, from the higgledy-piggledy jam-packed mass of a third class carriage. And I thought I was hot, dirty, itchy, dusty and uncomfortable!

At one point, having seen the conditions considered good enough for the personal servants, I suggested to Kali that he might like to sit for a while with us in our comparatively cool and dust-free compartment. He was genuinely shocked. He explained, carefully, that ours was not, and could never be, bearers' accommodation. With a courteous 'Salaam, Sahib' he left.

Thus began a relationship which lasted for years and which, I am proud to say, developed into a mutual respect as valued as any in my career. It ended just before the outbreak of war when my squadron was sent to the Far East. Over a year later, wartime security notwithstanding, Kali heard a rumour that my squadron would be returning, landing at Bangalore on a certain day.

Bearers' jobs, with the fluidity of war, were hard to come by and even harder to retain. Nevertheless, he gave up his precious job, travelled 400 miles at his own expense to be on the airfield when the first aircraft touched down. As the crew climbed out, Kali said, 'Please Sahib, you tell me which is Dudgeon-Sahib's aircraft. I am his bearer and I am working for him.' He was holding my bicycle, which I had given to him when we took off for Singapore, and a small cage containing my best pair of racing pigeons. The answer Kali got tears my heart, even now: 'Dudgeon-Sahib is not with us now. He has gone to England.' Kali stared, disbelievingly for some moments. Quietly, he said, 'You please, one day, tell Dudgeon-Sahib I came for him.' Then Kali turned and walked slowly away, pushing my bicycle with the pigeon-cage hanging from the handlebars.

# Chapter 8
# The Boy

Some people have nicknames, and some do not. Nobody, or so I thought, ever gave me one — except, if it counts, the diminutive 'Tony' for my first name. It would have done me a power of good if I had known what the airmen called me behind my back. I was grossly over-conscious of my status as an officer in the King-Emperor's Royal Air Force; as a pilot in sole charge of a mighty military aeroplane, cleaving the skies over the magnificent Himalayan ranges, I felt omniscient and very adult. I must have been unbearable. It transpired recently that one of the gunners, LAC Bolton, had christened me 'The Boy' — it caught on with all the other airmen, and stuck immovably. Of course, compared to me he was quite old; he was 22 and I was barely 20.

The cure for my big-headedness on the ground was easy. My colleagues just kicked my backside till my throat was sore. The dangerous aspect was that I thought I knew a lot about flying, and up there I was unseen, out of touch — and denied the close guidance so sorely merited and needed. It would be another five years, and well into a major war, before I grasped this fundamental and essential truth: 'He who believes his airmanship is adequate will probably die.' As a pilot, you never know enough.

We were into the hot-weather routine and the unbroken heat was terribly enervating. During one period of three weeks the lowest that the temperature *fell* to was at 3 o'clock one morning — that figure was 92°F (33°C), and air-conditioning did not yet exist. We worked from 7 am to noon and again from 4.30 pm till it began to get dark. During the baking afternoons, when the shade temperatures were around 110°F (43°C), we tried to rest and sleep. It lent point to the old pilots' adage 'Birds and fools fly', usually completed by the adjunct 'Bats and bloody fools fly by night'.

At Risalpur two junior bachelor-officers shared a big four-roomed brick-built bungalow. Each had a nice spacious sitting-room with, leading off it, bedroom and bathroom. There was an electric ceiling-fan which stirred the hot air around, making it fractionally hotter, but it felt cooler. Its draught gave one a choice: to lie in bed with a damp towel over your tummy, which kept you wonderfully cool and gave you diarrhoea for some weeks till the stomach became inured to it, or you might pretend you were cool without the damp towel, and keep the stomach quiet. We had running water, from a tap, which came out so hot that you had to fill the tin hip-bath in the morning and let it cool by evaporation. Then you could get into it in the evening without breaking into a muck sweat. More correctly, my bearer Kali would run the water in; not me. I, Pilot Officer, aged 20, paid for and enjoyed the full- or part-time care of six servants.

First there was Kali who, as well as giving me a personal service the like of which I have never known before or since, was the major domo of my entourage. He ran my staff with a rod of iron. He kept my household accounts. I never had to go to the shops for he would always produce some dealer or another to sell me what I wanted, on my own verandah. Doubtless he levied a small commission from everybody, but the results were wonderful for me. Second, to help Kali I also employed a young boy, a *chokra*, who for a pittance seemed to do 90 per cent of the manual work. Third was the *dhobi*, a laundryman who flogged flat stones with my rolled-up wet and soapy clothes. This, over a period of time, may have demolished a fair number of shirts, singlets, pants, trousers and stockings but at least it was possible to change my sodden, sweaty, smelly clothes for clean ones four times a day: two uniforms (for the morning and for the afternoon) and two civilian outfits — one after work, and another for dinner in Mess. The fourth employee was the *mali* or gardener whom I shared with my colleague in the other half of the bungalow. Fifth, the night-watchman or *chowkidar* who was supposed to ward off burglars and assassins. In fact I know he slept a lot of the night when he wasn't making great hawking and spitting noises. At least, the noises confirmed that he was there most of the time. Perhaps the local thugs and bad lads considered it unsporting to remove my belongings, so long as I was stupid enough to pay a friend of theirs to sleep. Kali was quite crafty enough to engage a real assassin for me who needed a respectable post as his cover. Whatever the reason, the fact remains that I was never burgled. The sixth and last man, the lowliest but maybe not the least important, was the Sweeper. There were no drains and therefore no plugs to pull. The two main jobs for which I paid him were to empty my bath-tub and the thunder-box. He also 'looked after' my colleague next door. We had an unconfirmed suspicion that he supplemented his meagre income by making a deal with the local farmers concerning the fertilisers he had available.

Six people to look after one 20-year-old is maybe extravagant but the caste system prevented any one of them doing another's job. Also, there were many seekers for every post — and any job is better than none. It assuredly made life very easy for me.

All mornings began in the same way. Kali brought me a cup of tea to drink in bed whilst I heard him busying himself in the bathroom. In a few minutes he was back saying, 'Ready, Sahib'. I dragged myself sleepily off my sheet. The enamel basin on the washstand was full of warm water. On its left, the cake of soap. On its right my razor, of which he changed the blade every four days. Beside that my shaving brush with half an inch of shaving soap forced on to it from the tube. I never discovered why tubed shaving soap went rock-hard in the hot weather. Next, a glass of cool water and, lying across it, my toothbrush with a neat section of toothpaste balanced on its bristles. Behind me a freshly laundered towel. I shaved myself for it was not my habit, as with several others, to have the local barber come and shave me in bed as I clung to the last vestiges of sleep. Nor did I require Kali to wash my back while I was in the bath.

In about 20 minutes I was ready to dress, having sponged off the overnight sweatiness and become, comparatively speaking, clean. In the bedroom Kali had set out my clothes. My shirt was over the chair, rank badges already buttoned in place on the epaulettes. One stocking was over each chair-arm with the feet folded in for easy putting-on. Shorts on the chair seat. Gleaming black-polished shoes on the floor with the laces undone. Brush and comb, coins, wallet and clean hankerchief in a line on the dressing table. Kali only produced and filled my cigarette-case for evening wear, as I was a non-smoker.

Kali held my trousers out for me . . . . as a good bearer he tried to do all he could for 'his' sahib.

At around 6.30, when dawn was rushing up with its yellow and golden lights in the sky, Kali said, 'I go now'. He shot out of the room, grabbed my bicycle and pedalled swiftly away in the direction of the Mess I gathered up my belongings and sauntered out. The garden was suffering too from the heat. The grass, though regularly watered, was sere and dusty. The only bedding-plants to survive were a few zinnias although the bougainvillaea creepers rioted up the sides of the bungalow in a blaze of reds, yellows and purples. I paused to have words with the *mali*. My Urdu was still practically non-existent but I did my best to make favourable noises for his efforts to help the parched blooms and withered grass to survive. I strolled gently up to the Mess, hoping not to sweat too much too soon.

The Mess, our home-from-home in a British cantonment, might by type have been lifted straight off an English airfield, except that it did not contain the unmarried officers' sleeping quarters. Brick built, obviously to the design of a British architect, its only concessions to country and climate were the high rooms, the big windows and the electric fans to lessen the ravages of the heat. I crossed the lawn upon which, of an evening, we sipped our *chota-pegs* (a half-tot of whisky with soda) and *nimbu-panes* (pressed fresh limes with sugar and water) like all the sahibs all over India. In the dining room, Kali was standing holding the vacant chair he had selected for me to sit in. On the table was the plate of bacon and scrambled eggs (called, believe it or not, *Rumble Tumble Unda*) which he had collected from the kitchen, just as he saw me nearing the front door. In the toast-rack, two slices of freshly made toast, with the marmalade, and butter in a dish with ice to stop it melting. Also, a glass of iced coffee with just the right amount of sugar and milk already in it. All that remained, after breakfast, was to repossess my neatly parked bicycle, and pedal restrainedly down the road between the casuarina and pepper trees to the hangars and my place of work.

Hardly surprisingly I was becoming mentally idle. Kali tried his damnedest to be a perfect servant, and to think of everything for me. I did not have to lift a finger outside the hangars and, accordingly, my thinking-processes were going to sleep. I was, without realising it, being set up for big trouble. Two sharp and salutary lessons came in a fortnight, not long after my arrival. Both occurred on training flights. The first was because I did not make enough effort, and my Black Dog produced the other. The atmosphere set up the trouble, and lack of close supervision from my superiors ensured that I dragged it down upon myself like a ton of bricks.

On 31 July, 1936, there was a training programme, primarily for the gunners. That is, the technicians who doubled up as rear-gunners. They were to 'shoot' with a camera-gun at a white-painted pyramid on the ground, built for the purpose, about forty miles distant — say twenty minutes' flying time — near a village called Akora. I saw on the notice-board that I was detailed last to use the aircraft and my gunner for the trip was LAC Leslie. Meanwhile, I could kick my heels around the tarmac and flight offices till my turn came. I was not bored. I could sit for hours on the tarmac with my back against a hangar door, studying and envying the sparrows and kites which flew so effortlessly and precisely, as I longed to do.

When my aircraft landed, I collected Leslie and my parachute. We walked out together, discussing the exercise. He told me: 'You know, Sir, I've never tried this air-to-ground camera-gun before. As you fly past the target it appears from under the wing, and then I've got to get the gun lined up, aimed and get my shot in, all in a few seconds. So, Sir, if you could fly past slowly, and as low as possible, and not too close, I could get the best results for my training record. If they're good enough this time, I won't have to do a repeat.' I nodded sagely, failing to admit that my inexperience was equal to his — it was my first time too.

The Hawker Harts used in India had three fuel tanks. Two fairly small ones in the top wing and a main tank in the fuselage, just in front of the pilot's knees. The pilot flying before me mentioned casually, as he climbed out without stopping the engine, that all three tanks had been partly used. No one of them, he said, had enough fuel to complete the exercise, but he reckoned it could be managed between the three of them. Only one had a fuel gauge — the main tank. It was a little rod with a bobble on its top which stuck up just in front of the windscreen; it was elementary and woefully inaccurate. Misguidedly accepting the previous pilot's word, we climbed in and started up, although the bobble was near the bottom, saying 'nearly empty'. The crackly roar of the stub exhausts as we took off was, as always, marvellous. Leslie folded his arms on the Scarff gun-mounting behind me and, using my head to shield him from the slipstream, watched over my shoulder.

It looked as though there was just enough fuel in the main tank to do the exercise once we had got there, and get home again. So, we would fly out on one or both of the top tanks and, when we got there, change to the 'main'. This way, when we were flying low, slow, and at greatest risk, we would be flying on the tank with the most fuel. In hindsight, my plan was sound so far as it went, but where it went was not far enough. Also, in hindsight, it could have been an equally somnolent flight commander who let his least experienced pilot go off with no pre-briefing, with three nearly empty tanks, and no way of telling even approximately how much was in two of them. The outcome was not inevitable, but almost predictable.

Blissfully happy with the drug of piloting, I headed for the target. I knew it was near a dried up rivulet leading into the Kabul River, a muddy river which could be traced on a map all the way back to Kabul in Afghanistan, and from which city it took its name. I studied the map carefully. Soon the great brown flow of the main stream came into view ahead. On its far side were the craggy Attock hills, dark ochre and uninviting. I thought about (but should not have) the partridge-like *chikkor* to be walked-up and shot. Delicious eating, I was assured. Also the *mugger* — crocodiles — to be stalked from the banks of the muddy Kabul and its mother, the Indus. To be stalked with infinite care and silence until the scaly knobbly reptile was well positioned. Then, for the kill, a bullet from a service Lee-Enfield rifle on loan from the Guardroom. The fascinating difficulty was that the *mugger* were always very close to the water. Even using every scrap of cover it was almost impossible to get near enough to drop them stone dead. If they heard the slightest sound, or even though the shot had wounded them gravely — two paces, one wriggle and slosh, into the river and they were gone forever.

At last the white pyramid appeared beside the dry stream-bed. Interesting scenery, and speculation, had totally supplanted fuel management in my mind. And Kali was not there to do my thinking for me. Leslie took up his stance and lined up the camera gun. I concentrated on positioning the target well for him — not too fast, not too close, and not too high. Low-flying is a marvellous thrill. The ground and the dusty green bushes sweep past. You can ride around or, should you prefer it, over the top of a bush or tree. You sense *speed* and things happen quickly. It is exciting — and damnably dangerous. You have no *time*! It is totally forbidden except for special tasks and it needs most careful briefing beforehand.

When the tank in the top wing ran dry, and the engine failed, my instant thoughts were fast and accurate. There is nothing like a bad crash in the offing to sharpen up the intellect and accelerate one's reactions. Instantly I leaned forwards and whipped the fuel-tank selector round from 'wing' to 'main'. At the same time I turned the aircraft slightly, towards the flattest space that I could see — the ridged and rocky bed of the stream. Low and slow, there was nothing else to do. I spent the remaining five to seven seconds cursing myself for an unmitigated idiot and shouting to Leslie to hang on and brace for the coming impact. I didn't think of, or have time to pray, but I hoped wildly that the carburettor was being refilled in time for the power to surge on before we hit. My hopes, unsurprisingly, were not realised.

I held off as long as I could and until she dropped right out of my hands. There was a brief period of crunches, graunches, thumps, rending metal, wires twanging and lurches before the aircraft was stationary on its belly in the stream bed. The propeller was splintered, the wings were warped and torn, the undercarriage had collapsed drunkenly to one side. Leslie and I, to my amazement, were unhurt. We were both very lucky.

I matured a lot in that quarter-minute. That is not to say I suddenly became a grown man and a wise pilot, but I took a large step forwards in that direction. And, too, a smaller step back from being a young lad playing with a wonderful and expensive toy.

My Flight Commander was very displeased with me, and so was the Squadron Commander. The Station Commander, however, was astonishingly generous. He was a little man, spare and with a pinched face, sandy hair and a clipped toothbrush moustache. I never remember him taking to the air in the pilot's cockpit, even though his chestful of medals showed he had gone right through World War I. He emphasised in his report that it was my first hot weather and the temperatures had been debilitating. He pointed up my inexperience, the ease of making such a mistake in all the circumstances and he directed that no further action should be taken against me. This, from the point of view of punishment, let me off completely.

When his report reached Air Headquarters in Delhi, they fairly jumped with rage. They pointed out (correctly) that I had been inexcusably incompetent, in that (correctly) I had mismanaged the fuel system, which (correctly) was an offence, which (correctly) ought to be punished, hot weather or no. They expressed great regret that my boss had pre-empted punishment and, though I was wholly to blame, had let me off. Once again, my good luck had held.

The second lesson came only five days later. This was a lesson in character, rather than in airmanship. It demonstrated for me that the world is not run by machines but by people — and people can be unpredictable, inconsistent, unfair — and sometimes downright wrong.

The Station Commander had decided that we should practise air-to-air attacks, as laid down in the Manual of Air Combat. Later, in World War II the scenario was shown to be sheer lunacy — but that was what the printed manual, written for World War I, said. One flight of three Harts would be playing at Bombers, and a flight of three from the other squadron would play Fighters.

First, one lone aeroplane would fly, in broad daylight, at a reduced speed, straight and level at 10,000 ft. This was 'The Bomber'. The flight of three fighters would approach from behind in close formation and pretend to fire their single, fixed, forward-firing machine gun. Then the flight would turn away. This completed Exercise 1. In real life, if the idiot bomber held still long enough, the attacking leader might fire. For his wing-men it would be impossible because you cannot hold your aircraft in the formation position, and at the same time point it at an enemy. The one contradicts the other. But no matter; that was what was written in the good book. In any case the question was academic since we had no forward-mounted camera-guns to prove the point.

Following on after the first 'attack', two Harts which had been standing off would pick up station on the lone bomber to make an Enemy Formation! The performance would then be repeated, formation attacking formation. And that would be it for the day.

In the gunner's cockpit of the leading bomber would be the Station Commander himself, seeing all and judging the Effectiveness of his Fighting Force, he hoped. My flight commander suggested, uncharitably, that he would helpfully provide a box for him to stand on, so that at least he would be able to see out over the Scarff gun-mounting.

Much of the pre-flight briefing for the crews was taken up with deciding how the bombers should comport themselves to be sure that they could be found by the fighters, without which there would be no attack. Being employed as a bomber pilot, cherishing a fervid intention of doing my best to avoid fighters, this seemed odd to me. Nevertheless, being a very junior cog, who was I to comment? In truth, having no radio, and as radar was uninvented, a bomber once lost to a fighter might never be seen again. And if the Station Commander wanted to play fighters with his bombers, it was not for me to reason why. I was slotted as one of the stand-off aircraft for the second pass. There was no job for a gunner but an LAC O'Connor, an Irishman, came along behind me for the ride.

The day was perfect. The silver aircraft with their coloured roundels and scarlet squadron markings looked beautiful as always, contrasting with the patchwork of little fields creeping past, two miles underneath us.

The first attack was as expected. The fighter flight came in and sat patiently in tidy formation behind the bomber, long enough for all three to have been shot down if, instead of the Station Commander, there had been a gunner in the target aircraft. Then the fighters pulled away and the target leader waggled his wings as a signal for us to approach into close formation. I began to come down and edge in towards him, quite gently. I concentrated totally on my leader but, with other aeroplanes in the sky nearby, a better pilot would have taken some time to keep a look-out all round. My Black Dog snarled and grabbed his chance to savage me to death. With about 50 yards still to go, there was an almighty bang and my machine promptly dived steeply towards the ground, two miles below.

I fought with the controls. I found I could hold the aircraft straight but nothing on earth would bring the stick back to raise the nose and arrest the dive. The elevators were jammed. With my left hand I tried to turn the tail-trimming wheel located below the throttle. This normally balances the aircraft by moving the whole tailplane but it seemed solid and I couldn't shift it. I closed the throttle, put both hands on the stick, my feet up on the bulkhead before me, and heaved for all I was worth. Still no dice. The machine continued its steady and nerve-racking dive. I grabbed the speaking tube and said to O'Connor 'She's going into the deck! Bale out!' To my horror he just said 'No, Sir. I'm not going to bale out. No.' This time I screamed the order down the tube but he was completely adamant. No bale-out for him. I screwed my head round to look at him. He peered back through his goggles. Deliberately and definitely he shook his head. 'No!' Then, as a helpful afterthought he picked up the speaking-tube and offered to stand up in the back while he pulled the ripcord. This would have wrapped his parachute round the tailplane spelling certain death for him and, if the aircraft went out of control, probably for me too. What I said is unprintable but he clearly gathered it was an unpopular suggestion and he abandoned the idea.

I thought for a few moments but time was fast running out. My lunatic passenger's hesitation had cost us dearly. We were already at 5000 ft, over half way down to the ground. We needed to be over the side before 2000 ft to give time for the parachutes to open. If he saw me clambering out, would he come to his senses and do the same? But, somehow, I simply couldn't metaphorically shrug my shoulders, and leave him to his own devices — although I felt he deserved it.

I let go of the stick and put both hands to my left to try another, stronger, heave on the tail-trimmer. It moved a tiny bit. Heave again . . . mightily. It moved a little more and the dive seemed to flatten slightly. Little by little and with sweat pouring down inside my shirt I managed to get her back to a level keel. And then, with judicious use of throttle, up into a slight climb. Gingerly, I turned towards home. We had been down below 1000 ft.

Fortunately I had ample fuel and so could unwind my tangled nerves and take stock quietly. By loosening my straps and craning my neck round I saw that the tailplane was distorted on its right hand side; its end was bent down and this accounted for the jammed elevators. What had caused the damage I had no idea — and O'Connor was not now on speaking terms with me, or perhaps he was mentally unplugged.

One of the other aircraft swung into formation beside me and I could see the pilot and gunner peering at my tailplane and making futile gestures, apparently trying to draw my attention to it. As if I had not noticed. There was nothing on earth that he could do to help me so I zogged him (using hand gestures to convey letters in morse code) a short message: 'TELL THEM STICK JAMMED'. The pilot nodded, put his nose down and went hell for leather towards home. I grinned at the vision of the turmoil on the airfield after he landed with the story. Just like digging a spade into an ants' nest.

I began to experiment and determine to what extent the machine was, in actual fact, flyable. The stick would move normally from side to side, but for up and down it was rock solid. I could move the tail-trimmer, but only by leaning down to my left and dragging on the little wheel with both hands; no landing was possible whilst doing that. A semi-controlled crash on our airfield, with buildings, hangars and thirty-foot casuarina trees on two sides, seemed at best an unwelcome prospect — and could be fatal. But, with a back-seat passenger who refused to bale out, what else? I tried some more. Using both hands, I experimented to find the setting which would give me the slowest speed for the likely crash to come. There was a middle position where she was flying level at half throttle; I could lose height gently with a little

*No. 11 Squadron, polished, gleaming and lined up ready for inspection on the airfield at Risalpur.*

*The author's aircraft, spruced up and ready for inspection. Even the tyres were polished!*

*Author's error. This shows the folly of forgetting to change the fuel tanks in good time when doing a low-level rear-camera-gun exercise. The camera-gun is the black tubular device seen behind the upper wing.*

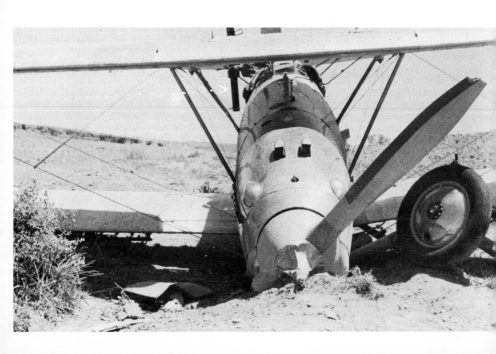

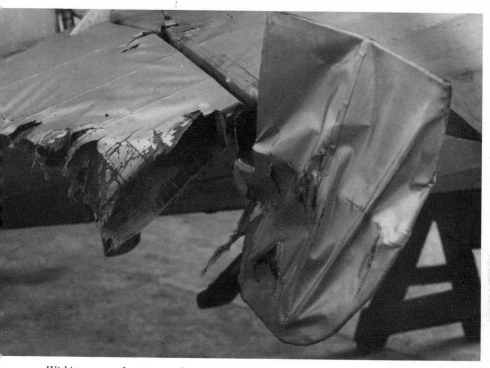

*Within an ace of a catastrophic two-aircraft accident. The wingtip of a following aircraft touched the tailplane of this one. It totally jammed the fore-and-aft control and this aircraft very nearly dived into the ground from 10,000 feet.*

*Coming in to land over the casuarena and pepper trees, towards the airfield to the right of this picture.*

*Flying Officer Johnny Betts, misguidedly, responded to our teasing that he played his flying over-safely, and landed too far up the airfield. **Good** pilots, we suggested, came in close over the trees and landed short. He tried it. He came in just too slow and hit the trees on the airfield's edge. He climbed out of this mess and offered to give me a black eye to match the one he had just received.*

When some tribes were considered by our political masters to be getting obstreperous, we were called upon to do a demonstration-flight over their area, in the hopes of persuading them to behave. We flew backwards and forwards over these hills for about three hours – and then went home.

Although No. 11 Squadron was a bomber squadron, Gerald Elsmie, Mad-Wally Rowbottom and a few others were endlessly trying to perfect our formation flying – the province of fighters. It always looks so easy, and is so difficult, particularly with no radio to facilitate advice and criticism. A 'Box of Four'.

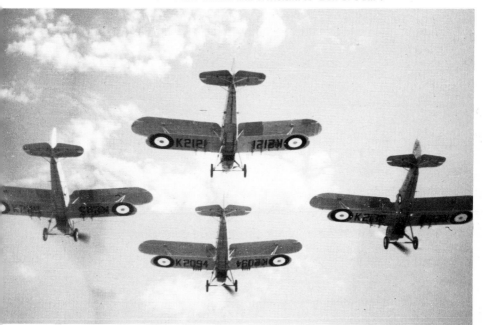

*Four aircraft over tribal territory, enlivening a boring reconnaissance by practising flying in 'Line Abreast', about 2 to 3 ft apart.*

*Mad-Wally tucks in to very close formation on the way back from a bombing sortie.*

*Supplies of bombs are trucked in by road, escorted by armoured-cars. The armoured cars were ordinary civilian Rolls-Royce chassis, with stronger springs and puncture-proof tyres – World-War I vintage – and fitted with 5 tons of armour-plate, machine guns and ammunition. They were still in use in World War II – at Habbaniya.*

*Bombs being winched up from their store underneath Miranshah Fort.*

*Part of the flight-leader's bomb-load. On the left, two 20-lb bombs used as 'sighters' to get the aim right. On the right, one 250-lb bomb, the other 250-lb bomb is under the other wing.*

*The local Wazir tribesmen used to come to the airfield quite frequently, hoping to sell us some of their out-of-date weapons and armour. Flight Sergeant Graham is holding an ancient muzzle-loader banded with silver. In his right hand is a particularly vicious weapon closely resembling a baby scythe. At his feet is a shirt of chain-mail whilst on his right a Wazir offers a studded leather shield.*

less power and climb slowly with a some more. Were throttle movements alone going to be enough to attempt a landing? The only way to find out was to suck it and see. The Bible mentions Faith, Hope and Charity. Faith was not strong. Charity towards O'Connor was absolutely zero; why in blazes should I risk my neck for this poltroon? Hope was the only thing left.

I started by going a long, long way back from the airfield and lining up to come in over the edge which had only a small ditch and no obstructions sticking up to catch me on the way in. Admittedly this approach took me towards the trees and buildings, but I presumed that by the time I hit them I would be going pretty slowly — if she wasn't wrapped into a small ball on the airfield before that. Very delicately I throttled back and began to lose height. We were on our way. Just as it did the week before, the prospect of a bad crash fairly pumped in the adrenalin. I felt the palms of my hands get sticky and a little trickle of sweat was running down between my shoulder blades.

It took me two tries to make it. On the first go we had not touched down by half way across the airfield, so power was slammed on for our miserable climb. We cleared the trees on the far side by a whisker, but we did manage to achieve a second shot. This time we just skimmed over the boundary ditch and the throttle was snatched shut as the wheels touched. It seemed forever before the tailskid grounded and, as it did so, I could begin to apply the wheel-brakes. We came to a standstill, in one piece. When my breathing had returned to normal I picked up the speaking tube. 'If there is another time,' I said, unkindly, 'when I say "go", you go. If you're not gone in five seconds, you'll be on your own. I'll go without you. Be warned.' O'Connor made no reply but he had the grace to look sheepish.

As I turned towards the hangars I could see that the news of a possible spectacle had gone round like wildfire. Practically the entire station complement had ghoulishly come out to watch the crash. Now, they were filtering disappointedly away, as there was no excitement. Excepting one person, that is. I was gratified to see that the Station Commander himself was to be my reception committee. Egotistically, I was flattered that the great man had observed how the life of my passenger had been saved by a practical demonstration of skill and competence. I parked the aircraft, climbed out, and waited smilingly for the applause.

His face was puce and he was angry beyond belief. At first he was incoherent but I soon began to get the message. 'You bloody young fool!' he shouted. I was dutifully silent, unbelievingly watching his bright blue eyes at about the level of my nipples. 'It was all your fault and I could see it perfectly. You stalled backwards into the flight behind and caused No. 2's wingtip to strike your tailplane. By the grace of God alone his machine is undamaged and we have avoided a disaster. But, no thanks to you! You are wholly to blame for this accident and I am initiating disciplinary action against you.' With that he stormed off, leaving me alone and lonely on the airfield's edge, with my mouth open. Everyone else, prudently was otherwise engaged.

I never did see what the great man wrote to Air Headquarters. But I did see their answer, following only a few days after the previous one. It was, I felt, incredibly magnanimous considering how they had bemoaned being unable to have me hung, drawn and quartered with my head delivered on a charger for the incident less than a week before. They said:

'The commander of the Attacking Flight says he saw Pilot Officer Dudgeon's aircraft taking up position ahead of him whilst he was inadvertently overtaking the slower-flying Targets. It is the inescapable responsibility of an overtaking aircraft to keep clear of the one in front. All the commander of the Attacking Flight had to do was to dive slightly in order to take his flight completely clear. Also, no aircraft in this command flies backwards, stalled or not.

'We must accept the Station Commander's statement, because he was in an ideal position to see what happened, so his report can stand. However, no action is to be taken against Pilot Officer Dudgeon and no entry will be made in his records.'

All in all, it was a very generous statement and my luck had held.

Again I matured, quickly. The Station Commander had had every reason to have been frightened; he had missed losing two aeroplanes and four people just by a hairsbreadth. It showed me, early, how a man who has had a very narrow escape and been scared to death can react in an amazingly unexpected manner.

I took singular care not to get anywhere near the Station Commander for a very, very long time.

# Chapter 9
# Frontier Force

How right my bosses were not to let me loose over 'The Frontier' proper before I had made my mistakes over the comparative safety of the plains! The tribal areas contained some savage additional risks. Only gradually, as I learned something of the Frontier essentials (such as accurate, reliable map-reading and navigation, so that I should never stray over to Afghanistan and cause a diplomatic incident) was I allowed to poke my nose, closely supervised, over Tribal Territory. This mountainous area, peopled largely by Pathans, lies up in the top left-hand corner of the Indian sub-continent. It began about 50 miles to the west of the airfield and went on from there to the Afghan border.

The Pathans are primarily farmers. They are blood-brothers to the Afghans and just as fiercely independent. Family and tribal disagreement is often settled by bullet or the sword; you might say that war is a hobby of theirs. In their chosen *metier* of mountain skirmishing, they are most adept protagonists. When we, the British, held sway in India we felt we should be responsible for keeping the peace — not exactly a popular move with the Pathans. Initially our Army, both British and Indian, held this responsibility. In the event of trouble a punitive column would be sent up into the mountains to put down the rising. They would march along the valleys, sending protective patrols up to the hilltops at the front; these would then come down and rejoin at the rear when the column had moved forwards. The final objective was to touch the pockets of the malefactors in the affected tribal areas — burning crops, destroying buildings, or exacting fines of money and rifles. Of these penalties, losing rifles was what hurt the Pathans most — their lives depended upon them.

These Army columns were not viewed by the Pathans as entirely disadvantageous. The cumbersome column of troops was a delightful target for skirmishers, and they used the mountains adroitly for cover. Moreover, an occasional protective patrol might be ambushed successfully and their rifles taken as booty — marvellous long-lasting Lee-Enfield rifles of phenomenal accuracy and which were worth hundreds of rupees. Not like the locally manufactured copy Lee-Enfields. Old railway-lines could be re-wrought to produce weapons indistinguishable from an original — on the surface; even down to the serial number and the Government broad-arrow on each one. However, railway steel was, in comparison, like cheese. The rifling was gone after the first 15 to 20 rounds had been fired — and without it all hope of any accuracy was gone too.

During the 1920s Air Chief Marshal Sir Hugh Trenchard, then Chief of the Air Staff, dreamed up the idea of using the Air Force as a method of keeping the peace. Simply, this was 'Control without Occupation.' The objective was essentially the same — touch the pockets of the malefactors. The use of aircraft was simple, just as effective, and much cheaper.

First, the political authorities decided that such and such a tribal area would be proscribed. Leaflets were dropped saying that any person or animal in the area would be attacked — and aircraft patrolled the area, keeping above the range of rifle bullets, from then on. The tribesmen couldn't farm. The crops were unsown or rotted. They lost money. Naturally, they did not risk people or animals for no return, so they moved to the areas next-door. This was not popular with the neighbours and added additional pressures for capitulation. Mostly, it was only a question of time before success came.

For some reason, probably the British tendency to understatement, the mighty ranges of mountains separating India from Persia, Afghanistan, Russia, China and Tibet were always called 'The Hills', even though these 'hills' rose to the eternal snows. The tribesmen's villages were in the valleys and their fields went up as high as the crops could be persuaded to survive. Each tribe lived in the valley and sub-valleys of a particular river and its tributaries. Flying over the crest of a hill took you above the area of another tribe. Two or three times a month we made 'reconnaissance flights', criss-crossing the areas.

The term 'reconnaissance of the tribal area' was only a figure of speech. To avoid damage from rifle fire and the possible loss of an aircraft we were not supposed to fly below 3000 ft from the ground. So there was nothing detailed to see; just the hills, a few fields and the occasional village underneath. Nevertheless, the vistas were magnificent, especially in January and February when the occasional rainstorm cleared the dust haze. Stretching as far as the eye could see were line after line of valleys and ridges, rising gently to massive snow-fields and crests in the distance. Most of the ground was in many shades of brown, except for vivid little patches of green crops in the appropriate season. A few of the lower hills had flattish tops but the majority were razor-backed.

The villages, tucked away in the bottoms of the valleys, were little clusters of drab brown houses made from mud bricks. They clustered together like boiled sweets in a glass jar. As evidence of the warlike nature of the inhabitants, every fourth or fifth building had its fighting tower. These, square in shape, stuck up twice or three times as high as the dwellings. The entire first storey was solid, giving the tower great strength. Above the level of the house roofs were the slits through which the rifles could be aimed. On its top, a low wall gave these farmers protection and concealment, coupled with a first-class all-round field of fire.

Although we flew above the range of rifle fire almost all the time, we were not out of danger. The consequences of an engine failure over tribal territory were not attractive.

The tribesmen were Muslims and true believers. They looked forward to the joys of Paradise after death. Not least of the pleasures in their Paradise are the ten thousand Houris who care for the inhabitants through all eternity. Houris are desirable maidens, black-eyed like a gazelle and possessed of perpetual youth and beauty. They provide foods, drinks and sweetmeats of surpassing flavour whilst cooling their charges with perfumed fans. If anyone craves more exotic delights, no wish will be refused and their virginity is renewable at pleasure. Another part of the belief was that you arrived to spend eternity, physically, as you left the earth below. This had its disadvantages for us unbelievers.

As the farmers became pretty frustrated by punishment with no sporting war to compensate, their resentment could be expressed harshly. We know that in the twenties they handed over a downed crew to the women of the tribe. They, with due care, removed what are known in colloquial French as the *bijoux de famille* — the family jewels. One portion was sewn into the man's mouth and other two were for sewing into his eye-sockets. Naturally, as the men would enter Paradise as they left the earth, the women took considerable pains to ensure they did not die before the operations were complete. This made certain that in spite of the best ministrations of any houris around, they were booked for a pretty rotten eternity — unable to eat, unable to speak, unable to see — and due for nothing else of much importance.

We, the aircrew, thought it would be both prudent and practical to dye our hair red. A red beard on a Muslim indicates that its owner has made the much desired pilgrimage to Mecca and, by kissing the Black Stone, has booked his passage to Paradise on an irrevocable ticket. We did not expect to be taken for Muslims — beards in the Royal Air Force were forbidden — but the maybe apocryphal story of a red-headed air gunner gave us hope. He had fallen in tribal territory and was handed over to the female villagers for treatment. It struck the ladies, however, that one or more red-headed male children were infinitely desirable. Not only would they make Paradise without fail but the pecking order for the mother of such a child would be astronomically elevated. So the gunner was put to stud.

It was more or less agreed that the unfortunate (or fortunate?) individual finally died. History did not specify precisely how or why he met his end. Nevertheless, we randy young pilots felt that such a death would be preferable to one from straight and sudden surgery.

At the time I was there, each aircraft carried, in a sealed pocket between the cockpits on the outside of the fuselage, a 'Protection Certificate'. It was known universally as a 'goolie chit' (goolie in Urdu=ball). This, written in Urdu, Pushtu and Persian, promised rupees beyond the dreams of avarice if the aircrew were brought in and handed over. There would be a significant reduction of cash if they were found to be emasculated, or dead, or both. Since the tribesmen could neither read nor write, we were not too sanguine as to its efficiency and thought that red hair would be a cheap and useful insurance policy. If nothing else, we hoped we could perform long enough for help to be forthcoming. The Squadron Commander (who hardly ever flew) was adamant — no synthetic redheads.

It did not escape us that a sealed and painted-down packet on the fuselage was a very stupid place to have such a vital document. One might have to bale out, the aircraft might burn, the crew might get separated if one was injured. I still do not know any good reason why a certificate should not have been sewn into the back-pad of each of our parachutes. Our pleas for this change fell on deaf ears. Perhaps it was a legacy from the olden days when parachutes were considered undesirable; the pilot was expected to try and save his damaged or burning machine at any cost, even if it killed him. The poor reason given was that the goolie-chit cash was paid out on sight, even if its bearer merely said he had a crewman to bring in — if he got paid first. So, it was contended that someone might steal a parachute, but they were unlikely to steal an aircraft. As any thief who got into the hangar could rip open the pocket and slip away with the chit, leaving the aeroplane behind, we were not impressed.

The question of getting down with the aircraft, and its precious chit, assumed crucial importance. Discussions waxed lengthy and heated. They began with the axiom that amongst the hills and over little winding streams with patchwork fields, a safe landing was impossible; a crash was inevitable. The problem was simply put: how to survive it and preferably how to stay uninjured? The main hope was that you could glide down on to some more or less flat spot, however small; you would drop the machine, like a pancake, from around twenty feet as slowly as possible. This would collapse the undercarriage, break the propeller, bend the wings — but the outfit would slither to a standstill in ten to twenty yards, you hoped. If you couldn't find any flat spot, the proposals became more hair-raising.

My reasoning was that if there was nothing flat enough on which to flatten it, the chances were that it would roll and slide down the slope or cragside till it reached the bottom. By which time the occupants, meaning the gunner and me, might be in a pretty parlous state. Therefore, after engine failure I would glide down to get as low and as slow as possible near the bottom of a ravine without losing full control. Then, down would go one wing which would slide into the hillside. If Allah was kind, the aircraft would cartwheel along the rocks — wing, engine, other wing, tail and last of all, me. By which time I hoped we would be travelling fairly slowly and, secondly, would not have too far to slide down till we reached the bottom.

Several of my colleagues favoured a more spectacular arrival. This was to dive down the side of the valley and then pull up to climb the other slope — preferably very steep. Speed would fall off rapidly and then, at the last moment, the aircraft would drop on to the slope when almost stationary. They remained convinced that sufficient of its rear-end would dig into the rocks to prevent it sliding and tumbling, over and over, down to the river. I was far from convinced on this latter point; also, could he get up enough speed in his dive to avoid flying slap into the hill in front? All this without engine in a manoeuvre never before attempted . . . it would need a very fancy piece of judgement indeed.

Mad Wally, of course, came up with the most scatterbrained idea of all. He seriously proposed, if he had engine failure over really difficult country, to make his gliding approach upside-down. Then, he claimed, the top wing would dig in and the machine would flip over, right way up and facing the other way. There he would be, he said, sitting comfortably and unhurt in his cockpit, ready to climb out in leisurely and composed fashion. There were no other takers.

Messrs Rolls Royce did us proud. In the four years that two squadrons of Harts flew round the frontier, we suffered only one engine failure over Tribal Territory. Of course, it had to be Mad Wally. Luckily for his gunner he was not over bad country. He was right at the edge where the hills were flattening out.

We were flying home from a reconnaissance, led by Flight Lieutenant 'Jonah' Jones. Wally and I were flying to his left and right side respectively. Suddenly, I saw Wally's prop slow down and he immediately dropped below and turned away. For ten to fifteen seconds I tried to attract Jonah's attention but he had his head 'in the office', so I too dropped away to follow Wally and pin-point where he hit. Later, Jonah said that when he looked up and took a casual glance right and left to see if we were OK, he first thought he must be dreaming when both sides were empty. His next thought was one of utter rage as he muttered 'What are those two crazy bloody fools up to now?'.

I waited with alarmed interest for Wally to slow roll on to his back and was much relieved when he did not do so. With considerable skill he set up his glide approach for a flattish spot between two streams in the foothills. Instead of pancaking in, he made a spirited attempt to put down a proper landing. And, what is more, he came within an ace of doing so. By exceedingly bad luck, right at the very end of his touch-down run, his lower right-hand wingtip hit a thorn bush which swung the machine round sharply. The undercarriage collapsed from the sideways strain and the aircraft tipped up on its nose. As I circled the crash I saw, joy of joys, the two crew climb out apparently unhurt. Then Wally climbed back into the cockpit, stood up and, as I flew by, semaphored with his arms the letters 'O-K'. I waggled my wings to show I had got it before racing off to drop a message on the nearest Army encampment, giving his location and summoning help urgently.

Wally was picked up and brought in to the Army camp before dark. He said his instant action after signalling OK to me was to take out the goolie chit and put it in his pocket. He could see tribesmen in the distance and approaching at a run. He was surprised and not a little relieved when they turned out to be very curious — and amicable.

Being Wally, he tried to get a percentage commission from the Government for not having nervously thrust the goolie chit into the grasping paw of the first tribesman to approach — thus, he contended, he had saved the authorities large sums of money, and he deserved a reward. Hardly surprisingly, that bird did not fly.

Wally's crash was officially described as 'a good forced-landing in difficult country' and he had to be content with that.

# Chapter 10
# Proscription

RAF Church used to be compulsory. Church, that is, for all who belonged to the Church of England denomination. Sunday Church *Parade* was for everybody — atheist, agnostic or otherwise — and after Parade the outcasts would be sent away, ostensibly to their own places of worship. Having got everybody lined up and inspected for immaculate turnout, in best uniform with medals, the command would be given 'Fall out Roman Catholics and Jews' (except for one splendid day when the words came out 'Roam out Fallen Catholics and Jews) and those so qualified would be excused joining in our devotions.

In the 1930s, as the result of World War I everybody with any length of service had medals. Sometimes even now, at a Memorial Service for example, when the congregation responds to the words 'Let us pray' there is the delicate chink of chest-metal as an elderly sea of blue-clad forms kneels in unison. My first burning ambition was to be a qualified Service pilot but my second and almost equal ambition was to have two medals, so that I also chinked. I was fortunate in that I achieved my second ambition while I was still a Pilot Officer.

On the Frontier, if our station took part in operations, everybody got a campaign medal. If you spent only one day on a station at 'war' you qualified. It was known as the 'Sweeper Medal' because everybody, but everybody, got it. Staff officers from Delhi used to come and visit a station 'on ops' for a day, if they had not got the medal already. Sweeper Medal it might be — but it chinked like any other.

Wars begin in August or September and have done so since time immemorial, everywhere. That is when the crops are in, money is available and food stocks are at their best. The Frontier tribesmen were no exception to this rule. One tribe would attack another, or re-open some blood feud, or hijack a post-lorry, or (most frequently) unearth some religious reason. Any excuse would do. Often, as a result, the political agents for the area, after entreaties and fruitless threats, would call upon us for help.

Although the word 'war' has been used, it is barely appropriate. Everything was done in a very gentlemanly manner. The first step, usually, was to proscribe or deny the area belonging to a tribe. The usual leaflets would be dropped saying that the valley being farmed by the wrongdoers would be patrolled from dawn some two or three days hence. After that, any living thing found in the valley could be attacked. Everyone had plenty of time to get clear.

The tribesmen were not stupid. They got out, and stayed out, with all their herds, women and children. Meanwhile, to economise on hours and effort, we would move to some nearby airfield deep into Tribal Territory. It would have a substantial fort on its edge and an ample garrison of soldiery to protect us. At night we, the aircraft and the soldiery, would be bundled inside the steel doors of the fort for safe keeping. Apart from the odd bullet whistling over the fort at night, fired by some indignant tribesman, life was very placid. It wasn't very expensive compared to sending out an Army column to gain the same end. Nobody got hurt. Once, in four years, I saw a creature in a proscribed area. It was a grey donkey. The unfortunate beast was trying to find food in a very parched and inhospitable area. And who the blazes wants to kill an inoffensive donkey which has had the misfortune to drop its halter or slip its hobble? I made some dives and fired a few front-gun rounds fairly near it. It paid not the slightest attention and merely swished its tail. Then I went away for half an hour and when we came back it had vanished. Obviously some brave owner, holed up in a cave for the day, had made a swift dash to get it out of sight. My gunner agreed that for our sortie report we would forget it had existed.

At the end of a sortie we were encouraged to fire our guns at blank and imaginary targets in the area, just to remind the tribesmen that we were there for business.

Flying round and round up there, three hours each sortie, day after day, week after week was excruciatingly boring. Particularly as the proscribed areas were comparatively small. Smaller usually than, say, London Airport. Imagine flying backwards and forwards over Heathrow (or even driving a car, when you would see much more detail) three hours every day for six weeks? And with no living thing to watch and nothing useful to do? I got through several novels, and the sight of a grey donkey made it a red-letter day.

All this does not mean that we did not see tribesmen. They paid us the remarkable compliment of believing that we knew what we were about, and that we kept our word. They knew perfectly well which valley was taboo and that its boundary was the crest at the top of the slope. Five yards down the other side was safe ground. So they would squat up there like a row of swallows with rifles, sitting on a telegraph wire, just on their side of the crest, so that they were as close to us as possible in the hope of getting a pot-shot. Sometimes we would fire a burst in front of them, just on our side of the crest; they didn't even take a pace back, and usually fired at us hopefully as we pulled up and away. It was all very sporting and fairly harmless.

It was discovered early on that our tribesmen farmers were evading our embargo on farming; they were working at night. An answer was quickly forthcoming — long-delay fuses on bombs. The delays were for several periods — two hours, four hours, twelve hours and so on; whatever you chose that would meet the case. The fuses were made with a glass phial of acid and a copper strip. Dropping the bomb broke the phial and when the acid had eaten the copper, Bingo! Up she went. The fuses were pretty hit-and-miss affairs. The delay often was anything from half to three times the advertised figure. It was not at all unusual on a sortie to see one of yesterday's bombs suddenly explode in the area. We thought the 24-hour delay was a bit stupid anyway; why drop it today and have it go off tomorrow? Go and drop it tomorrow when you would be there anyway. We parked the bombs in various spots with various delays so that they would go off at odd intervals somewhere, sometime, in the dark. This, we hoped, would discourage the farmers. And it helped to pass the time.

On the whole, we pilots preferred sorties other than the first and last of the day. More time in bed in the morning, and no loss of drinking time in the evening. It was not difficult therefore to get my Flight Commander to slot me for both the dawn and the sunset trip. He thought me insane, and said so. Six hours in one day, looking at nothing? Of course, I was known to have an insatiable appetite for flying; perhaps that was something to do with it? I forbore to say that a nonsensical personal record was in the making.

We had no night flying equipment and in that latitude you could only get off safely about 40 minutes before dawn and land safely by the same time after sunset. To the discomfort of my ground crew the aircraft was prepared in the dark. Then, as the very first lightening of the sky showed in the east they opened the fort doors and pushed the machine out onto the gravel airfield. This was even less popular with the team in case an early rising tribesman might be in the vicinity. The two of us clambered in, strapped up and did the simple pre-flight checks. Someone wound the starting handle and the engine caught. The ground crew scuttled back behind the steel doors and slammed them shut.

Spurts of blue and yellow flame sprouted unevenly from the stub exhausts as we taxied out. After lining up, the throttle was eased wide open and, tail up, we raced over the bumpy gravel. The flames changed to twelve evenly vibrating nine-inch long blue tongues, jutting six from each bank of exhaust stubs at the sides of the engine cowling. We lifted away and climbed at full power to our area.

The pre-dawn sky went through its wonderful routine as we got higher and higher. The faint grey-green tinge in the east changed to soft pink and then to red, merging into orange and finally yellow for the sunrise yet to come. The blue flames gradually faded as the light improved and, when the dawn came, they would be gone. Soon I could distinguish salient features on the ground beneath; river from earth, rock from sand. Suddenly at 14,000 ft in the east came the brilliant orange spot heralding the sun itself. I kept on climbing, hard. Rapidly the disc rose and in two or three minutes it was clear into the sky. Below, the earth was still in deep shadow.

At the instant the disc cleared the lip of the mountains I swung over on one wing and dived almost vertically towards the earth. The sun, naturally, started to disappear below the mountains as I went down into their shadow. As soon as it vanished I pulled up and climbed like mad to make it reappear. Harts were not very powerful machines, even for their era, and there was no way to regain quickly all the height I had dived away. And the sun was climbing inexorably. Nevertheless, I managed to make the sun drop below the horizon three times before it had risen too far for me to play with it any longer. I settled down to the remainder of my three hours, watching the shadows being chased down the mountain sides and into the valleys, changing the colours on the ground from velvety blue to mauve, then to ochre and at last to drab sepia in the pure daylight. Then, nose down for home and breakfast.

That evening I did the same thing in reverse. Floating around at about 16,000 ft the shadows on the ground showed that, down there, the sun had set. I rolled her over on one wing and dived vertically down, partly to get up as much speed as possible for the ensuing climb and partly to make the sun disappear. Then pull back on the stick and zoom up at full throttle to make it reappear. Down again. Up again . . . Three times my long-suffering Hart made the sun come up in the West before finally it was too low for me to get my playmate back.

Acute boredom makes simple things seem fun. I doubt that my achievement will ever be considered for the *Guinness Book of Records*. Still, not many people have seen the sun rise three times in the west, and set three times in the east — all in one day.

The ultimate sanction for extreme naughtiness was to knock down a village belonging to the tribe concerned. Usually it was the collection of a few buildings which contained the headman's house. A bit spiteful perhaps, but common sense. The thick mud-brick walls took an incredible amount of explosive without collapsing or being really beyond some effective mud-and-wattle patching. Also, the villages were very small and therefore difficult to hit when using our somewhat primitive bombsights. Therefore, we would try to expend the least explosive for the most psychological effect.

The procedure for us to inflict the punishment, decided by our political masters in India was strictly regulated and most proper. First, having been given the map reference of the village we took aerial photographs of it. This had two objectives. First, so that we could be reassured by our civil overlords that it really was the village they wanted knocked down. Second, so that our bombing leaders could each carry a copy, to be sure they also got the correct village under them. Although the maps we used were remarkably good in general, there tended to be some inaccuracies in the fine detail — presumably because not many surveyors had spent longer than they absolutely had to on the ground amongst the tribesmen. It would have been highly embarrassing to knock down the wrong village, not only for us and the politicians but also for the villagers themselves.

Having identified the right, or wrongdoing, village we were given leaflets. These said that, saving immediate capitulation, bombing would start any time after the next 48 hours. They, their livestock, their children and their wives (the order of priority is interesting) had better be removed, lock, stock and barrel. I never heard of capitulation between the leaflet-dropping and the bombing. Perhaps the Fakir of Ipi had something to do with it.

Since time immemorial religion has been closely linked with armed conflict or brutal behaviour. Consider the Spanish Inquisition in the name of Roman Catholicism, or the modern feuds between Muhammadanism and Judaism, or even the Protestant versus Roman Catholic factions in Northern Ireland. The list is limitless. The North West Frontier Province ran perfectly true to form. The Fakir, or holy man, from Ipi was endlessly stirring up trouble. He was a wily old bird, and unlike his devotees he could read. He also had an excellent intelligence service and, when the leaflets were printed in Peshawar for us, he very soon had a copy in front of his steel-rimmed spectacles. He lost no time in visiting the headman concerned in order to stir up some good old-fashioned anti-British rancour. At the same time he did not miss the opportunity of improving his own status. As a first step he would claim to know, by supernatural powers, that we had unreasonably decided to drop explosive bombs on a particular village. Nevertheless he, the almighty Fakir of Ipi, had a wonderful power which was greater than ours. This, graciously, he would exercise in the tribesmen's favour. He would frustrate our efforts and turn our bombs to paper. He then paid us a considerable compliment by staking his personal safety on our good faith and moral rectitude. He camped out in the village selected as a target, so as not to miss the fun.

When our aircraft approached overhead on the appointed day, he would perform his mumbo-jumbo with appropriate incantations. Then he would point to the leaflets showering down as evidence of his benificent power. Since the tribesmen could not read a word of what they said, he was on a good wicket. His stature was enhanced by leaps and bounds.

Next, after a spell of praying and meditation, he would receive another supernatural message saying our aircraft were returning in a couple of days to drop more bombs. He found it most upsetting but he was exhausted by his efforts; his magical powers were somewhat spent. He feared that next time the bombs were released his paper-transmutation act might, conceivably, not work so well. Perhaps, in the circumstances, it was best that the villagers should make a dignified retreat.

Wonderful to everyone but himself, he was dead right the second time too. The day, and the bombs, were precisely as he had foreseen. He was no fool and could turn almost any situation against us and to his own advantage.

After a long-drawn-out summer of proscription we reached the knock-down phase on 12 November. We had planned to hold an Airmen's Ball on the 11th, the evening of Armistice Day, in one of the hangars at our home-base. Every wife and nubile daughter had been given a bidding to attend. All fourteen of them. We could not possibly disappoint their partners, two hundred and fifty airmen, starved of female company and craving for a dance with a real live woman; we would fly off to our operational base the next morning. Officers, of course, were put under strict orders to stand back and let the dogs see the rabbits. Instead, they consumed a great deal of beer, chatting with the airmen who had lost out in the stampede across the hangar at the beginning of every tune, trying to get the chance to say, 'Excuse me, Ma'am, but may I have the pleasure?' It was a marathon for the girls, and the evening went on and on and on.

One of the wives (with a couple of daughters on the floor) had a figure that was unmistakably 'motherly'. Late in the evening she was dancing with a corporal. She was enchanted when he, courteously gripping her ample figure and with a beer-breath that nearly knocked her off her feet, said confidentially, 'Do you know, Ma'am, I can't think why a nice girl like you doesn't get married.'

The whole affair was a great success and when we closed the bar it was well into the small hours and shortly after the last exhausted and generous-hearted woman had dragged herself home on swollen and aching feet. With a stopper on the beer supply, the hangar was soon empty. Tottering off to bed I got two hours' sleep — and that was about twice what some of my colleagues achieved.

At dawn we were down at the flights with our small-kit ready to be stowed by the crewman for the flight of 130 miles to the advanced airfield. I felt terrible. I had a monumental hangover. My mouth felt like a farmyard. My eyelids seemed to be lined with sand and my eyes, when I shaved, looked like eggs poached in blood. The ear-splitting roar from the engine was too terrible for words.

The bomb-aimer flying with me was a fresh-faced individual with a ready smile called Aircraftman Reed. He was superlative as a bomb-aimer and always had the best results in the squadron. He held the lowest rank in the Air Force — Aircraftman, 2nd Class. In that rank he remained for years. He could not pass the exams to Aircraftman, 1st class because in tests he froze up totally.

When World War II broke out — to hell with exams — they promoted him straight to Sergeant because of his exceptional talents. A great pity that it was so long delayed.

The take-off and flight there was worse than poor. It was in no sense a squadron-formation; it was nine aeroplanes more or less pointing in the same direction. Each swooped and weaved as the pilots tried to get their eyes in focus. Even after an hour in the air (which, normally, was an infallible hangover cure) my stomach was still full of jumping frogs. We came in to land and she felt as if it would be a nice touch-down. The only thing amiss was that I didn't feel any ground under the wheels. Realising instantly that my eyes were deceiving me, I quickly did another landing, ten feet lower down. Still there was no ground. I tried a third but by then I had run out of airspeed and the machine fell clean out of my hands, banging and bouncing, wheels-to-tailskid, along what seemed like miles of rough gravel surface. Luckily, nothing broke.

Reed, in common with all the crewmen, had a touching confidence in 'his' pilot. Nevertheless I felt very shamefaced. What must he think of my horrible performance? I picked up the speaking tube to say 'Not a very good landing, I am afraid.' That was the understatement of the century; it had been awful! Reed's gentle reproof came back, quick as a flash: 'That's all right, Sir. You'll be yourself again tomorrow!' The Squadron Commander, however, was not nearly so restrained. He expressed his displeasure to us in no uncertain terms.

The bombs we used were kept in the explosives magazine which was underneath the fort. Access was from the airfield, down a hole like a square well with a sheet of metal as a trapdoor on its top. There was also a little crane, with gears and a handle. Someone, down below, hooked on a bomb and someone else wound the handle to get it up. It raised a question as to the sanity of the architect who planned this system. Having a trapdoor outside the steel doors of the fort made me nervous. We had little faith that some unnaturally bright tribesman could not get his hands on some explosive, lift the trapdoor, and drop it down. Armament specialists always assert that bombs are quite safe till they are properly fused and armed. Nevertheless, there were several hundred big bombs down below us and, if they had gone off, the departure of the fort and its inhabitants would have been more than spectacular. And, whatever the original cause, or whoever the perpetrator, the Fakir of Ipi would have claimed it for himself.

The technique of bombing fascinated me. The bomb-aimer had to do two things at the same time. First, he had to direct the pilot so that he was flying precisely towards a spot above the target because, once you have let a bomb go, it continues travelling forwards at exactly the same speed and direction until it reaches something which stops it — and nothing can change that. Second, he had to release the bomb some distance away so that, under the influence of gravity and ever-gathering speed downwards, it is just over the target when it gets there. Simplified like that it does not sound too bad but, in addition to the basic calculations, there is a host of other things to inject errors — side winds, up- and down-draughts, speed variations, barometer readings, height, temperatures and dozens more. Reed was kept very busy.

We bombed in flights of three aircraft in close formation. Having no radio, our pattern bombing was done by using a standard procedure coupled with some hand signals. Each aircraft carried two large bombs and, after take-off, we climbed as fast as possible to get above tribesmen's pot-shotting height. We dropped salvoes of three bombs, one from each aircraft. The leader flew as accurately as he was able, to give a really steady aim on the target. The bomb-aimer lay on his tummy, on the wooden floor, just below the pilot's knees. Sliding back an aluminium trapdoor, he peered out through the hole in the floor and passed his corrections to the pilot through the speaking tube. Finally, about fifteen seconds before release, the aimer said 'Stand by!' The pilot, flying with one hand, put the other arm above his head. This warned the other two pilots who, also flying one-handed, grasped a brass handle down by their right thigh. Then, the instant they saw the leader's bomb fall, they yanked the lever and their own bombs dropped too.

At this point, from the outside, it must have seemed crazy as all three pilots heads disappeared. Each was peering down between his knees, through the hole in the floor, to watch the bombs. The three crewmen were doing the same. Three aircraft, sailing through the sky with nobody looking out. Why we didn't collide remains a mystery.

The bombs, moving along forwards with the same 100 mph speed as the Harts, appeared to us as if they were going straight down, ever faster and faster. Far below, the ground unrolled, moving backwards across the square hole like a panoramic cinema screen. Hillsides, bushes and streams went steadily past as we strained to keep the bombs in view but, painted drab brown, they soon vanished against the moving picture of drab brown earth. They took just over 22 seconds to drop the one and a half miles, and it seemed like forever. At first, one was convinced they must be almost there and the target was not yet in the picture; they were going to undershoot. Then, the target appeared and the bombs had not hit; it must become an overshoot!

Then, suddenly, and with no sound that we could hear, the walls and buildings would erupt into three puddles of dirty smoke and dust. Aircraftman 2nd Class Reed (who couldn't pass his exams to Aircraftman 1st Class — let alone to Leading Aircraftman, Corporal or higher) had got all his complex calculations dead right once more.

Nowadays, with radar and computers feeding the autopilot, it is a bit different. Then, it was remarkable that, from about a mile and a half up, we could flatten a target about the size of two tennis courts.

After the first salvo, round we would go in a wide circle to make our second and final run for the sortie. We kept well clear of the highest hilltops, on which sat angry tribesmen with rifles. The thick mud walls and the fighting-towers could take an incredible amount of punishment before they fell. It would go on, day after day until the village was beyond a mud-and-wattle patching operation; it would have to have a full rebuild.

These were the times when one really feared an engine failure. On the ground there would be nowhere to hide, and would a tribesman who had just lost his house pay much attention to a goolie chit — particularly as he couldn't read a word it said?

During 'ops' normal squadron life had to go on, of course. Reports had to be submitted. People had to get paid. Letters had to be answered. Most of this burden fell on the Squadron Adjutant. It was a thankless task on the whole, except that the Squadron Commander could sometimes offer as a sop some flight or task that was more attractive than most. At this time it was Flying Officer 'Ritchie' Richardson who was taking his turn.

One day he was being driven frantic by a string of requests and impassioned pleas for his undivided attention. He mopped his brow as the caterer wanted this, the sweepers wanted that, an airman wanted something else. And as if that was not enough, outside there was a never-ending queue of individuals, each waiting his chance. When the office messenger came in and said that even some of the locals had a request to make of him his comment was blunt: 'I'm very busy. Tell them to wait.' 'Why is it,' he thought, 'that nobody ever comes to see me unless they *want* something?' Doggedly he carried on through the morning and it was not long before he forgot about them altogether.

At last, blessedly, lunchtime arrived. He picked up his topee as he got out of his chair and stretched. That lunchtime beer was going to be like nectar. He went to the door. There, the messenger politely reminded him that the peasants were, as he had instructed them, still waiting to speak with him. Irritable at this delay to his needed beer, he reluctantly said he would give them a few moments. There, under the awning over the verandah outside his office, were four tribesmen squatting patiently. They stood up and made obeisance to him. Ritchie was glad to see that their rifles (from which *any* tribesman is most reluctantly parted) must have been taken from them at the main gate to the fort. Attentive eyes studied him from dark craggy faces. They shifted their weight nervously from one foot to the other.

The office clerk, doubling as interpreter, explained that the men said they had found something belonging to the Sahib. They had carefully brought it to him, carried on a bed to avoid damage. The clerk pointed to a rope-strung wooden bed on the verandah, up against the wall of Ritchie's office. Further, they had saved it from going bad by covering it with damp banana leaves. Perhaps they could expect some reward for their efforts? Carefully they removed the banana leaves. There, on the bed, was a long-delay bomb big enough to blow the whole headquarters to smithereens.

As Ritchie saw it his eyes bugged out of his head like door-knobs. And to think that he had kept it sitting against the wall of his office all the morning! It says much for his self control that, stifling a mad urge to drop everything and break into a frenzied run, he nodded sagely at the bomb. 'Mr. Mukkerjee,' he said to the clerk, trying to stop his voice squeaking, 'tell them to take the most valuable item, on its bed, to the far edge of the airfield where this important device belongs. At once. I will discuss a reward when they come back. That is, if they are quick, and if I have not by then left to have my lunch.'

With beaming smiles the four men leapt into action. Grabbing the legs of the bed, one each, they positively sprinted away with it and its lethal burden. Ritchie offered up a brief prayer that they wouldn't drop it before they had done at least 150 yards. Irreverently, at the far edge of the airfield, they tossed the bomb into the ditch and came running back, with the bed. Solemnly, Ritchie thanked them and gave them a few rupees each. They seemed delighted. He hoped to high Heaven that he had not given them too much, in case they went looking for, and brought in, more 'important devices'. He tottered weakly up to the Mess. He did not have his longed-for beer; he ordered a treble whisky, without water, which barely had time to touch the sides of his throat as it went down.

One hour later the bomb went off.

# Chapter 11
# The Roof of the World

To the north of our station lay a region of contrasts which ranged from the arid deserts of the Indus plain to the perpetual snows of the High Himalayas.

Since time immemorial caravans of camels, mules, donkeys and porters have crossed the many passes from China, Russia, Tibet and Afghanistan into India, bringing goods for trade. Perhaps the best known, by name, of these passes (because of the unlikely fiction attributed to it and then filmed elsewhere by Hollywood) is the Khyber Pass, used by travellers between Peshawar and Kabul. In fact, although the craggy hills on either side look impressive, it barely merits the name 'pass' for it rises to only 5000 ft, and even 45 years ago it had a motorable road. It made a pleasant outing to drive there for a Sunday afternoon picnic and take a look into the enigmatic territory of Afghanistan. Other passes are of sterner stuff. They cross the area which has been aptly named 'The Roof of the World'. Several mule- and foot-tracks rise to nearly 20,000 ft — much higher than we could fly with safety having no oxygen, and without the time to get acclimatised to that altitude.

However, where traders can travel, so in principle can armed forces. Protection against this eventuality was the task of the Army. Other than the Khyber with its motor road, the Army-in-place usually consisted of one or maybe two British officers, rented by India from Britain for the job — like us. They enlisted enthusiastically ferocious tribesmen from the local area whom they uniformed, armed and trained as 'Scouts'. Their force was usually stiffened by some of the very high-calibre Indian non-commissioned officers. These tiny isolated outposts, stationed in some narrow valley on one side or the other of their particular pass, had the daunting task of repelling the advance of any hostile enemy column bent on invading the Indian sub-continent. As no vehicle of the time could conceivably have come over the passes, in their steep valleys it would not have been surprising if those disciplined, tough mountain-men had stopped any intruders in their tracks.

In winter the high trails into the North West Frontier Province were mostly impassable. The snow was too deep and the cold too frigid even for a Tibetan mule, camel or porter — let alone an armed column. The outpost could be cut off for months at a time except for the ticker-ticker of the telegraph operated by the Indian postal service. Therefore, where possible, landing grounds had been built near the detachments for emergency reinforcement, communications and if necessary, casualty evacuation.

Doing a stint as Squadron Adjutant, particularly for a somewhat sober-minded CO from World War I, was hardly a job to inspire and thrill. But, sometimes there was a pay-off. Like this one. I looked at the names on the list. Four pilots: Flight Lieutenant 'Buck' Buchanan (the leader), Flight Lieutenant Tony Tinker, myself and Sergeant Parsons. I could hardly believe my eyes.

This was a very special perk. It was a trip to do a half-yearly visit to a landing ground, far up into the Himalayan mountain range. It had been built beside the fort at Drosh in the Chitral area. It was barely 600 yards long and at an altitude of 4000 ft. The pass to be guarded by the garrison of Chitral scouts was the Lowarai, one of the lower passes — only 11,400 ft high at the saddle. Nevertheless, even this route was closed for four months of the year. Personnel were changed round in the summer and to get up, over and down you trudged for about four days. And that included the wife of the Commanding Officer — if she wanted to take advantage of her permission to live with her husband. Although we could fly there in an hour, passengers were taboo except for reasons political, operational or medical. Wives did not come into these categories.

We were permitted to make these fly-in inspection visits six-monthly and to be selected for even one of these flights was much envied. Besides the excitement of going amongst the normally forbidden high mountains it was a landing away from a recognised base, which in itself made it out of the ordinary. There was an element of risk to be surmounted by showing some personal piloting skill. Two squadrons shared the task and, twice in a year, three or sometimes four aircraft went; say six to eight pilots a year needed from the 36 available. Allowing for Squadron Commanders' and Flight Commanders' choices it was odds-on that you never made the trip at all.

Lucky Flying Officer Dudgeon was lucky on two counts; not only to get the trip but it was the winter one and in January/February the visibility can be superlative, making the scenery and vistas almost unbelievable. It might be the flight of a lifetime.

The first item on the agenda was to send a telegram to the CO at Drosh, telling him the approximate date of our arrival, weather permitting, and asking his advice on what we should bring with us. Most of our available load would be taken up with official supplies together with our toolboxes and spares, in case we had to make any repairs up there, but we would have some space left over. The request we made for the CO's 'advice' was a euphemism for his list of what he would like us to bring, space permitting, that he would not otherwise see from one year's end to the next; items that were not essential or (before the days of refrigeration and food processing) food that would go bad on a plodding porter's back. Bananas. Fresh sausages. Kippers. Apples.

Our plumb ignorance and blind faith in those days was horrifying. We would load up our poor Harts with tools, luggage, spares and personal kit in the back cockpit until the unfortunate gunner was practically sitting cross-legged on the top, and the machine's weight and balance would have made its designer hysterical. As if that wasn't enough, we also slung metal-gridded crates underneath the wings, attached to the bomb-rack mountings, and filled those up too. Even with full nose-down trim we often had to hold up the tail by shoving forwards on the joystick as well. I used to carry a couple of strong elastic cords (one wasn't strong enough) which I clipped round the stick and then under the lip of the dashboard to do some pulling for me, thereby taking some of the load off my muscles — which otherwise ached like hell after a couple of hours. Luckily for us, Hawkers always designed forgiving airframes and our Kestrel engines from Rolls-Royce were superlative.

At last, panniers fixed, stores packed, perishables in the Mess ice-box, we were ready to await good weather, for in those days with no radio or oxygen, one's eyeballs were crucial. The appointed day turned out to be a humdinger. We had no weather forecast — just a general area forecast sent from Delhi 600 miles away — and even that was of dubious accuracy. However, even from the ground we could clearly see, gleaming in the sunlight, the snow-capped mountains 70 and more miles away. Conditions promised to be very good. Eyeballs said so.

In addition to my share of the stores and perishables, the chieftain, or mayor, of Chitral was on the gunner's seat behind me. We took off and climbed steadily towards the cleft in the hills which was the valley of the Panjkora river, and from the upper parts of which the summer trail would lead over the Lowarai Pass. Thence it would wind down the mountainside to Drosh on the Chitral river, which flowed south-east and carried the trail into Afghanistan. With the drag and load of the crates hanging under the wings, and with unsupercharged engines, we were hardly making more than 1000 ft of altitude in each minute.

The patchwork of scrubby fields below was in its winter brown, waiting for the shoots of green to poke through in March. As we slowly got higher and higher, range after range of snow-covered mountains came into view. Ahead and to our right they towered to more than 20,000 ft. We could not see over them to others, even higher, that we knew were beyond. Even so, a marvellous panorama of mountain after mountain, tops nearly all higher than we could fly, stretched clearly visible in the gin-clear air from nearby to over 100 miles distant. As we got closer they became blindingly white in the sunshine. Smoky blue shadows nestled below us in the crevasses, glaciers and valleys. Only down in the deepest valleys, far below the snowline, could be seen brown earth and rocks spattered by occasional touches of dark evergreen bushes.

The mayor behind me was obviously terrified, on this his first flight. He crouched on the gunner's jump-seat, staring steadfastly at his feet, patently convinced that his last hours had surely come. I first spoke, and finally shrieked down the voice-tube but got no reaction. I offered a short prayer that Messrs Rolls-Royce would, as usual, keep the prop turning. I would never be able to get him to grab a slender chance of life by baling out, for a crash-landing in some parts of that terrain would be without hope.

The bed of the Panjkora river, a few thousand feet below us and now frozen solid, was climbing fast towards a source somewhere up near the rim of the mountains, a rim notched in front of us by the Talor Shoh Pass which carried the line of ridges down to 18,750 ft; even if we had wished, trying to get over that gap would be fatal without oxygen. We had now reached about 14,000 ft, safely clear of vicious currents and wicked turbulence, as we swung left towards the Lowarai Pass, our lower notch through which we could escape down into the Chitral Valley.

With the Flight Commander's permission, my station was a

loose No. 4. The vic of three Harts in close formation looked beautiful as they slipped over the saddle, 2000 ft above it and half a mile from either side. The machines were doped silver with polished aluminium cowlings reflecting the sunlight. They had squadron markings of twin scarlet bands round the fuselages; the spinning noses of the propellers were blue for 'B Flight', as were the painted discs of the wheels contrasting with the black rubber of the tyres; the RAF roundels were a glossy red, white and blue. Those three splashes of mixed colour, heaving gently in the up- and down-draughts, were against a back-drop of that cobalt-blue sky belonging to high flyers, the gleaming white snow and ice, the blue-grey shadows; the Himalays were vast, the machines were tiny — the beauty was exquisite. Nosing down, we dived towards Drosh, two miles below and ten miles ahead.

The mediaeval-looking fort of Drosh reared its battlemented outline on a rock promontory, hugged by a bend of the steep and tumbling Chitral river flowing through a shallow gorge at its feet. Its solid mass towered over one end of the crescent-shaped landing ground which was cradled inside the next bend of the river downstream. It dominated and, from our point of view, completely blocked the valley beyond it. The landing was to be made on the first part of the crescent, facing and furthest from the fort. Parking was on the section off the landing-run and round to the left. It was, as you might say, a one-time-only airfield. Landings only towards the fort and take-offs away from it. If you made a nonsense of it at that height above sea-level with a 600 yard maximum run, and a heavily laden aircraft, you could forget being able to open the throttle to go round again for another try — unless you wanted a sporting chance of flying in through the Fort Commander's bedroom window. You would just have to crash it on the airfield as gracefully as you could, and await your CO's wrath in due course.

It was a funny feeling coming in to land. The normal approach, to which we were accustomed in that era, was impractical. It put more faith in your judgement than in the reliability of your engine. It had some good points for engines were not so reliable as now, and an engine-cut on the way in to land could drop you short and literally ditch you very nastily. One was assumed to be better than the engine. The story of a landing went like this: 'Begin by flying downwind at 1000 ft above the airfield; close the throttle; make an about turn with no use of engine as you line up for the final approach; glide in a little high, still with no use of engine; at the very end, sideslip off your surplus height — and land in the normal manner.'

In fact, if your colleagues heard a tell-tale rumble from the engine during an approach, one suffered unmerciful teasing for imperfect judgement. My chum Johnny Betts, who had once been a Canadian fur-trapper, tried to get away without rumbling on an unsatisfactory approach at Risalpur because of this teasing. His machine ran out of gliding speed near the edge of the airfield and sank into the top of a casuarina tree. It lurched out of that and fell on to the tarmac in an ungainly heap. The aeroplane was a total loss, and Johnny was very lucky only to have a black eye. The gunner was lucky too; he only hurt his knee.

At Drosh, with no second shot up one's sleeve, no road access and no hospital, we simply dared not trust pure judgement for a total commitment so far back — flying the wrong way, in an unusually heavy aircraft, and at an airfield four thousand feet up to boot. No Sir! *Any* engine was more trustworthy in that case — particularly one made by Rolls-Royce. So, having had a good look at the situation, one by one we pushed off down the valley for a mile or two, high enough for a safe and relaxed turn back between the hill-slopes and straighten up on the line of landing. Then, rumbly-rumbly gently along the rising valley, using a whiffle of engine or sideslipping as necessary to adjust the height, and getting lower and lower. One go, one only, and it *had* to come out right. For an inexperienced pilot, like me, it felt like flying into a bottle. All too quickly the hills seemed to crowd in from either side. The looming bulk of the fort directly in front was coming up much too close for comfort. Finally, over the edge, drop her fully stalled — and get the brakes on. It was an approach that made the hands go sticky; but after ten times you would probably wonder why you worried over the first one.

We stayed on the ground for roughly an hour before the return flight. Time enough to unload the paralysed mayor, unpack the stores and the welcome goodies — and then up to the top of the fort for a look down the valley into Afghanistan. I learned I would have another passenger for the return journey; he was a sick Chitrali Scout on his way — his only way — to hospital for an operation. We took off one by one in the opposite direction, away from the fort. Comfortably down the valley we formed up into tight formation for a fly-past as a salute in gratitude to them for their hospitality.

The hills of the Lowarai pass climbed far faster than we could, so we gained our necessary height by flying up the Chitral valley, northwards, for about 30 miles. Ahead, a further 30 miles away before we turned, the snowy outline of Tirich Mir was silhouetted against the clear blue. By Himalayan standards a good, but not remarkable mountain, mainly because there are 16 peaks higher in the same range. Nevertheless, to we Europeans, it was more than striking; its domed shape is nearly *two miles* higher than Mont Blanc — which is the highest peak in Europe. Seen with its brilliant white mantle of eternal snow and ice, broken by dark slashes of rock-cliffs and shadows, towering above nearer hilltops unworthy of the distinction of even a name amongst the giants, but which were themselves thousands of feet higher than Mont Blanc . . . yes, we considered that it merited the term 'remarkable'.

Finally, reluctantly, and for my part semi-drunk with the beauty of it all, we re-crossed the Lowarai Pass and set course back over the drab fields towards Risalpur, an ambulance for my passenger, and lunch.

# Chapter 12
# Even Higher

There was a certain amount of rhubarb-rhubarb among my brother pilots when I was selected for yet another landing-ground inspection. This time it was to Gilgit, which is even farther into the Himalayas, to the extreme north of Kashmir. The Gilgit garrison guarded against access through the very highest passes leading from Russia and the Sinkiang province of China.

Personally, I felt this access to India was for the birds rather than for any human invaders. Not one of the gaps between the mountain peaks was under 14,000 ft and some of the passes, like the Talor Shah, pushed their oxygen-starved travellers to over 18,000 ft. Only in the best summer months did these sky-scraping passes show a foot or mule track. For nine months of the year the winter ice and snows blocked them totally. In the good weather, any hardy survivors who got over the saddles would have to scramble a long way down the river valleys till they debouched into the green and fertile plains below. Moreover, to follow a rocky and boulder-strewn valley was no sinecure. For example, the Kilik pass (16,500 ft) provided access from the Chinese border near Russia, followed by no less than 22 days walking or riding to the plains; there was no feasible track for any species of vehicle, let alone something which might call itself a road.

The cluster of houses called Gilgit village was strategically placed roughly half-way from Kilik to the plains, beside a river of the same name and under the great peaks either side. It had been judged a good place to halt an enemy so, true to pattern, the British had enlisted and trained some of the enthusiastically tough tribesmen to form the Gilgit Scouts. Their commanding officer was Major David Cropper. He lived in a more or less European-style house', built by local labour. With him were his wife, baby son and one of the more adventurous English nannies. The baby had been carried there but the adults had walked and ridden along the mule track from the plains for eleven days, camping on the way.

About four miles downstream from the village, the Gilgit river is joined by the Hunza. Thence, as one stream, they plunge and cascade down to join the Indus, already 700 miles old, on its remaining 1200 miles to the sea. Where the Gilgit and Hunza rivers meet, in the crotch of the Y formed by the junction, 5000 ft above sea-level, there was a small flattish space. On it the powers-that-be had had carved out by manual labour a little airfield or, to be more precise, a landing ground. By dint of much raking, scraping, shovelling, and man-handling baskets of gritty earth, a cross of two 500-yard-long strips of levelled ground had been created. Towering over and almost blocking off two ends of the cross was the rugged brown shoulder of rocky mountain that separated the two rivers. There were no buildings, no staff, no radio, no servicing and no fuel. This was what we were to land on, and inspect. We carried enough fuel to go there and back, but with not much to spare. So there would be no mucking about making little diversions to goggle at mountain scenery on the way.

Major Cropper knew we were coming and, as expected, we got the telegram wondering in a polite way if we would have room for those non-essential but very welcome goodies which he could not reasonably authorise to be carried up to him by porters on an 11-day trek. We loaded the aircraft and waited for the weather. This time we would have to weave and turn to follow the valleys so the weather had to be satisfactory all the way. On this flight even the smaller mountains on either side were too high to climb over and get out of trouble. The big boys went above 25,000 ft.

Finally the right day dawned and soon we were clambering up the hand- and foot-holds on the fuselage sides, settling ourselves into the open cockpits and checking the instruments. Behind, over my shoulder was my fitter, Aircraftman Kerr. Kerr was a little man and I doubt he was more than 5 ft 4 ins. Being my fitter, whose job was to look after the health of the engine, I hoped he had given it particular tender loving care for I had some idea of the terrain we would be crossing. He gave me a grin and a 'thumbs-up' to indicate that he was in, had his gear stowed, and had attached his harness to the short steel cable which anchored him to the floor. This would let him move about in the rear cockpit but would save him from being chucked out of the aircraft if we hit a big bump. He was ready for the off.

I smiled as I thought of the unusual items (for 1938 bombers) stowed in the iron crates under the wings. Oranges and bottles of orange juice for Master Cropper. Lengths of dress material chosen by Mrs Jones, the Squadron Commander's wife, for Nanny and for Mrs Cropper. For the household, tins of sausages, sardines, cows' milk, butter (a welcome change from that of goats and sheep), jams, sugar and kippers. And, for the Major, an 8 mm cine-projector specially modified by Kodak, a 12 volt car battery, a 12 volt car dynamo and the essential guts of a bicycle. Plus a couple of crates of beer. Our station workshops had done some very fancy re-fashioning of the bicycle, certainly unforeseen by its manufacturers, so as to create a one-manpower electric generator. I gathered that the projector, showing the Major's films, would run off the battery, as it was kept charged up by the dynamo, which was being driven by the bicycle gears — all kept in action by the strenuous pedalling of one Gilgit Scout . . . while the Major drank the beer. It seemed an admirable arrangement to me. I taxied out and lined up.

With the throttle wide open and the ear-splitting crackle from the stub exhausts six feet in front of me, the Rolls-Royce Kestrel engine dutifully provided its maximum 475 horsepower. The heavily laden machine was painfully slow to accelerate. I thought the tail-skid would never come off the grass. However, at last she lifted off and, with a necessarily gentle turn at that weight, we set about catching up the Squadron Leader.

The first 60 miles cut north-east across the cultivated plains irrigated by the Indus river. Visible were a mass of tiny fields, which were mostly brown because it was wintertime but a few had something showing green to break the drabness. Steadily we climbed to reach our cruising height of 12,000 ft. High enough to be clear of the treacherous updraughts and whirlwinds that lurk amongst the highest mountains; low enough not to become stupid and ineffective through lack of oxygen. I wound the movable radiator in a few notches to keep my engine properly warm — and me too, for air came through it into the cockpit. We were flying 'in company' rather than 'in formation'. Close-formation flying may look very pretty and it is satisfying; it takes great skill to maintain a precise position in relation to your leader. However, the continuous and essential movements of controls and adjustments of power are wildly extravagant in fuel. So we flew near enough to keep a watchful eye on each other in case of trouble such as engine failure, and far enough apart to be relaxed, to navigate properly and to monitor the instruments. But mainly to be certain of having enough fuel to get home safely.

After about 30 minutes I could see the gap in the mountain range where the Indus came out and into which we were going. The nearest mountains were drab brown, fawn and grey. Rocky, inhospitable, ugly — and they were not yet impressive. Their tops were only about 10,000 ft, but beyond them there were others much higher. We turned along the river and went into the mountain valley, northwards. We would follow the Indus roughly in this direction for about 50 miles. Then, as it turned round a mountain spur to the east, we would follow it for another 70 miles in that direction till we branched off north again, away from the Indus, to follow a smaller valley to Gilgit.

On this first leg we got a taste of the real Himalayan massif. In ten minutes the hills on either side were higher than we were. The tops became snow covered. The little fields and orchards on every flat spot by the river, however small, became sparser. The great river itself tumbled through defiles and, even from two miles up, we could see its white froth as it plunged round and over rocks in its bed.

Soon we saw below us the tiny villages of Sazin and Gayah. The clutches of little brown mud-brick houses with beige, maize-stalk-covered roofs were barely visible against the dark fawn-brown earth and rocks. It was the sun's inky shadows beside the buildings which picked them out for us. We, and the river, turned eastwards towards the slightly larger village of Chilas.

As we followed the river round the 18,000 ft peak to our right, a view unfolded which beggared description. Now we were amongst the big boys. Below was the foaming Indus river. Here and there on any passably flat spot far below were tiny pocket-handker-chiefs of fields or orchards, delineated by their terracing or walls. We could not pick out the sheep and goats which we knew must be there. On both sides of the river, steep beyong belief, the mountains rose jaggedly right up to our level and beyond. They spread out, ridge after cleft after shoulder after abyss. At our height to right and left, patched with ice and snow clinging to the ledges, were sheer cliffs thousands of feet high. The incredible size of the mountains made them look as if they were just beside my wingtips; the fact that they seemed to go past slowly proved they were a several miles distant. To my left the other aircraft, themselves maybe almost a mile away, looked like models flown by minuscule dwarfs and in imminent danger of striking the cliffs on their side; my map said they had two or three miles' clearance.

*The final moment of a bombing run. The author, having turned on to the run and been guided finally by the bomb-aimer lying on the floor, has been warned that there are only about 10 seconds to go. He has therefore put up his right arm to warn the two pilots in formation with him that his bomb is about to go. They, in turn, have put their hands on their bomb-release levers. The author's left-hand bomb can be seen falling and the pilot of the machine from which this picture was taken is also releasing his own bomb so that all three drop in salvo.*
*The right-hand bomb, still on its rack, will be dropped on the next run.*

*Smoke and dust clearing away from Shankai Village after the bombing attack. Note, on the left a typical house with its inevitable fighting-tower. Another fighting-tower may just be distinguished on the crest of a hill in shadow, silhouetted against the cloud of dust.*

Mad-Wally's 'good forced-landing in difficult country'. A couple of locally enlisted scouts from the army cantonnment at Bannu have been put on guard and are doubtless gaining a lot of credit from their curious civilian compatriots. Wally's gunner (note his leg) sits up in the rear-cockpit to guard the Lewis machine-gun of untold desirability to the tribesmen. Two practice bombs, for use as sighters, are under the fuselage.

When our political masters wished to lay down the law – before or after punitive action – they would call a Jirga. This was a meeting with all the elders of the tribes concerned. This particular Jirga was held in the garden of the Officers' Mess in Miranshah. The proceedings are managed by the Political Agent, who is half in shadow at the table and wearing a topee. The senior military commander is beside him. The P.A's assistant is to his left, wearing a homburg hat. A few armed Tochi Scouts are dotted around. The elders of the tribes, with their guns safely parked outside, are squatted in front of the great man to hear his dictat.

*The Lawarai Pass is ahead of us, but we must be still higher before crossing to be safe from the dangerous air currents. The saddle is at 11,400 feet.*

*The Lawarai Pass is crossed at about 14,000 feet and we begin the let-down to the airfield. The Karkoram is in the background. Flt Sgt. Parsons is the pilot.*

*Thirty miles north of Drosh landing-ground we could see the sugar-loaf mountain Tirich Mir – seventeenth highest in the world – 23,230 feet.*

*The unsettling view that the pilot gets over the aircraft's nose as he lands on Drosh landing-ground – he does **Not** try to open the throttle for a second shot.*

*In the valleys we could not climb out of, having no oxygen. The rock-faces are several miles away from the aircraft.*

*Up amongst the big mountains. The Indus River can just be distinguished at the bottom of the valley in the centre of the picture, two miles down.*

*Twenty-five to thirty miles to our right the mighty Nanga Parbat, carrying a plume of cloud and snow-crystals, rose to 26,600 feet – far, far higher than we could fly without oxygen. (P.89).*

*Circling Gilgit landing-ground before making the approach. It is the light coloured cross-shaped area to the left, nestling under the hill. The Hunza River is on its far side and the Gilgit River is in the foreground. The two possible directions for landing are towards the hill, so the approach and touchdown must be dead-right the first and only time. Landing over a small cliff towards a block of granite is scary.*

*All the aircraft safely down and parked on Gilgit airfield. Unloading our kit and stores.*

*The main street in Gilgit village.*

*Two Gilgiti scouts filling the catalytic-heaters which would prevent our engines and radiators freezing-up overnight. Note horses in background for the ride to Gilgit.*

To my right towered the mighty Nanga Parbat, 26,600 ft high, sixth highest mountain in the world. I looked at it, hardly believing in its reality.

It was 25 miles away and it seemed like five. Its spectacular quality was magical. Between me and it were sharp peaks, ice and snow fields, rocks looking black in contrast and, down in the clefts were mighty glaciers streaked and wrinkled as they inched along their beds. There seemed to be no vegetation up there though I knew that some lichens can be found at enormous altitudes. Anyway, the tree-line was several thousands of feet below us. The snow and ice were tinted gold, silver and grey in the morning sunshine, then changing from blue to purple in the shadows. From the peak, a plume of virginal white powdered ice streamed against the cobalt-blue sky, ice stripped off the crest by the gale force winds. This whole region, 'The Roof of the World', was aptly named.

Chilas village went by miles below. Down there, on the muddy ugliness, insignificant beings eked out their scanty living; up on the crests with the ethereal beauty, nothing but the screaming of the wind. Between them, me; held suspended by a shape of metal and fabric, driven along at a hundred miles an hour by whirling ironmongery, wood and petrol. It felt unlikely.

I switched my attention from the peaks to the valley underneath me and looked at it curiously. It was not reassuring. After careful consideration I came to the conclusion that if Kerr's engine did not keep turning, he and I were going to die, quickly, or slowly. No ifs and buts; not perhaps; nor maybe.

There would be several options available. We could glide down in the aircraft and crash it into the foaming icy river. Or it could be cartwheeled against a precipitous, snowy, rocky hill-face which fell away at a crazy angle straight into the river at the bottom. Maybe it would wedge on an outcrop, or maybe it would roll and slither down into the water. Alternatively, we could 'take silk'. Coming down in a parachute would either land us in the river or, at best, drop us on the hillside where we might lodge, hopefully without broken limbs. None of it made a damn of difference because we would almost certainly both be frozen to death the first night, clad in our thin clothes and cotton flying overalls. If not during the first night, then it would be the second, or third, because it was a four-day trek, at least, to reach us — even if one of the other pilots told rescuers exactly where we had gone down.

It is remarkable how the prospect of death in the immediate

future sharpens the senses, often falsely. Had the oil pressure fallen a pound or two? Was the exhaust sounding a little rough? Was the radiator really hotting up? Charles Lindbergh, when he flew solo across the Atlantic, stuck a piece of paper over his oil-pressure gauge, because there was nothing he could do about it and it would only make him worry. I wished whole-heartedly for some sticky-paper. The previously exquisite beauty of the scene around me became a trifle soured. It was very scary.

Flight Sergeant Graham swung over from the left to pull into close formation with me. My heart pounded. Was this impending trouble? Then I saw he was grinning. His aircraft looked beautiful against the mountains with its silver fabric wings, the red, white and blue roundels, the polished aluminium cowlings blackened round the stub exhausts, the two scarlet-painted bands round the fuselage that were our squadron markings, blue shadows — the whole moving smoothly and gracefully against a gigantic backdrop of rocks, ice and snow. Graham had removed his helmet and was wearing only his goggles. His black hair was blowing in the slipstream. 'Clot!' I thought; it was common knowledge that the tearing bellow of the stub exhausts, only feet in front of your face would quickly damage the hearing in unprotected ears. He would have to be spoken to later.

With no radio, we used our complete language of signs. He put one hand to his eyebrows in classic Red Indian style and moved his head from side to side to convey 'I am looking' — and followed with thumbs-up. I returned him a thumbs-up and nodded. I had answered as clearly as by using words: 'Yes; I wholly agree with you. It all looks wonderful.' He then made little jabbing motions with one finger pointing downwards, followed by holding his nose with one hand whilst he made plug-pulling movements with the other. I nodded again, briskly and firmly this time, so as to tell him, 'Yes, again I agree. What we have below us stinks to high Heaven.' Graham grinned again and swung away to return to his cruising position.

Some 45 minutes later we arrived over Gilgit landing ground. Instantly all the rough running, low pressures and high temperatures vanished as if by magic. It had been a very long 45 minutes and the only 45 minutes I can remember when a simple uncomplicated loss of engine power would have resulted in no chance whatever of rescue or survival.

Up the Hunza valley to our right was yet another monument of snow, ice and rocks. It was almost more breath-catching than

Nanga Parbat, for this time the sun was behind me and it lit the mountain's faces brilliantly with direct light. This was Rakaposhi in all its glory, only 1100 ft. below its big brother and eleventh highest mountain in the world. So; we had seen two of the greats in one morning, close up. Now there was that ridiculous little cross upon which a landing was to be made. Forget the past 45 minutes. A new problem was on hand.

The Gilgit Scouts had lit a smoke-candle to show the wind direction. I assessed the options carefully. The valley opened out a bit to one side, and this gave two directions for landing. One possibility was to approach along the valley towards the shoulder of the mountain; the other choice was to swing round and across the valley, over the Gilgit river and towards the mountain on the other side of the Hunza. Unequivocally, it was a one-shot affair. It had to be right first time. No going round to have another try. If you got it wrong, put it on the airfield somehow and break it there when you were going slowly. If you tried to fly away with an overloaded aircraft at high altitude, with its engine suffering from low power due to thin air and lack of oxygen, you would fly into one or another mountain-side for certain. Better by far to incur the wrath of the boss, Squadron Leader Jones, than to enrage St. Peter by having him open the Pearly Gates for you ahead of schedule.

I did a couple of circuits to weigh it up carefully. I chose 'up the valley and towards the mountain'. It looked a very big mountain; a very solid mountain; seen over the aircraft's nose as I approached it at 65–70 mph it looked a very close mountain; it was most positively a nerve-racking mountain. Of course, such is the ludicrous resilience of youth that once the machine had been put gently on the ground, and I had brought it to a standstill by careful and steady braking, there was nothing to it. I remember looking round and thinking, 'Two hours' flight equals eleven days' walk; rather them than me.'

I climbed out stiffly and shook hands with Major Cropper who had come out to meet us. Then I started helping Kerr to unload and anchor the aircraft down for the night. All the way he had been kneeling on the gunner's seat with his arms crossed on the cockpit rim behind me and looking over my shoulders. Out came the screw-pickets like giant steel corkscrew tent-pegs which we twisted down into the earth before roping the wings and tail to them. Finally, with all our kit out, we fitted the green canvas engine and cockpit covers, and laced them up tightly.

That done, Kerr said to me, 'You know, sir, those mountains are quite something, aren't they? As we were coming along, I was wondering where you were going to land, if the engine had stopped.' I thought for a moment as to just what I could say. Then I looked him straight in the eye: 'You're the fitter. It's your engine. If it had stopped, the only thing I could have done was to send you climbing out on to the wing with your toolbox to try and get it started again. Of course, if you had preferred, you could have hung on out there, turning the starting-handle very quickly.' He grinned at me. He understood.

While all this was going on Major Cropper moved around interestedly but tactfully keeping out of our way. His face was sharp with a jutting chin. A strip of black moustache showed on his upper lip. He wore breeches rather like plus-fours with stockings, ankle-socks and sandal-type shoes called *chapplis*; these are very tough, made locally and are superlative for mountain walking. His rank badges poked out of slots in the shoulders of his khaki sweater. On the top, in conformity with the orders of the time, a fawn solar topee with the regimental colours on its ribbon. He was very much the Army officer, ramrod straight and immaculately turned out, compared to us Air Force types, somewhat creased, a bit oily after landing and very relaxed at work except in the cockpit itself. He came up to me. 'When you are ready,' he said, 'we are going to the village. It's about four miles.'

# Chapter 13
# Not Quite Smith's Lawn

When the last cover was laced in place on the line of neatly parked Harts, and the last screw-picket had been tugged and heaved-on to check its strength, we had a final look around Gilgit airfield. On one side of the valley of the Gilgit river, with its snow-capped hills, wound away to our left; the Hunza valley went to the right. In the middle the massive shoulder reared up, its lower slopes coming right down on to the landing area itself. The aircraft, snugly bedded down for their two-day stay, looked very puny and fragile in these surroundings. The third valley, behind us, was the one through which we had flown.

Major Cropper took his cue. 'Now, Gentlemen,' he announced, 'there is a gravel track to the village which is some four miles or so away. If you want to ride, I have eight spare horses for you. If you don't like riding, or you would prefer some exercise after your long flight, it is a very pleasant walk along the valley and beside the river. I am leaving a patrol of Scouts who will camp out on the airfield as long as is necessary to keep a guard on your aeroplanes. Who would like to ride? Please do not feel you have to; the Scouts who rode them out will be only too happy not to have to walk back!' The eight aviators chose to ride. It may have been bad luck for the Scouts for them to walk back in their *chapplis,* but it would have been a tough trudge for us in our ordinary shoes.

The rocky, boulder-strewn, gravelly track wound along the foot of the mountain while the muddy Gilgit river waters sloshed below the bank on our left. Major Cropper, looking very smart and at ease, took the lead, only dropping back to chat when the path was wide enough. Those Scouts who had not been left on guard strode purposefully along behind, laughing with each other and talking animately in their incomprehensible language. They were men to be admired. Hill men with powerful frames and muscles showing through their sweaters and socks. Clear brown eyes twinkling with enjoyment of the non-routine job. Their faces showed a mongol strain, probably a trademark from the invading hordes of Gengis Khan, when that conqueror ruled from the Yellow Sea to the Black Sea in the 13th century. Their brown-skinned faces gleamed; I wondered if they needed to shave? The ponies clip-clopped as they picked their footsteps neatly between the rocks.

After a time, 'Halt,' said the Major, 'and dismount. You see before you the longest suspension bridge in Asia, which we are going to cross.' We all looked at it with respectful awe. He continued, 'The stone for the supports on each side of the river was quarried locally, but the steel cables from which the bridge hangs were carried up from the plains, by porters. Long lines of them with cables on their shoulders, moving along the track beside the river like immense caterpillars.' Maybe in 1938 it was the longest suspension bridge in Asia, but it wasn't much of a bridge. It must have been barely 50 yards long. Two fairly insecure looking grey stone support towers rose about 40–50 ft on each side of the river. The two rusty supporting cables swung across the mud-coloured torrent, 20 feet below. Hanging from equally rusty and knotted vertical steel wires were wooden slats, grey with age, which made a pathway roughly four feet wide. It gave me no confidence.

A notice-board was on one of the stone pillars. It too was suffering from the elements with its chipped black paint and flaking white letters. It said:

By Order–Limit

6 men
1 camel
2 horses
3 cows
10 goats or sheep

No one should cross the bridge mounted.

Nothing on Heaven or earth would have kept me on my horse across that bridge; it would have felt safer crossing Niagara in an open dinghy. Solemnly, one by one, we led our ponies across the loose and creaking boards as the bridge swayed uneasily in the wind. Between the boards one could see the foam-flecked rapids. The ponies were totally unconcerned.

The village of Gilgit was little more than one street of mud-brick and stone two-roomed houses, one up and one down. Most of them had a verandah or *stoep* towards the road and on which little brown toddlers played and women did household chores. In front, at the road's edge, brown men in brown clothes squatted with their goods for sale spread out before them. Some sold grain and seeds; others sold household goods like candles and dishes, tin kettles or cooking pots, unrefined sugar and rough salt. An occasional shop had hand-woven rough cloth and some cloaks and garments of sheepskin. These sheepskin coats, *poshteens*, were attractively embroidered but the tanning left much to be desired. If they got wet, the smell rose to high heaven.

I looked carefully to see if there was anything of interest or value to my more sophisticated western eyes, but this was the simple life. The people there, by our yardsticks, were poor. In their world there were no precious metals, minerals or gems for the seeking. To extract an agriculture-based living was rough and tough. The market stock reflected the economy and the communications. Only small light things which could be grown, boiled down or carried there on porters' backs were on offer. Probably made locally, but without the use of refined products like mineral oil or electricity. It was a far cry from a flight I had made some months earlier to coastal villages on the Arabian Gulf where, in the 1930s a visiting RAF pilot could buy real pearls for pennies; small ones, anyway. Here we could find no treasures to buy; only the wonderful scenery to marvel at.

The Squadron Leader and I were staying with the Croppers. We were introduced to Mrs Cropper and to Nanny, and we duly admired the baby. All were delighted and full of thanks for the air-transported goodies. The major offered us a drink before dinner. Squadron Leader Jones opted, rather tactlessly I thought, for a glass of the precious beer we had carried there. I chose a glass of *nimbu-pane,* the ubiquitous fruit juice made from crushed fresh limes. Housekeeping cannot have been easy for Mrs Cropper. No electricity, no oil or paraffin, so naturally no refrigerator and no ice for our thirst-quenchers.

When we were all seated, Major Cropper turned to Squadron Leader Jones and asked 'Do you play polo?' It was fairly certain that my boss, who was an engineering specialist in the Air Force, hardly knew which end of a horse went first. Indeed, a four-mile ride from the airfield had sorely taxed his thigh muscles already. He explained, courteously, that polo was not one of his strong points. The Major turned to me: 'Do you?' I explained that I could ride a bit, and I had tried now and again to hit a polo ball about. I was not, however, by any stretch of the imagination a *bona fide* polo player who owned, or had owned, even one polo pony — let alone a string of the beasts. A little smile twitched round the corners of his mouth. 'Would you like to join in and have a go tomorrow?' That smile: was it amusement, or scorn? Was the honour and reputation of the Royal Air Force at stake? Were we all poltroons? I took a deep breath and said I would be pleased, nay honoured, to play a chukka or two if I could be loaned the necessary horses. I added that, bearing in mind my inexperience, I hoped he would brief me comprehensively before the game. 'Excellent; excellent!' cried my host. 'I'll just get things organised for you, and then we shall have time for me to explain the local rules before dinner.' He capped his hands and the immaculate bearer appeared. The Major reeled off about 30 seconds of local language before the bearer bowed slightly from the waist, gave me a long startled look, turned and departed.

Beaming, Cropper turned to me saying 'Fine, fine! That's fixed. I can lend you the riding kit and you'll have a horse at 11 o'clock tomorrow. Unless your head's simply enormous you can wear my wife's topee. Now, I'll explain the game to you so that you will know what to expect tomorrow.' I listened attentively.

'Polo,' he began, 'was invented in these valleys. It is the local game which all the men play. They are natural horsemen and they all ride. As children they cut sticks from the willows which grow, here and there, beside the rivers. They do this by selecting a wand which is pretty well straight for about three feet or so. Then they cut off the thicker branch from which it grows a few inches above and below the joint. This makes the mallet head. Naturally it is at an angle to the wand, or handle, which is why the heads of polo sticks in the Western game are always at an angle to the shaft.

'As soon as the children can run they play "polo" on their little short legs, beating a woven wickerwork ball back and forth along the village street using their home-grown polo sticks. No one has a watch, so no one times any chukkas. They just go on until they are exhausted. To keep things fair and to eliminate advantages of the ground such as up and down hill, corners of horses, gullies and drains, market stalls, gossiping grown-ups and so forth, they change ends after each goal, and play the other way. They get remarkably good and by the time they can sit on a horse they are already experts with a stick. Their eye for a ball, moving or stationary, has to be seen to be believed.

'The polo played by adults — such as tomorrow — has almost the same form except that a needle match (even between rival villages) does not go on from dawn till dusk. Also, we do not play in the village street; it causes too much damage. We therefore have a proper polo ground just like they do at Hurlingham and Cowdray, but there are some differences. It's only a couple of hundred yards long, and its width is like the village street, roughly 15 yards wide. To keep the ball in play there is a three-foot wall of hard mud-bricks either side. The goal posts at each end are about half the width of the field apart. Spectators sit on the wall, excepting on one side in the middle. That space has a raised earth platform, the same height as the wall. On it sits the Mayor, in a chair. He is the starter, because he throws the ball into play. He is the timekeeper, because the game stops when he says so. He is also the umpire, but no one would be spoilsport enough to stop a good game in the middle. Beside him are any honoured guests, such as Squadron Leader Jones tomorrow. I will be playing on the opposing side to you. In front of the Mayor, on the wall, is the village band. Primarily there is the big drum, but with pipes, whistles, local bagpipes, tambourines, little drums and some twangy stringed instruments thrown in. They play all the time but, the more exciting the game, the louder and more frenzied the music. It comes to a violent crescendo every time someone scores a goal.

'The game normally lasts about an hour, as long as the timekeeper is not too excited to say "stop". None of these pansy seven-minute chukkas and then change horses. The Gilgiti horse is made of tougher muscle; he goes right through the game non-stop. At each end of the field is stationed a strong-armed Scout; his job, if the ball goes past the goal and not through it, is to pick it up and throw it as far back into the field as he can. The game can then continue with minimum delay. If the ball scores a goal, two things happen. First, of course, the direct of play changes. Second, a *Tambruk* is taken. This means that the Scout gives the ball to a designed member of the scoring side. He then gallops up the field with the ball in his hand. When he gets opposite to the Mayor, he tosses it in the air and tries to hit it with his stick as it comes down. I told you these chaps had a good eye for a ball; they will score a goal, wham, right down the far end of the field, a hundred yards away, about two times in three. If he scores, he will get another *Tambruk* back up the other way again. If he misses, the game goes straight on from there.

'I think that is about all you need to know, really. Oh no — one more thing. If you can catch the ball, drop your stick and gallop flat out through the goal to score with it for your side. If anyone else catches the ball, drop your stick, try to get to him, and pull him off his horse.

'Don't be alarmed. Tomorrow's game will be reasonably quiet. Last week we played our annual match against a Hunza village; two men broke an arm, and one horse was killed. They won't be bringing out their best horses.'

By this time my eyes were bulging out of my head like snail-shells from Burgundy. The very last thing I remember that night as I snuggled down between the sheets was making a solemn promise to myself that I would not in any circumstances succeed in catching the ball during the game.

Ten o'clock next day saw me self-consciously kitted out in jodhpurs, white shirt, green sleeveless sweater, my black uniform shoes and Mrs Crocker's topee, firmly anchored as a crash-hat by its strap under my chin. I made friends with my horse. It was obviously built for work rather than for speed and agility. I was pleased that it gave indications of having been sired by a billiard table; a solid body with a good flat back and short strong legs. It seemed to have a slightly long-suffering look in its eye, as if having seen all this before.

I was introduced to the Mayor. My courteous greeting and thanks were duly translated by my host. What he said I know not, but the Mayor was plainly delighted. Gently the band played that wavering eastern music, full of semitones, which sounds mournful to western ears. I hoped it would not be a dirge for me. Along the walls on either side hundreds of spectators squatted. The Scouts were in their drab uniform. The civilians wore their jackets, blanket-cloaks, baggy trousers and most of them had bare feet. In best Muslin tradition, there were no women. Every male from the village who was not incapacitated must have been there. I got a strong impression that, for them, this bird-man on a horse was a first showing. Were they expecting some species of Pegasus, lifting his horse and soaring over the other combatants? Would the ball be thrown in the air to be caught there and whisked through the opponents' goal, yards off the ground? Aeroplanes still had a strong aura of the occult in those days.

The Mayor indicated that the teams should mount. We all gathered in a great gaggle before the rostrum as he threw the ball amongst us. From that moment on my recollections are very hazy. Almost every time I got near the ball, galloping down the field, some Gilgiti figure showing all the characteristics of a reinforced concrete Centaur would lean his horse against mine at an equal speed and just push us away. Luckily, my horse, clever beast, would exercise his initiative and very sensibly clap on the brakes in the nick of time before we hit the wall.

Whenever, just occasionally, I did manage to get into position beside the ball, my horse found himself thoroughly confused. He knew his normal drill to perfection; he had to hold his steam till, with a swish of the swung polo-stick, his rider would hit the ball ahead; then, after the swish, his job was to gallop flat out down the field so that the chap on his back could hit it once more, neatly between those two little posts at the far end. The only snag to all this, from the horse's point of view, was that his other riders didn't miss the ball first time round. Swish — and the two of us would then speed off like an across towards and through the goal, leaving ball and game far behind us. The band reached giddy heights of impromptu composition and the spectators cheered wildly every time I scored a ball-less goal.

At one point in the game, after my side had scored a goal without my assistance, I was accorded the great honour of hitting the *Tambruk*. 'Don't,' said Major Cropper, 'gallop too fast. A smart canter is plenty.' I nodded. The ball was thrust into my nerveless grasp and I set off up the field at the recommended smart canter. 'Please,' my prayer went up to the Almighty, 'let me just hit the ball, even if it doesn't score a goal for my side.' Opposite the Mayor I tossed the ball into the air, raised my polo stick and swung it round and down to intercept the ball rather too far out. I leaned to the right, and as far forwards as I could, to reach it. The horse suddenly saw the brim of Mrs Cropper's topee about to prod its right eye. It, therefore, swerved smartly to the left. I continued to the right.

In my early days at a cavalry riding-school I had learned one salient thing. When you fall off, don't let go of the reins and then you won't have to walk home. So, lying on the dusty field, I still had my horse which was looking down at me with a distinctly jaundiced air. The spectators were dancing on the wall, cheering to the echo. So! The bird-man could fly; maybe without his horse, but so what? The band was in an ecstatic delirium, breaking all decibel records. The Mayor stood up and clapped. For the first time in living memory the game came to a complete standstill before the end. They picked me up, dusted me off, and put me back on my horse. The game then went on unabated till the Mayor/Umpire/Timekeeper said 'stop', aeons later.

It was not, on my part, a very glorious performance, but I felt that the honour of the Royal Air Force had been partially vindicated.

We were due to leave next morning. The weather proved to be poor. The difficulty was that we had not got enough fuel in hand to fly down the valley just for a look-see, and then to come back if it was unsuitable. When we went, it was to go all the way home; otherwise, it was not to go at all. Our hosts were kindness itself, but neither they nor we relished the prospect of eight frustrated men hanging around, just waiting for the weather to look up. On the other hand, with those craggy mountains sticking up far higher than we could fly, and hidden in the clouds to boot, we were not playing games. We decided to ride out to the airfield and have a look.

It was one of those maddening days when the weather is called 'marginal'. Your time is up; you want to go; they want you to leave; it will probably be all right. It all hung on the leader's personal lonely judgement which went like this: 'If I decide to go, and we get through, that is just our normal job completed. If I decide not to go, we surely will be a burden here, and am I being unduly nervous? If I decide to go, and get it wrong, it could easily cost the lives of seven other people who trust me.'

We passed some of the time loading up and preparing the aircraft. The Gilgit Scouts stood around, laughing like children, chatting and kicking pebbles. The four pilots discussed the matter together, while Major Cropper listened intently. The visibility was good; it was not raining. No top of any hill was visible for all were in the clouds; to the south, along our route, the valley was a triangular tunnel and we could see down it — flat clouds on top and the two mountain sides sloping steeply down to the river. The wind blew gently towards us, along the valley. How high were the clouds? 2,000 ft? 3,000 ft? We could see down it for 10 miles, and it was big enough to fly along — but, if the weather got worse and we had to come back, was it wide enough to make a turnabout in emergency? And what was it going to be like when we met the Indus for our turn westwards? Would the light wind, then blowing across the valley, roll the clouds down into it? It could become a very hairy situation very quickly indeed.

If the clouds did fold in on us, and we managed to get back

there would then be, to make matters worse, the problem of getting more fuel flown in somehow, bringing with it more of the same sorts of decisions and risks for even more people. I said I was game to give it a go — but that was easy; it wasn't my final decision. The boss hesitated. Graham and Parsons said they were ready to try it. The Squadron Leader looked intently at each of us, and at Major Cropper. Nothing was said. He fingered his chin and looked down the valley again. Now, after many years and many such decisions I know the mental agony it must have been for him. It has been called 'the loneliness of command'. On the one hand an inner fear that his competence was being judged by us, and we might think him scared at his job; on the other hand, the certain knowledge that he was betting seven lives beside his own on his personal say-so. Abruptly he turned. 'OK. We'll go.'

Airborne, having taken off away from the mountain, we formed up quickly so as to make a low pass in salute and thanks, over the village and the longest suspension bridge in Asia. We opened out a little to conserve fuel, but not too far. We might have to tuck in quickly if the leader suddenly decided conditions ahead were unsafe and he started to do a turnabout. We entered the tunnel.

The fates were kind. The weather did not close in and the clouds did not come down. Indeed, as the river went further and further downhill we got more space under the clouds. Two hours from take-off we were all safely on the ground back at base.

I have often wondered if the 'Onegilgitscoutpower' cinema-projector worked well

# Chapter 14
# Temptation

Sitting in the driver's seat of an aircraft is something very special. You take it off and, largely due to your personal skills, you can put it down again safely. It is quite a responsibility, getting your machine to do what you want it to do. Your life, and perhaps those of a crowd of others too, hangs on your capability. Managers everywhere are exercising another kind of responsibility. That is to get people, as opposed to machines, to do what they want them to do. It is different, and can be equally satisfying. Outsiders sometimes think that military leaders get their results by barking out orders. This however, does not get very far; if the recipient has to stick his neck out, even so far perhaps as to get it chopped off, he has to have a very special trust in the man giving the order. And getting Service individuals to produce outstanding results, when you have no direct control over their salary, promotion or place of work, becomes an art in itself. Successful results in command can be deeply satisfying, but command is not all good clean fun. My first command promised well, but like the curate's egg, it was only good in parts. It began during a holiday in Kashmir.

Women, it was believed, were physically incapable of taking the heat without falling sick. As we had no air-conditioning they, therefore, were sent up into the hills to luxuriate in the cool at one of the summering stations located throughout the Himalayas. Most of these were little townships set up in the mountains and which, over the years, had grown almost into resorts. One of these was a large floating village of houseboats on Negim Bagh lake, which laps the town of Srinagar in Kashmir. I had heard that their situation was idyllic. Lotus and other water lilies were beside your window. Across the lake was the superb skyline of the eternally snow-capped Himalayas. Merchants brought carpets, silks, flowers and goods from far off Cathay to your gunwales and if shopping was needed you went by boat. Even better, dances every night in Nedou's Hotel to a band playing smoochy music. One got there and back in a *shikara* boat with the damsel you were squiring for the evening, lounging on plush upholstered seats behind a discreet curtained awning, paddled gently by silent Kashmiris who would take as long to get there, or back, as you wished.

There was, as may be imagined, a certain competition amongst the lonely ladies for the comparatively few male escorts available. First choice, of course, would be their husbands when they could get time off from the plains. If no husband was available there was a steady trickle of steaming bachelors on leave, who were only too enchanted to have female company after the boozy all-male population of the messes. In such a situation anything could, and frequently did, happen. Two middle-aged gentlemen in Bangalore on a spring evening were sipping their *chota-pegs* in the Mess. One asked 'Are you sending your wife up to the Hills this summer?' After a thoughtful pause the other answered 'No; I'm keeping her here, and sleeping with her myself for a change.'

Being a young bachelor and holding only Flying Officer rank, in my second hot-weather I had some difficulty in prising myself loose. Older men were senior and married; they got there first, and stayed longest. It started with the fact that the Station Commander was on home leave in England and my Squadron Commander was standing in for him; two of our three Flight Commanders (married) had sinecure jobs running hill-stations, up there with their wives for the whole hot-weather; the third had been 'borrowed' by Air Headquarters to teach the Afghans how to fly British-built Hawker Hinds, because their Air Force was being equipped with them. I was Squadron Adjutant, keeping the Squadron Commander's chair warm and expecting to be forbidden summer leave till the autumn when all the rest had come back. However, by dint of much pleading and many crocodile tears, an all too brief two-week break for a little cool air was achieved.

Srinagar it was to be. Kali was equally delighted to be going on leave. He packed up my clothes, my bed-roll, my travelling washbasin and goodness knows what else. Then, on the appointed day, for a ridiculously low payment he produced a large taxi which was an American four-seater tourer. Junior officers, mostly, could not afford a car for themselves. There was no railway, and no airline — hence the taxi. Everything was stowed away somehow and we set off on the 300 mile drive to the fleshpots. Kali was in front with the driver and I sat regally in the back.

Leaving on one side the fact that the driver was a speed maniac and his taxi felt as if it were held together by faith, the drive was a wonderful experience. First in the searing heat, we crossed the parched plains, leaving behind us a vast column of dust and the imprecations of all other road users. Then, up into the hills and the resin scent of pine trees. The Indian Works Department had hewn out a gravel road, curving and winding over hills and along valleys. The more we climbed the cooler and more pleasant the trip became. Kali, from somewhere, produced a cardigan for me. Then, down a thousand feet or so, to reach Muzaffarabad which was the Kashmiri frontier town. Get out of the car for passport and Customs check.

Kashmir is a very strict Hindu state, so all beef is totally forbidden. In response to polite queries I assured them I had no beef, nor Bully Beef, nor Bovril, nor Oxo cubes, nor tinned steak and kidney pie. No — no beef whatever. I took care not to emulate an earlier colleague who had thought to take the Mickey out of these white-suited Customs-wallahs. Politely but firmly they searched his baggage down to unfolding his last handkerchief. They practically reduced his car to its component nuts and bolts. They refrained only from giving him a complete body-search. After all, had he not inadvertently but clearly let fall the information that he was carrying beef products? And who could believe his ridiculous cover story (obviously invented on the spur of the moment when he realised the enormity of his offence) that some black-and-white-striped peppermints in a glass jar were what he meant by bull's-eyes? . . . That little joke cost him about six hours.

We went swooping and swirling along the gravelly road snipped perilously from the precipitous slope cut by the Jhelum river far below. The driver appeared to place his trust equally between Allah and the horn button. I, looking down at the foaming torrent a hundred feet below, was not so sanguine. My frequent and plaintive cries of 'Asti! Asti!' (which I understood to be Urdu for 'Slowly! Slowly!') fell upon deaf ears. No Jehu, however, could impair the superb, cool, pine-scented lungfuls of clean air replacing the hot, dusty, enervating atmosphere of the plains behind us.

Suddenly, as we came round a bend, we could see a monumental queue of cars, post-lorries and horse-drawn tongas, stretching far ahead. 'Landslide, Sahib; I arrange' said Kali with perfect unconcern. About fifty yards of road ahead had slipped from its tenuous hold on the hillside before sliding and tumbling down into the river. Already there were gangs of workmen who would have a new road in place within a few days. The foreman squatted on a convenient rock, under a large black umbrella. He directed with shrill cries hundreds of coolie-labourers who dug, pulled, hacked and carried rocks and earth. With the patience of the East, most of the vehicles would wait unconcernedly till the new road was open. We were more fortunate. Kali could do better. He picked his way from boulder to boulder till he reached the corresponding queue on the other side. There he selected another taxi with whom he negotiated to take us to Srinagar, while our taxi took his load back in the other direction.

Then began a lengthy discussion as to which driver had come the further, and therefore would have to go back the furthest. That man deserved an adjustment (and how much?) from the other driver who had been paid for a whole trip, but was only going to do two shorter bits, each less than half. Both, I gathered, were swearing on oath that their fares (meaning me, for one) had been so niggardly that any transfer of funds was out of the question. At last Kali, acting as Solomon, extracted some extra rupees from me, and from my counterpart on the other side, and got things moving again. Both drivers remained utterly convinced that each had had the worst of the deal. When I asked Kali if we had really been fair, he just shrugged his shoulders scornfully.

Having got the taxi problem sorted out, Kali then gave a tip to the foreman. Immediately all work on repairing the road halted; for some more coins the repair gang became luggage porters and downed tools to carry our kit from one side of the landslip to the other. We, the two fares, sauntered across, unencumbered, at ease and making noises of gratitude to the foreman on his rock. We loaded ourselves into the new taxi, which was not only just like the first one, but apparently driven by the first one's soul-mate. In another 50 miles we had left the steep-sided valley and were rushing along straight poplar-lined roads. We were still some four to five thousand feet up, but it was a great flat valley floor which, because of its altitude, grew summer vegetation almost like Europe.

At the lakeside we were besieged by hordes of Kashmiris, each of whom had the finest, most convenient, best furnished, best staffed houseboat with the best cook on the lake. Served, of course, by the best and most voluptuous shikara with the softest cushions to paddle me wherever and whenever. While Kali made the detailed arrangements I looked over the many shikaras whose owners craved my custom. I wondered who had had the knowledge of double-meanings to suggest their names, and if the owners knew what could be inferred. One was called the 'Love — On Spring Seats'. Another had a skull and crossbones above its name-board, on which was 'The Jolly Roger'.

That evening I revelled in the relaxations of my temporary home. Kali the major-domo already had it well organised. For the first day in months I had enjoyed a *hot* hip-bath. When I had dried and put my wrist-watch on again, its metal back had felt cold instead of hot. The floor was cool and slippers were welcome. I even wore the cardigan over my shirt. As I sat in my deck-chair, sipping a beer and waiting for dinner, it was all to good to be true. The sunset sported a myriad colours, turning the snows to pinks, mauves and blues. The lake was flat calm and looked like molten lead. Somewhere from across the water floated the strains of a popular tune, played on a portable gramophone. Little wavelets from the shikaras gliding past gently slapped the sides of my houseboat. One of them stopped and I learned that news travelled fast in this community, or someone had a pair of binoculars; the boat had brought an invitation to drinks, at a houseboat a little further up the bank, for next evening. If, I mused, half the stories of Kashmir were true, the Muslim Paradise, with its ten thousand houris, was going to have competition. The immediate future was overflowing with possibilities. Kali turned up the oil-lamps and announced dinner.

Next morning, during my breakfast, Kali was summoned by someone outside. He returned with a telegram. Its message was simple. Trouble on the Frontier; Squadron going on to operational basis; Flying Officer Dudgeon to return forthwith; or sooner if possible. Unwillingly I read the paper twice and wondered? A wicked little devil was telling me that there might be a chance for the world to be persuaded it had never arrived. I cursed everybody and everything at length, comprehensively, fluently, and particularly I cursed the postman who had so astutely discovered my whereabouts. But, with the aid of Kali's unfailing capacity for organisation, I was back for duty on the station next morning. On the way, as we had been driving through the deepening darkness, I could not help wondering what I was missing at that drinks party.

It is an ill wind . . . If I had to forfeit my leave it was some compensation that as senior officer on the spot I, a mere Flying Officer, was going to command my squadron on real, live operations. Proscription was not a tough assignment, which doubtless was why I was allowed to get on with it. Really, it only entailed making out a daily programme so that one aircraft would be over the specified area from dawn to dusk. I took it very seriously but while the weeks ticked by, something less pleasant was in brew.

Down in Delhi it was hot and humid. Delhi and the Frontier endlessly claimed each to have the more unpleasant summer of the two. Both were vile. In his office, the Command Navigation Officer, Flight Lieutenant George Nelson was bored to tears. His wife was at Simla, up in the hills. Anyone who could fix it was up there also. Little was happening. He ran his fingers through his fair hair in frustration and frowned. When he put his arm back on the desk, the sweat under his forearm smudged the ink and made his signature run on a letter. He simply must get out, up in the air and away for a break, somewhere. Anywhere would be better than this steaming cookpot. He pondered a while and then went along the passage to see the Senior Air Staff Officer. He had a plan.

SASO was sympathetic. Yes — it could be an excellent idea if he did a staff visit to the Squadron on ops. Good thing to let the front-line see that Staff did not suffer from Office Constipation. He could check up on how seriously they took their navigation problems; very important with the Afghan frontier so close. It would be OK to take the Communications Flight Hart for the trip. And one of the better clerks could go as a passenger, as reward for good work. Excellent idea . . .

Nelson's blue eyes sparkled. It would be an interesting flight. He would leave Friday and return Monday. That way he would get four days away, but no one could take him to task as he would only miss two working days. Oh yes — and he would qualify for a bar to his Sweeper Medal!

# Chapter 15
# Dangerous Dust

Friday dawned clear, slightly hazy and hot as usual. Flight Lieutenant Nelson studied the Met report for his long cross-country flight. No cloud, light winds, some dust haze. Nothing to worry about. As a Navigation Specialist, he completed his flight planning meticulously and with great care. His knee-pad log was full of detailed entries, noting to the nearest half-minute his calculated ETA at each one of his check-points.

Easting, George Nelson's clerk in the office, was bubbling with expectation. He had been taken up for the occasional flip but he had never before done a long flight like this one, to another airfield for a purpose. Nelson took off, and set course. His first proper check-point was Jalalabad on the Sutlej river and to his intense satisfaction it came up right over the nose, spot on time. Life was good. The dust haze was irritating, but it wasn't too bad.

For the next 150 miles — about an hour and a quarter — he was crossing a wide plain, partly irrigated by four rivers. The nearest was the Sutlej; in the middle were the Chenab and the Jhelum; right on the far edge was the mighty Indus. Below him was a vast patchwork of tiny fields, criss-crossed by hundreds of small roads, tracks, irrigation canals and ditches. In mid-summer many of the watercourses were dry and difficult to pick out as such. Occasionally there was a long straight railway line, but these did not give much help in the way of pin-points. The mass of petty detail, most of it too insignificant to be marked on his map, was confusing. He reckoned his map reading was in hand, but the haze made it difficult to be precise. The nearest town large enough to be distinguished from the dozens of little hamlets — Mianwali — was at least twenty-five miles away to the north of him. He came down to 1000 ft to see better. Beyond the Indus he would be into the mountains and over Tribal Territory. It was the bit after the Indus that he was looking forward to — away from this flat featureless stuff, little better than desert. Especially as he had not flown over the mountains before.

As the time for crossing the Indus neared, he found himself between the Devil and the Deep. The visibility was getting really poor and he had to fly very low to see the ground clearly. On the one hand he knew that he was approaching the hills and he would have to go up sooner or later; sooner would be more prudent. On the other hand the Indus would be his last unmistakable landmark; it was essential to pin-point himself accurately, so that he could set up the precise final run-in to his destination, Miranshah. He decided that staying low as far as the river was the correct choice. The uncertainty irritated him. He glanced round at Easting. He was in the classic Hart gunner's position of arms folded on the cockpit edge, looking over the pilot's shoulder. Easting grinned, and Nelson forced a smile in return.

He checked his fuel calculations. They too were uncomfortable. He had plenty to reach Miranshah but barely enough to go back to Lahore, his diversion airfield, in comfort — particularly in this lousy visibility where he might have to search around a bit when he got close to it. This damnable dust haze; below him was the brown earth merging in a mile or so to featureless brown air which went right up, over the brown sky above and down the other side with no sign of horizon. It felt like flying under a pudding-basin lined with brown velvet. Sometimes, above, was a pale disc of sun. Luckily, he could still distinguish the small circle of ground around and below him, if he kept low enough.

Abruptly the Indus appeared, meandering its muddy way across his track. He glanced at his watch — spot on. He tried to identify the river bends quickly and surely. However, the river-bed was a mile or so wide and, being summer, was made up of indeterminate and temporary narrow muddy streams with sandbanks between them of similar colour. None of them on the ground would, nor could, fit on to his map. He had no means of telling but, after 350 miles of flying over those unidentifiable details, he was only two miles north of where he hoped to be. It had been an extremely competent and accurate piece of pure navigation and piloting. He was, however, out of practice in applying commonsense airmanship to the task as a whole.

He peered ahead. To his horror, ahead of him on the far edge of the river bed was a dirty great brown cliff of sandstone, rising almost vertically till it lost itself in the brown sky above him. He yanked back on the stick and slammed open the throttle. The engine responded instantly and the nose went up as the sandstone cliff raced past under his wheels. Then, as fast as it had appeared, it was gone. He now had the nose pointing somewhere up to the sky, speed was falling disastrously and he had no horizon to orient him in the brown murk. He was, to put it mildly, somewhat poorly placed.

Nelson kicked on rudder bringing the nose across and down as he lifted the wings to try and level the machine in order to fly her out. Harts had fairly rudimentary blind-flying instruments and the skills to use them effectively needed continuous practice. He fought the turn-and-slip needles trying to get and to keep them central. His speed was still dangerously low so he eased the nose down a bit to accelerate before she stalled and fell out of his hands.

For an instant he glanced out of the cockpit. He saw, right in front of the dipped nose, a brown river and beyond it a brown sandbank. Easting, probably, had been thrown to the floor by the crushing forces when Nelson snatched back on the stick. There is a slim chance that he might still have been looking over Nelson's shoulder. If he was, that piece of river was the last thing that either of them ever saw as, with a mighty splash, the Hart went straight in. In less than one second they were both extremely dead.

At Miranshah it was a filthy day. The dust made you sticky and your eyes smarted. Your sweat felt like a thin layer of gritty paste. We had stopped all flying except for the one aircraft flying round and around the proscribed area. Its pilot had nothing to see in the dust haze except the circular patch of ground right below him, but the tribesmen hearing him would not know that. He was under very strict and unequivocal instructions to nip home smartly if it got any worse — and long before it became dangerously bad.

We were a bit surprised when a visiting Hart from Delhi was signalled to be on its way to us, and somewhat relieved when it didn't arrive. We assumed its sensible pilot had turned back or diverted to some other airfield. Our seemingly careless attitude was normal. Aircraft were signalled out upon departure; when they arrived, as 99.9 per cent of them did, that was the end of the matter. This kept unnecessary signals off the air and needless panics were avoided. If it didn't arrive, one took action as soon as it became probable that something could be wrong. Most minor emergencies and diversions sorted themselves out anyway before people started to get excited. So, an hour after its fuel would have run out, we sent a formal 'request news' signal.

During the night I was awakened to receive a message that the Delhi machine really was missing. Admittedly it could have landed somewhere safely, miles from any telephone, but also it might be down amongst the hills and in Tribal Territory. Did they carry goolie chits on HQ Communications Flight aircraft, I wondered? It would be very unlikely. And, we were proscribing a tribal area so the locals were likely to be unfriendly. If it was out in the plains it would soon be reported, but HQ wanted an air search of the hills in the morning, weather permitting.

I had never seen or practised an air search but we planned as best we could. We only had nine of the twelve squadron aircraft with us, the fourth from each flight being at base for maintenance on a rotating schedule. We got all nine ready for take-off as soon as the sunlight would reach the bottoms of the valleys. Silver dope and coloured roundels of the missing aircraft would then show up better. The weather was still pretty lousy but all the pilots said they would give it a go if I wanted them to. This was my first really important judged decision in a command situation. On one side of the balance, two men lost. They might be in Tribal Territory, they might not. They could be dead and past help, or wounded and in dire straits. It might be possible to rescue them, or they could be totally inaccessible. On the other side, with no imponderables at all, nine aircraft and 17 men would go out at considerable risk to themselves on my say-so. It was for me alone to say yea or nay. It was my first taste of 'the loneliness of command'. It was horrible. The eight pilots watched me quizzically while I thought. I said, 'We'll go.'

The search would be in line abreast, one mile apart, 2000 ft above the hilltops, flying back along his intended path over the hills, and as far as the Indus. Beyond that was friendly population and he would already have been found. My aircraft would follow the centre track, with four aircraft each side, spread out one mile apart. Control would be by coloured flares, fired from a Verey pistol. Any flare seen would be acknowledged by firing one of the same colour. Instructions could thus be passed along the line. If anyone saw the missing aircraft they would fire a green Verey flare. If the weather improved, a white flare fired by my gunner, Reed, would be an instruction, to be passed down the line, for the search to be opened up to two miles between machines. If for any reason the search was to be abandoned he would fire a red light, and we all would come home. If nothing had been seen when we reached the Indus, close-up formation for the return flight. Once back at base we would have another think or — with luck — we would have news of him having come down, safe and sound, on the plains.

When we set course over the airfield I could only see one aircraft on each side. The others were totally hidden in the haze. It was much worse than I had foreseen. I peered intently down at the semicircle of ground I could distinguish on our left; Reed was peering down at the other semicircle on the right. There was no horizon and I was flying largely by instruments. I picked up the speaking tube. 'The chances of actually seeing an aircraft,' I said, 'even if it's down there are poor as hell. What to you think?' His voice came flatly into my earpieces: 'Bugger-all, Sir, really.' I decided reluctantly to abandon the search and stop risking everybody's necks, including my own. If by some miracle we spotted him and went down to see if we could help him, it would be only too easy to meet a hill suddenly, with fatal consequences, in that weather. Reed took out the Verey pistol and fitted the red flare cartridge.

When I looked out towards the nearest aircraft, they weren't there. They had vanished into the dust haze, which was thicker than ever. The flare made a great arc into the sky. There was no answering red from either side. Urgently, two more reds were fired. Still no reply. My thoughts raced, as this contingency had not been foreseen and briefed for. Too late I realised my inadequacy, having not said, 'If you lose contact, close in as much as is necessary to keep in sight. If you lose contact entirely, go home immediately.' To my alarm and despair, nothing would come into my mind to rectify my failure. They had been sent off into dangerous weather and they had vanished from all control. I turned about and concentrated on getting myself back to Miranshah. Luckily, we picked out the small Tochi river and followed its twisting course till it ran past the Miranshah fort and airfield. I landed, and waited for the others, keeping my fingers crossed.

That wait was one of my most unhappy experiences. Five hours later, for certain, they were all down on the ground — in one or in several pieces, alive or dead — because by then they were all out of fuel. Not one of my chickens had come back to roost with me. Drafting the 'request news' signal for the eight aircraft and crews conjured up appalling visions of smashed machines and bodies strewn all around the Frontier. My request to them had been unreasonable and poorly planned in the circumstances prevailing; though they had backed me up, it did not absolve me from direct responsibility for any deaths — or worse — that might occur. I should have thought more clearly, planned more completely, foreseen more cleverly. The price of success is eternal vigilance. I had not been up to my task. It went on and on . . . It was a very distressed 22-year-old junior officer who lay awake that night.

Signals began to filter in during the small hours. First one crew, and then another, were reported down safely. By morning, six of my eight Harts were accounted for and none were damaged. Most were on airfields and one pilot had skilfully managed to get his Hart down safely on the Army's polo ground at Bannu — a mere 300 yards long; we later learned that the Colonel there had been incensed with rage because its soft surface, which they had recently and lovingly watered, had been deeply scored by the tail-skid. He expressed his views in no uncertain terms and the pilot's plea that he had been weathered-out on a life-saving mission was no excuse; airfields were for landing on, not polo grounds cherished and cossetted as much as any fairway on a golf course. He should have taken his infernal machine elsewhere.

The day broke as bright and pretty as the one before had been dull and ugly. By nine o'clock they were streaming back and, to my unutterable joy, the other pair came back too. These had gone down on two little landing-grounds with no facilities, when conditions became absolutely impossible. All my chickadees were back at the nest, safe and sound. Nothing could matter now. Not even the tartly worded signal which came from the Squadron Commander, asking how on earth I had managed to lose his entire squadron in one fell swoop.

There was another message. Some river dwellers on the bank of the Indus had heard a roar and big bang coming from the dust-shrouded river. Going out in a boat to investigate, they had found something silvery sticking out of the water. They could not move it. They had told the police, who gave us a pin-point. We plotted it. It was just two miles north of the dead-straight line from Delhi to Miranshah — and just where an isolated escarpment reared its ugly face almost 600 feet from the water's edge.

I took my Hart and went to have a look. It was only 92 miles and I was there in three-quarters of an hour. The wreckage was clearly visible. A length of the starboard upper mainplane and part of the aft fuselage were sticking out of the water. Both were a bit muddy from the throw-up. The rest, including both cockpits, was under the brown stream. I flew past a few feet up and read the number on the tail-fin. It was Nelson's machine. With nothing else I could do, I set course for base to report the details. Also, to help the Powers That Be decide what they needed for the task of salvage. I wondered if there were crocodiles in that part of the river? We had better be quick on the draw.

Another Flying Officer, a friend of mine, got the salvage job. He was Michael 'Poppy' Kane from our rival squadron. He managed superbly for he only had ropes, pulleys, hand tools for dismantling, two airmen and a lorry. Anything else had to be improvised on the spot. He got several local boats and across these he strapped long poles. Then, with this pontoon, pulleys and plenty of local labour, he got the aircraft clear of the river bottom and to the bank in three days. The interior, after being submerged in the teeming lukewarm water for that amount of time, was not pleasant. He looked inside, was violently sick, and then he got on with the job in hand.

Poppy (why 'Poppy' I never found out) rang me up from the local police-post. Could I fly down and land there immediately? There was a field, harrowed and ready for an autumn sowing, which he hoped would be long enough. It had been a bit soft but he had driven his lorry up and down thirty or forty times and reckoned the tyres had beaten down a pathway long enough and hard enough for me to manage a landing.

From the air it looked very short indeed but Reed said he was game if I wished to have a go. So down we went. Once the wheels were on the soft dust it felt as though the brakes could never grip enough to stop in time, but they did, just. Poppy was very grateful that I had come. He was feeling very isolated and badly needed some moral support. He explained that one body had been very badly smashed up. The bacteria in the river had caused it to putrefy and swell horribly. There was no advantage or sense in trying to get it back to a military cemetery. It wouldn't go into a Hart and another three days by road, in a lorry, in that heat, was not practical. He therefore had got the local carpenter to make an outsize coffin before conducting the best Burial Service that he could compose. He and the airmen, with the Muslim villagers in silent and respectful attendance, had said the Lord's Prayer, and such part of any others that he could remember. The grave was next to a Muslim burial ground and had been marked. Some parson could come and give it a proper blessing some day, and perhaps someone would erect a gravestone. Did I agree with what he had done so far? If there was anything better to be done we could always dig him up again. To me, it seemed that Poppy had done an unpleasant, unhappy and praiseworthy job.

Meanwhile, Poppy asked, would I fly the second body back to base right away? It was tied up in a sack and, as yet, was not too foetid but there was not much time to be lost. If I would take him, he could have a proper military funeral, with Honours. Of course, this posed no practical problems for me, so we fed him in through the gunner's cockpit and laid him on the floor with his head by the bombsight and his legs down the back of the fuselage.

Then came the question of Reed. Even after two years I had not yet fully grasped the down-to-earth sense, realism and moral fortitude of my Air Force colleagues in unpleasant situations. Rather diffidently I suggested that if he would prefer not to share the back with a niffy corpse, I could easily come back for him on a second trip. Reed, very gently, taught me my lesson — not to underestimate people. Without a flicker of expression except a slight raising of the eyebrows he said, 'That will be quite all right, Sir. There's plenty of room for my feet.'

We were all delighted at some news a few months later. In recognition of Poppy's exceptional perseverance, initiative, commonsense and good judgement in handling a difficult and often obnoxious task they gave him a medal. A proper one. He was awarded an MBE.

# Chapter 16
## Munich Aftermath

One of the subsidiary tasks of the RAF squadrons on the Frontier was to reinforce other RAF elements in different parts of the world, both to the east and to the west. Each year, in our Harts, we had made a practice flight to Singapore or to Cairo. In our touching inexperience we imagined our outdated short-range biplanes would make a significant attacking force. Luckily, the Powers That Be were not so deluded. Even before Neville Chamberlain had come back from Munich, waving his ineffective 'Peace In Our Time' sheet of paper, the Air Force was growing and re-arming at an unbelievable rate for the war with Germany that we thought was inevitable. Now, in India, we too were to be re-equipped with new aeroplanes.

We also got a new Squadron Commander, Bill Spendlove, and he was like chalk from cheese compared to his predecessor — the World War I pilot who was a quiet man, doing his job methodically and spending very little time in the air. Bill was utterly different; tall, slim, vital, an international hurdler, and A.1 instructor (the best) and marvellously entertaining at a party. He had a jutting chin, the steeliest of blue-grey eyes — and he could out-fly us all. He demanded quality in our airmanship, brooked no nonsense, and he got results. I was one of the first to be hauled over the coals; a slap-happy young pilot, thinking himself an ace and unused to any supervision from the top, I cleared by a foot or two the trees on the edge of the airfield as I landed, beside the tarmac. But, unlike his predecessor, Bill was not in his office chair. He was out there, watching his pilots fly. He beckoned to me and, following the precepts of good man-management — praise in public and reprove in private — he led me to his office. There, he treated me to one of the most shattering reproofs I ever received. With his eyes looking even steelier than usual he started off, 'I was so angry out there that I didn't dare speak to you in case

I lost my temper in front of the airmen . . . you risked your aircraft unnecessarily . . . there were other aircraft refuelling and any error could have resulted in a major burn-up . . . ' There was much, much more and he finished up '. . . and if I ever see you do that again, I will instantly put you under arrest.'

It was a deeply shaken young man who crept out of his presence. His rocket shook me to my very roots, but it made me a much better pilot and probably saved my life many times thereafter. It had a sideline advantage; later, when eventually some responsibility came my way I dished out the same rocket several times to my subordinates, with equally salutary results.

Bill had told us that our first new machine would arrive overhead at about 11 o'clock from Karachi, where the necessary parts had arrived from England on a boat and several aircraft were being put together. One was to be flown up to Risalpur in three hours non-stop. For us, an aircraft which could do that was intoxicating stuff! It took our Harts a whole day, and needed a refuelling stop on the way.

In ample time every single pilot on the place, and most of the other station staff as well, were out on the edge of the tarmac to see this modern marvel. The Bristol Blenheim arrived travelling at what seemed to us to be an unbelievable speed. But sadly, instead of being lovingly polished aluminium, it was black, buff, and bullet shaped. The glossy red, white and blue roundels with distinctive brightly coloured squadron markings were changed. The shiny colours in the roundels were now dull matt. It looked hard, evil, efficient — and exciting to fly; on the ground it was downright ugly compared to our gleaming Harts.

I turned to Bill who was stroking his chin and looking at it very thoughtfully. I asked, 'How is the conversion going to be done, Sir?' He took a few moments to answer; then slowly he said, 'By guess and by God, I suppose. There is no aircraft fitted with dual controls for instruction. We've got no handbooks. I have heard that a chap who made his name flying seaplanes has flown one, and has written a foolscap page of tips, so I am trying to get a copy. A man called Tapper is coming sometime from Bristol's to tell us about their engines which, it seems, are not so placid as the Kestrels we are used to in our Harts — but he is not a pilot. And that's all we've got; from there on it's going to be a question of climbing in and doing it. However, we must be thankful for small mercies. I gather that it is possible for someone to stand beside the pilot; then, holding the stick as the pilot climbs out of his seat, they can actually change places in the air. So, it is at least possible for someone to get a "feel" of the beast before he does his first take-off. I'm going to do a trip with the delivery pilot this afternoon. When I've had a go, I'll show you the taps and knobs before I do the same for you.' This was exciting news. I was longing to get my my hands and feet on it, even if a lot of desirable information was missing.

By this time I knew Bill Spendlove very well and we had a valued mutual trust and friendship. I was not, however, expecting him to drop me a blockbuster. 'You're going to be busy for the next week or two. Your job will be to convert the other pilots in the squadron. It shouldn't be too bad and we can work out the finer points together, later. You fly the chap around and show him the ropes from take-off to landing, including giving him a spell at the controls in the air. Then, when you think he's competent enough, you give him the all-clear to have a go at the whole thing from the pilot's seat. You then stand beside him while he does it, to tell him if he's getting it wrong. Meanwhile, most of my time will be spent concentrating on pressing Headquarters for more Blenheims. OK.?'

I goggled at him in disbelief. Was he joking? It was an exhilarating challenge to pass out to solo stage all the remaining pilots in the squadron by standing beside them and talking fast. It was a considerable compliment that the boss seemed to think I could do it. But, with no dual aircraft, no proper written guides or instructions, no mentor who really knew the aircraft to advise us first, and me not being a qualified flying instructor, the prospect was on a par with getting into bed with Cleopatra — and her asp. The results could be rewarding — but fatal. I swallowed hard and said 'OK . . . Sir.'

While Bill was having his check-out I sat on the tarmac, sipping a mug of tea provided thoughtfully by the squadron 'char-wallah', and studied the Blenheim during its comings and goings. Sitting in the sun on that hot morning I, naturally, could not appreciate fully the great changes coming to our Air Force; yet changes obviously were going to be esential, and we were going to be guinea-pigs. The days of personal touch and finesse were vanishing. The days of make-and-mend on the spot were in irresistible decline. The magic days when you had your 'own' machine whose fitter and rigger talked about 'our' pilot were numbered. Hard-working days when, if an aircraft was unserviceable, its pilot considered it his normal duty to work on it in the hangar, as a general assistant to 'his' mechanics, till they got it right again. We were entering an era of quantity before quality. To change a whole piece rather than to repair the one you had. Nostalgically, I thought about the vanishing past.

A rigger was intensely proud that his aircraft flew exactly as its designer had hoped. It should never be one wing heavy, or try and turn to one side or the other. LAC Crouch would ask me after every landing, 'Did she fly all right, Sir?' And, if any substantive comment was made, he would promptly twist and turn the bracing wires to make it perfect, using spirit-levels and rigging-boards to measure all the angles if needs be. RAF mythology tells of an early biplane designed with so many bracing wires that a good rigger kept a canary as part of his toolkit. This was not, as a coal-miner's bird, to trace poisonous gases but to be used during the daily pre-flight inspection. He released the bird each morning between the wings; if it escaped, the rigger knew he must have a wire which was not quite taut enough.

Untrue maybe, but there really was a grizzled Flight Lieutenant with a wooden leg who had his being at Halton, where mechanics were trained. He was a great 'character' of whom there were many stories. He made his pairs of sock suspenders last twice as long as normal by using one only, and holding the other sock up with pins. Over a drink in a pub with strangers he could cause faces to blanch when he solemnly drove a drawing pin into his shin, through his trousers, by striking it with his clenched fist. At work he used to give viva voce exams to the apprentice riggers. A favourite question was: 'Let us say that you are doing a daily inspection on an aeroplane and you see that the elevator wires are crossed. What do you do?' Almost inevitably the quaking lad would answer, 'Er . . . I'd uncross them, Sir.' With a roar he would bring his wooden leg up and bang it on the table. 'Ho! Would you, you bloody idiot,' he would cry, emphasising each word with another thump. 'How in hell do you imagine I got this, you unthinking nincompoop? They *should* be crossed! Think, boy, *think!* Your pilot's life depends on it and don't you ever forget it.' It might have frightened some poor youngsters out of their wits, but it made very good mechanics.

Now, the Blenheim flying round the circuit had no wires to the elevators; only push-and-pull rods which could never be inter-changed. And the wing had no bracing wires to tweak and twist; its shape and angles were set immutably by the makers in the factory. LAC Crouch was wondering what had happened to his trade.

My fitter, LAC Kerr, prided himself on being an ace at whipping out the 24 sparking-plugs of the Kestrel engine, cleaning them till they shone in his hand and then setting the gaps within a thousandth of an inch. The Blenheim's plugs were of a new type. They were beautifully made, partly of platinum, and obviously were very, very expensive. Kerr was visibly shattered when he learned from Mr. Tapper of Bristol's that after every few hours flying he had to replace them with new ones *and throw the other ones away!* To win the coming war it was doubtless right for the technicians, but to them, at that time, it seemed wrong somehow.

The pilots were taking an enormous technical leap. They were to quit their simple biplanes with only one engine, a wooden propeller, undercarriage which stuck out in the breeze, cockpits with not too many complicated instruments and controls. They would transfer to monoplanes, with two engines, metal propellers with swivelling blades, undercarriages which went up and down, a host of other innovations they had never seen before — and a cockpit with 84 different taps, dials, knobs, buttons, switches and levers to cope with. To boot, the beasts had twice the speed, twice the range, twice the bomb-load — and two crew members from some other place instead of one's own personal mechanic that you yourself had trained to fly with you.. All this to be done with no instructors on the new techniques, no books on the arts needed, and no one with sound experience on the machine who could tell us what to do. Somebody, somewhere must have decided that it was good enough, but to the thinking pilots it also seemed wrong, somehow.

Soon, in all innocence and ignorance, we got down to the job of becoming modern multi-engined monoplane pilots. First we read eagerly, trustingly and avidly the foolscap sheet of of notes purporting to tell us 'How Best To Fly A Blenheim'. Later we discovered it merited another title: 'How To Manage A Twin-Engined Aircraft To Be Sure Of Killing The Entire Crew If Something Goes Faintly Amiss!'. To start with, its take-off recommendation was to climb very steeply at a low speed with full power. Now we know that if either engine had lost power momentarily, the low speed would have resulted in a spectacular cartwheel, crash and explosive disintegration as an absolute certainty. We got no engine hiccups, but in England they did, and many crews died in consequence. As for the chap standing beside the 'pupil' and doing the fast talking, not strapped in and with nothing to hang on to, even a minor crash would almost assuredly have killed him.

Allah must have looked down on us with a benign smile. The malevolent Black Dogs must have been completely in love with some gloriously attractive bitches for none of them even snarled. How we achieved the conversion of all the pilots without mishap remains a minor miracle. We got the norm of quantity, but it would be false to pretend that our quality overall could be preserved.

Over the next few weeks the pace of work was hectic. Once we had been converted — if the word is not too presumptuous for the blind leading the blind — some of us flew our beloved Harts to the depot at Karachi and returned with Blenheims. Others boated on a P & O liner — a beautiful first class government-paid holiday because there was no work to do — to Egypt and flew Blenheims back from there. Navigators appeared. So did Wireless Operator/ Air Gunners. In an incredibly short time we were outwardly transformed into two squadrons with modern aircraft.

'Right,' said the Powers That Be, 'now go to Singapore like you did two years ago in your Harts.' There were, however, certain differences in the two tasks. In the Harts we took six days and landed eleven times on the way; in the Blenheims we were to land five times in three days. We thought that, with our navigators and wireless operators, it would be easier than in the Harts. We were wrong.

Normally, the Blenheim had a crew of three but for this trip we would be taking two extra men each — technicians mainly — for we could expect no servicing facilities en route. There were no seats for these men but they could lie on top of the baggage stowed in the middle of the aircraft, looking out through the front between the pilot and the navigator. Napoleon said an army marches on its stomach; our technicians brought the tag up to date by flying on their stomachs. The only 'passenger' was David Tapper, the Bristol company's engine specialist. He was to fly in Wing Commander Bill Anker's aircraft. Ankers was the new Station Commander in succession to our little-man-who-never-flew. He was a strong character, a go-getter and he had been flying enthusiastically for many years. He announced that he would pilot one of the Blenheims to Singapore, selected from our sister squadron. His conversion-to-type was the same as for everybody else.

We were, as may be imagined, pretty raw and not much

beyond the 'gentle turns in good weather' stage, whatever we might have thought. We knew we were going across India and along Burma during the monsoon but the prospect of bad weather no longer worried us; we had a new and wonderful instrument for cloud-flying. It was called an 'Artificial Horizon'. Its workings were explained on our precious foolscap sheet. Instead of chasing those little bubbles in glass tubes and blind-flying needles quivering on their dials as of old, there was one new dial with a little aeroplane and a cross-wire on it. The little aeroplane was you and the cross-wire was the (artificial) horizon. You merely watched the dial and flew its little aeroplane towards the cross-wire; it was as simple as looking out of the window and flying towards the real horizon. So our foolscap sheet said. But it was a half-truth. The first half was that this new dial was in many ways far better than the bubbles and needles. The other, missing, half of the truth was deadly. Alas, no one there could add two crucial pieces of knowledge. The first gem was that if you banked or manoeuvred too steeply, the cross-wire got moved to a false position and your 'horizon' became tilted to an impossible angle. This turned your instrument into a murderous liar, and it gave you not the slightest indication that it had happened. The second vital piece of information that we lacked was just how violent and unmanageable were the air currents in the monsoon clouds. They produce turbulence which can throw any aircraft about like a falling leaf in an autumn gale — to positions far beyond those which would turn your blind-flying instrument into a killer. Unwittingly, we compounded those two perils with yet another one. In order to concentrate servicing resources on the ground, we proposed to fly both squadrons — 24 machines in all — on the same hops each day. Eight flights of three, spaced half an hour apart. The first machines would be off at dawn and the last machine would be landing a thousand miles away at dusk. No one said, or maybe they didn't appreciate, how much those great, big, bubbly, pretty monsoon-cloud-castles build up in the afternoons.

I was scheduled to lead the first flight each day; the squadron commanders were in the middle and Bill Ankers as the senior officer would take off last. We reckoned that his senior rank might be useful to get delaying problems out of the light and keep us all on our way. Early during the first day we found that our green, recently acquired navigators and wireless operators were wholly unreliable. They had not been trained for and had no experience of the different terrain, the landmarks, the type of maps used and the very primitive radio aids. They became confused and got lost almost at once. Most of us, therefore, kept down fairly low, underneath any poor weather and doing all our own map reading and navigation as we did in the Harts. On the second day Bill Ankers had been rushing around and he was hot, sweaty and uncomfortable. He decided to fly high, in the cool air. He aimed to fly through any clouds he encountered by using the new instrument, and arrive the other end cooler and better. That was why he went into a cloud which, today, a modern pilot would know deserved a gigantic flashing billboard saying 'KEEP OUT'.

It must have taken them between a half and one minute to hit the turbulent core of the cloud. They would have been tossed about like a Shrove Tuesday pancake. The crew members and passengers, being chucked around and bashed against the inside of the aircraft like peas in a whistle, were probably concussed and had broken limbs; some might even have been killed. Ankers, strapped to his seat, would have been fighting all he knew with the controls to get and hold that little aeroplane on to the cross-wire. And, if he succeeded, the cocked-up and lying device would ensure that he never flew into clear air safely. The result was inevitable. In a minute or two the machine was seen by witnesses on the ground to pop out the bottom of the cloud at an impossible angle. Before it could be righted it had struck the ground with a mighty explosion and a black mushroom-cloud of burning petrol. At that instant we needed replacements for one Station Commander and four valued colleagues.

Our troubles were not over. On the way, one aircraft got lost and landed on its belly in a paddy field; another slid off a landing ground because the smooth tyres did not grip on wet grass; someone else pulled the undercarriage up while he was taxying in. The two squadrons finally reached Singapore, one with eleven aeroplanes and the other with nine. The journey had not been so incident-free as we had expected. The guinea-pigs still had a lot to learn.

# Chapter 17
# Mac

Wing Commander John 'Mac' McFarlane was what the Air Force called a 'character'. The Service used to be full of them but, with the passage of time and escalation of costs, there was no room for those charming and amusing individuals who ran things their own way and seldom by the books. He was full of ideas. He was the first person to wangle RAF pilots into the cockpits of the early airliners, thus giving them their first glimpse of what Europe looked like from above — just in case one day they had to go there in anger. He taught on flying-boats and it was he who launched the idea that learning to handle a craft on the water could be done as effectively, more simply, less dangerously and much less expensively by using a boat driven by sails rather than by petrol engines and whirling propellers. He therefore persuaded a grudging Treasury to buy a fleet of sailing dinghies; and, if the pupils wanted to practise during weekends by going on picnics and holding regattas, that was cheaper still — it was in their own time. For years the Treasury searched high, low and assiduously for the catch; there wasn't one.

Mac had never been known to let the chance of a 'swan' around the world slip through his fingers. He had done it in ships, making some of the earliest tests in seaplanes from Naval vessels. He had gone right round the British Isles in his flying-boats. He had flown to Malta and to Norway. Towards the end of his career he exceeded his own best efforts by leaving his station in Northern Ireland to run itself happily while he hitch-flew many thousands of miles to Montreal, to New York, South America, Ascension Island, Africa and back via Gibraltar. His stated purpose, of course, was to ensure that all the facilities in these places were in good order.

His boss, the AOC, had about as much sense of fun as could go in your eye without making it water. Also, he had been caught napping; he only learned of the monumental joy-ride after Mac got back. His ego was dented because he hadn't been asked first. He kept repeating, 'It was most improper. As AOC my prior permission should have been sought. And, in the circumstances, I should naturally have refused.' Which, naturally, was why he had not been asked in the first place.

In 1939 Mac McFarlane was Station Commander to the force of transport aircraft in India. When they were given the task of lending support to a couple of newly converted Blenheim squadrons going off to Singapore, guess who decided to fly one of the Valentia aircraft?

A Valentia was a large biplane with two engines and a fuselage shaped like a cigar. The two pilots sat in an open cockpit, right out in the nose. It wallowed and had the agility of a pregnant sow. It sailed along at a splendid 80 miles an hour, which is slower than many people drive on motorways. It would take anything anywhere, provided you could get it inside or hang it under the wings. Normally, the crew entered by a door in the rear, walked along the fuselage and through another door into the cockpit. One day, a pilot called Firpo Chichester went to his machine to find a ladder propped up against the nose. On asking why, the groundcrew answered, 'She's a bit full inside, Sir.' Having climbed the ladder and gone over the nose into his seat, Firpo found that the door to the cabin behind him would only open an inch or two. She was indeed 'a bit full inside'. He called through the crack, to the airmen lying on the packing cases, 'Will the rear door shut?' On getting an affirmative reply he said with complete unconcern 'OK — let's go.' And they went. It certainly was a long-suffering aeroplane.

Mac and his colleagues of course had no way of keeping up with the Blenheims. They followed the route that we had taken two years earlier in our Harts. From Lahore, their home base, they passed Delhi, Agra and the Taj Mahal on their right. First night-stop, Allahabad. They were flying over the great plains of the Punjab and Uttar Pradesh which lie to the south of the Himalyan massif. The plains are watered by a mass of slow-moving sludgy rivers that were born amongst the eternal snows and which eventually combine to make the Mother-Ganges. Mac, looking down, could see uncountable little fields, tended by the peasants to make a near-starvation living. Fields which the peasants seldom owned because they had been mortgaged up to the hilt and beyond when famine and hard times struck.

After Allahabad and a night in its rest-house there were six hours more of patchwork cultivation before Calcutta, with a stop half-way at Gaya for fuel. Gaya just had one short strip for landing, with no buildings or facilities in use for feeding. The crews sweated as they used the hand-pump to fill the tanks from fuel drums provided by courtesy of Shell. Dum-Dum, Calcutta's airfield, was hardly welcoming and restful. Two grass strips in the form of an L and, on one side, a double row of tents. At first they were encouraged by the fact that there was a well-appointed airport building, but Mac's No. 2 discovered that brutal and licentious airmen were rigidly excluded. Mac, who was not prone to having his men treated like outcasts, first spoke gently to the No.2, and then less gently to the Airport Manager on duty. This rat-faced little man was adamant; some fare-paying passengers were due in on an Imperial Airways Atlanta aircraft and they took priority. In no way would he let them be incommoded by hot, tired, unwashed, hungry and thirsty Air Force individuals, even if, in the final analysis, they were working to protect those self-same passengers. Mac fought a wordy and lengthy battle but, on seeing his second in command pass behind Rat-Face with a thumbs-up sign, he suddenly ceded gracefully.

Mac had his supper with the others from a trestle table behind the tents. A cook with a charcoal stove was producing fried eggs by the acre, backed by those only-if-you-are-very-hungry skinless, tinned sausages. Fortunately, there was unlimited beer. It was not long before Rat-Face, now promoted to Purple-Rat-Face, was jumping up and down in front of Mac. An Imperial Airways passenger had gone to the Airport bar and demanded ale. He had been refused and it transpired that while Rat-Face had been talking to Mac, some treacherous officer had snuck into the bar, unseen by Rat-Face, and bought the entire stock. R-F positively demanded that some bottles be surrendered, so that he could satisfy the whims of his passengers. Mac, emphasising his points with waves of his beer glass, indicated that if Purple-Rat-Face had been co-operative, the so-called treachery would not have occurred. As it was, the beer was purchased legally, and that was that. If the passengers were so damned important, and thirsty, let them drink champagne.

From Calcutta the route lay over the Ganges delta. Below, for over a hundred miles, there were thousands of little streams into which the great river had been split. From height it looked like a net on the ground, made from a light-brown wool which had been knitted and then unravelled. In each little loop was an islet of brilliant green vegetation and the spots of a few huts. After the delta they crossed a stretch of the Bay of Bengal and so down at Chittagong for fuel. Chittagong was only a grass landing-ground to which fuel had been moved but the few local English inhabitants were kindness itelf. They had made sandwiches. They provided beer for which payment was refused. They begged Mac and his team to shelve their programme and stay one or more nights if possible. This was an entreaty to be repeated at every halt from that point onwards. But no; the Blenheims in Singapore were calling.

From Chittagong and almost all the way to Singapore the country overflown is almost without exception, to put it gently, inhospitable. Over Assam, Burma, Thailand and Malaya there are two consecutive problems, should you come down inadvertently. The first is a tough one; it is getting down alive. The second one is even tougher; it is staying alive afterwards and reaching help.

Mac looked down from his Valentia at the jungle below and pondered. The hills, with occasional clouds in the valleys, looked as though they were covered with giant parsley gone mad. Rolling greenery as far as the eye could see with never a glimpse of the ground. It had a beauty, of a sort; in fact it was an unending counterpane of branches and leaves reaching for the sunlight at the tops of trees with bare trunks 200 ft high. If he glided down, the big branches might fillet the wings off his aircraft and the fuselage would streak like a plummet to the earth below. On the other hand they might get stuck up there, and then getting down 200 ft would be a pretty problem, even if they were uninjured. Valentia pilots had no parachutes so the problems of catching them in the high branches did not arise. Assuming the first hurdle had been surmounted and Mac was on the ground, alive and mobile, what next? The only advice that had been offered was 'walk downhill — all water eventually reaches the sea.' It would mean struggling through near-impenetrable jungle, only to reach a coastline bordered by mangrove swamps, populated by crocodiles, leeches and poisonous water-snakes. Furthermore, even then you still could not be seen from the air or from the sea. The prospect lacked attraction. Mac, as we all did, toyed with the idea that if he was coming down, failing the miracle of a clearing or sandy beach, it might be best to drive the aircraft fast into the treetops. The result would be just as certain and it would have the advantage of being quick. He wondered if his co-pilot had thoughts on the matter. He made no comment and turned his attention to the flight in hand.

Day after day the Valentias plugged their way along the edge of the Bay of Bengal and the Andaman Sea. At Akyab the local rubber planters took Mac swimming from a little sandy shoreline. At Rangoon, wholly forbidden on religious grounds, Mac circled the Shwe-Dagon pagoda whose 80-ft roof-spire was alleged to be covered in gold as thick as a sovereign. At Mergui he had to land over 60-ft rubber trees and land on a slippery grass surface before refuelling by hand from two-gallon petrol cans. At Victoria Point the approach was over a 250-ft hill, followed by a steep glide on to a grass airfield only 650 yards long. Alor Star, wonder of wonders, had a 1000 yard runway and a comfortable rest-house with proper beds, and sheets! Finally, after six days, 45 hours' flying, doing their own servicing, refuelling from drums and cans, humping their luggage, putting up and taking down their camp-beds. they rumbled safely and thankfully into RAF Kallang, Singapore. Unloading the Blenheim spares and kits began.

'Nice to see you, Mac,' said a local station commander who had come over to see if we needed help. 'Hope you had a nice trip. I expect you heard about Bill Ankers on the way. Bad luck that. When you've had a bath and a drink — or, to get your priorities right, a drink and a bath — they'd like to see you in AHQ. I'll get you a car when you're ready.' Death was indeed our familiar; although Bill Ankers had been a good and popular CO the Air Force was a dangerous game and, when it claimed a victim, the matter was played down to the point of apparent callousness. 'Oh ho!' thought Mac. 'How are Neta and the girls going to get down here?'

Mac could read between the lines as fast as anybody. Air Headquarters in the same breath as Bill Ankers. He was a station commander, and he came from India. The Blenheim squadrons came from India. Who better to take Bill Ankers' job? It stood to reason. His wife Neta and their two young daughters would, somehow, have to pack everything up, on their own, and travel by train and boat from Lahore to Singapore to join him. There were no charter flights or Transport Command to help in those days and Treasury was parsimonious. Poor dears.

Two weeks later, Mac sent for me. 'You,' he said, 'are going to be my Station Entertainments Officer. I have acquired the unfettered loan of an empty warehouse, or godown, just outside the camp gates. I want it to become an airmen's club. On camp the airmen are not allowed spirits, or girls, in their Canteen. So they go off-camp to buy the spirits, and they collect venereal disease along the way. The club will have a bar and, being off-camp, spirits may be sold. You can put down a timber dance-floor on the concrete. On Sundays there will be a church service so, as it is ostensibly a church, I can get chairs free from the Air Force. You will have to get your own tables somehow.

'The club will be open seven nights a week for the airmen, and respectable girls. How you eliminate the whores is your pigeon. I expect a formal entertainment — revue, play, sing-song or some such — every second Saturday. And the place is to be cleaned up before church every Sunday. Water and electricity are available.

'Get an Entertainments Committee together, make plans and tell me how much money you need within the next ten days. Any questions?' I felt as though I had been sandbagged. The brief seemed comprehensive and the project could be fun. No questions came. I went out to try and find two or three enthusiastic airmen who would be ready to collect volunteer labour and run the outfit in due course.

Roughly a week later I requested audience with the great man. 'Our committee is formed,' I began, 'and we have made an estimate for materials. We want to build a bar at the outset, for that is where income is made. Also a stage, for the shows and the concert parties. And a dance-floor for the respectable girls. We start there with nothing at all — just a concrete floor and walls, with an electricity meter and a tap by the road. Labour is free from the volunteers and here is the estimate for the bare materials to build with — timber, nails and screws; paint, distemper and brushes; electric cable, sockets and lamps — and you will see it comes to 1,289 Singapore dollars. I think the team have planned very well, to get the club going for only just over £160 sterling.' I waited for the applause.

Mac looked at the bill of goods. He scratched his nose thoughtfully. Then he looked me straight in the eye. 'You say that $1,289 is the least you can do with? Is that correct?' 'Yes, Sir,' I answered stoutly. 'In order to build the club that you sketched out last week and get it going.' Mac nodded sagely before saying, without a flicker, 'OK. You can have ten dollars.' I couldn't believe my ears. Even in 1939, ten Straits dollars would only buy a couple of planks, a roll of cable or a tin of paint. Mac looked at me keenly as I tried to find an acceptable phrase for 'You must be mad . . . Sir.'

'I mean it. Ten dollars. And this is what you do. You go and buy Housey-Housey [Bingo] tickets and you run sessions in the Airmen's Canteen. You take ten per cent of the pot — more if they will let you — and you do the sums on a blackboard in front of them. As you collect the money, they build their own club. And how fast they get it done depends on them.'

Mac, of course, was absolutely right. The airmen's money funded the club and then they built it themselves. The decor, in gold and black, turned my stomach but they loved it. They were proud of it, they owned it and they policed it jealously. Drink, compared to the Singapore clip-joints, was fabulously cheap. The Committee ran the bar and ten per cent of the turnover came to me for banking. The barmen, all of them airmen, took a small cut for themselves but if anyone's take became too big an aggrieved client could be relied upon to give him a black eye. That kept things nice and straight with no effort on my part. As promised, the Entertainments Committee organised a revue every other Saturday with a dance on the Saturdays between. Someone traced the Singapore Magic Circle who generously put on a conjuring act to start off every show. The rest — piano-playing, songs, comedy turns and so forth, with encores — spun the concert party out to a couple of hours, and all for 50 cents.

The airmen were fanatically determined that the reputation of 'their' club should never be queried by the boss. Indeed, any airman who escorted in a girl who had the misfortune even to look 'fast' was politely invited to escort her out again, pronto.

The tale of the Amateur Dramatic Society was sad. The stage itself had been a major part of the outlay and they needed to recoup. So, under some pressure from the Financial Manager (me) the first couple of shows were actor-proof farces. The airmen turned up in droves and the cash came rolling in. Actors run to type the world over and the Society then insisted on doing something worthy of their thespian prowess — *Hamlet*. It may have been a masterpiece but the house was almost empty because, as forecast, most of the airmen didn't want culture. They wanted belly-laughs. As the actors couldn't then get the Management (including the airmen's committee) to let them do *King Lear* without first recouping the loss on *Hamlet,* and they didn't want to do popular stuff, the Society died an early death.

On Sundays, at 11 o'clock, a church service was held. Although Church Parades were a thing of the past, the congregations were excellent. I often wondered if the parson congratulated himself on his capacity to 'pack-em-in' with such a large and regular congregation. Mac, being Mac, found it extremely easy to have his church well supported. He merely announced that 'Church is, of course, entirely voluntary. But, if you don't go, I'll make it compulsory.'

Life continued under this benevolent but resolute despot for the next ten months. Perhaps the place should have been called 'RAF Mac' instead of its official title.

# Chapter 18
# Miss Mac

The two teenage girls were wildly excited about the move to Singapore and chattered like parakeets as Neta, stoically, packed up all their belongings. With some misgivings she buried Mac's personal revolver, a legacy of World War I, deep amongst her underclothes. Pig-headedly, he had always refused to register it. Thus, about two months after Mac's departure on his intended 'quick trip' to Singapore and back, the three of them set off on the first leg. This was a three-day journey by train to Calcutta, pulled by the usual chuffing, coal-burning, smut-belching steam behemoth. Inevitably, the scampish younger daughter broke the tap in the shower-cubicle on the first day. She also soured the elder daughter by using all her newest and treasured lipstick as a drawing-crayon. Neta blanched visibly when, boarding the ship in Calcutta for Singapore, she saw a large sign saying in enormous letters, 'Penalty for smuggling firearms — forty lashes!' You might say that the passage to Singapore was as incident-free as any other family journey.

A few Sundays later I was voluntarily at the church service in the Airmen's Club. Nosily I looked around to see how well the place had been cleaned up after the revels of the previous evening. The sermon was boring beyond belief. Up at the front, as befitted his status, sat the Station Commander. News had circulated that his family had arrived from India, even though we had not yet met them. The back view of three strangers was pleasantly intriguing. A fidgety flaxen-haired seven-year-old was firmly pinned in place by Mac on one side and a large, comfortable, motherly figure on the other. On Mum's other side was, obviously, the elder daughter. This was much more interesting than the church service, or the droning parson. It was a nice dress. A little black job, with short sleeves. Pulled in at the waist. A nice waist. Nice figure altogether, really, what one could see of it from the back. Attractive small handbag. Nice shoes. Where on earth did she get that terrible big-brimmed yellow straw hat? Mum bought it, probably, being 'suitable' and she had to wear something to church. Wonder what colour the hair is underneath? Might the hat look better from the front, framing the face? To be checked out after church, definitely.

The Mac family were run to earth in the Ladies Room of the Mess, having a pre-lunch gossip and a drink. The contents of the black dress looked even better from the front than they did from the back. The hat, thank goodness, was gone and her hair, unlike her young blonde sister, was mouse-coloured. Rich mouse, I decided charitably. Soft voice. Attractive face. Eighteen? Get to work, fast, before the snakes among my bachelor colleagues can work faster. Chivalry burgeoned in my breast — chivalry being the desire of a man to protect a girl from everybody but himself. I took my courage in both hands and lined up before the great man, her father.

As from a distance I heard myself say, 'May I invite your daughter to lunch with me at the Singapore Flying Club on the other side of the airfield? Also, if she would like it, take her flying afterwards in one of the Club aircraft?' Mac gave me a long look and it seemed quite obvious that he was going to say 'No' to such a ludicrous first-acquaintance request. My heart sank. What he did say was, 'What does she think about it?' Feeling extremely foolish, the only reply possible was, 'I don't know, Sir, yet.' To my astonishment he followed up with, 'Well, you ask her. If she wants to go, you have my permission.'

There is not the slightest recollection in my mind of what we had for lunch, but the flight afterwards is deeply engraved. The Club had a Percival Gull, a cabin aircraft with the two seats in front side by side and fitted with dual controls. Within one hour, we had not only been able to see the town and fly all around the island but she had also had a go at flying the tiny machine as well. And she said I could use her Christian name, which was Phyl.

The next morning was spent biting my nails and wondering what would be a courteous interval before getting back in touch. Tuesday, twenty-four hours later, I rang up the boss's house and asked to speak to Miss McFarlane. The boss said he would fetch her. So far so good. Would she like to come out to dinner on the following evening, Wednesday? She would; even better. So might I come and pick her up in my serviceable but somewhat elderly limousine of American manufacture? It was far from slick, grand or exciting. It had been bought, originally, for two reasons only; it was cheap and it worked. She accepted my offer nonetheless.

The shortage of English girls was severe and, moreover, the Mess was brimming with competitive bachelors. Although I was 23, the previous four years in India had done nothing to turn me into a smooth Don Juan. There, mostly, girls had been conspicuous by their absence and the few available tended to favour the swains with the deepest pockets. It was the greatest pity that the car wasn't my earlier fabulous, scarlet, sports, two-seater speedster; other ways would have to be found to keep up the pressure . . . Flowers? A suitable bouquet might provide some favourable groundwork. Moreover, Wednesday afternoon was the 'sports' afternoon, so one could slip away unnoticed to buy it.

My car nosed through Singapore town between the rickshaws, past the myriad street-vendors and under innumerable poles stuck out of every house and tenement window, put there to hold the laundry while it dried. Then, into the lush countryside for a few miles. Running north and south from the town to the causeway which joins the island to the mainland was the Bukit Timah road. It was not a particularly built-up area and on either side were several flower nurseries ablaze with colour from tropical plants of every imaginable variety. These, in the equatorial heat and nearly 100 per cent humidity, flourished and bloomed like something out of a science-fiction story. It was alleged that, as a gardener, you pressed a cutting into the ground and jumped back before it climbed up your legs. I drove into what seemed to be a likely looking nursery, and got out.

The proprietor, no more than five-foot two and thin as a rake, was beside me in an instant, bowing and smiling. Rubbing his wrinkled hands over one another he asked what would be my pleasure? The realisation dawned that never in my entire life had I bought flowers. My mind was a total blank. The little man tweaked at his white singlet and hitched his black cotton shorts as he waited with his expression growing steadily more nonplussed. Frenzied bashing of my stunned brain finally extracted two straws to clutch at. The old black-and-white movie dramas of the pre-war era had indicated that orchids were special for girls. Second, from somewhere, sometime, my memory dredged up a phrase that a flower named spider-orchid grew on the island. I blurted out, 'Spider Orchid'.

The proprietor beamed, showing a full rack of gold teeth, bowed even lower and pointed to some little white blossoms no larger than my thumbnail. Admittedly, they were beautifully formed and tinted a delicate pink or yellow at their centres; however they were tiny blooms and on dull, leafless, brown stalks about 20 inches high bearing roughly eight to each stalk. These flowers were elegant, plain, and totally unimpressive.

'How many you want?' asked the gardener.

'How much?' I countered promptly, beginning to lose my nerve. They were so *small,* and I understood orchids were pretty expensive too! How in blazes could I now retreat with dignity, to identify and settle on something better?

'Ten cents.'

I took a deep breath and began to do some mental arithmetic. Two dollars had been my target but at ten cents an orchid that would only run to two or maybe three twigs — and three brown sticks seemed to be a parlous sort of bouquet, even with the little white flowers. Trying to look like a man of the world but feeling scared witless I bravely said 'Five dollars.' The little man fairly leapt into action. It soon became apparent, and then I lacked the moral guts to retract, that the 'ten cents' was for five *sticks* and not merely one bloom.

Numbly I tottered back to my car, clasping to my chest a great faggot of two hundred and fifty sticks. One might suppose there should be an entry in the *Guinness Book of Records* for the simpleton who arrives to take a girl out, on their first evening date, and weakly thrusts at her a bundle of 2000 orchids.

That was just the start. For the next four months, whenever I could beat my rapacious comrades to the draw, we had the most enormous amount of fun together. We picnicked. We swam. We watched flaming multi-coloured sunsets as the fast-falling tropical night enveloped a hill named 'The Gap'. We went night-flying over Singapore, high in the velvety sky with a zillion stars over the million flashing lights and garish signs, looking like a constantly turning living kaleidoscope. We danced at Raffles Hotel, very close together, to a tune called 'Deep Purple', played by the band at our request in an outrageously slushy tempo. One night, Mac gave me a monster rocket on his own front doorstep for bringing her home too late; dating the boss's daughter had its problems.

On 3 September 1939, World War II broke out. That night there was an almighty party in the Mess. Most of my colleagues, so long as they retained the power of speech, were cursing their ill-fortune at not being in England to join in the ephemeral (they thought) thrashing of the Germans. Others, including me, thought our chances of seeing the other end of a major conflict to be fairly slim. We were right; the survival rate for experienced aircrew who flew for most of the war turned out to be one in seven.

In October the Powers That Be decided on some re-sorting of the Far East resources, which included me. My squadron would fly, via India, to the Middle East. Mac would return, with his family, to India. I, having already done nearly four years abroad, was to go back to England by boat and fight from there.

The sad parting from Phyl was formalised in the back seat of my elderly Dodge Sedan one afternoon. I explained, as impersonally as I could, that some weeks hence I was setting sail for England, just a few days after they left for India. The war, from England, was likely to be ruthless and deadly. No; there was no question of a hasty wartime wedding; I would take no chance of leaving her a teenage widow. She said, in a very small voice, 'But, I'll wait for you — I want to.' That remark came within a hairsbreadth of cracking me, but her offer was refused, just. I extracted a promise from her to go out and have more fun, wherever and whenever she could. No holds. No ties. No pacts. No commitments. Then, in the future perhaps, if I lived, if we were both unfettered, if we met each other again — a lot of if's — we could see if the threads might be picked up again from where we had put them down.

For the remaining weeks we continued to enjoy the simple things together but the atmosphere, unsurprisingly, became a bit strained. Finally, as the Mac family was embarking on their boat for India I said to Phyl, 'I'll wave to you. Wave goodbye back to me, will you, please?'

'What do you mean?'

'Just, please, wave back to me when I wave. I want to remember it.'

After the poignant standing on the quayside as the liner pulled away I went back to the airfield to find Freddy Gill. Freddy was a chum of mine and he commanded the Communications Flight. He had a Walrus. A Walrus, in that context, means a rather ungainly, ugly but effective amphibious aeroplane. As arranged, we climbed aboard, took off from the airfield and set course for the Singapore Straits. The liner by this time had got well out and was heading into a gentle breeze at around ten knots. Perfect. A couple or three circuits round the ship made sure that the staccato clatter of the stub exhausts and the beat of the four-bladed pusher-propeller had assuredly got everyone on deck. Freddy then double-checked that the wheels were safely tucked up out of the way before alighting gently on the water about 100 yards to one side. Then, at a fast ten knots taxi to keep abreast, he gradually came in closer and closer to the ship. I left the co-pilot's seat, scrambled along inside the fuselage to the nose-gunner's cockpit, slid back its metal lid and popped up. We were then about 30 yards away. After a few moments searching I saw Phyl, high above me, hanging over the rail and waving madly. As promised on the quayside, I waved my final goodbye.

I bobbed down again, closed the lid and scrambled back to the co-pilot's seat as Freddy opened the throttle wide for take-off. In half a minute we were gone.

# Chapter 19
# Fuka

On the same day in early June 1940 that my Troop Transport docked in Port Said, Mussolini decided that the moment was propitious to join Hitler on the winning side. The Mediterranean was therefore closed to unarmed traffic. The ship would now have to reach England by sailing back down the Suez Canal and then all round Africa via the Cape of Good Hope. Someone, somewhere, must have said, approximately, 'What is that Flight Lieutenant Blenheim-pilot doing on board? We need Blenheim pilots. Get a doc to take a squint down one of his lug-holes and, if daylight doesn't show through from the other side, pass him as fit to start a new tour, here.' So the ship sailed without me and I went as a flight commander of 45 Squadron to the Sudan.

Promotion and change, in wartime, tends to be by inheritance. It can, accordingly, be rapid. That was how, after a couple of bombing raids over Eritrea on Asmara airfield, 55 Squadron in the Western Desert got me as CO with the rank of Squadron Leader. I was 24 and younger than the majority of my pilots, but hardly any of them looked down their noses on that account. From the very first day they gave me the most wonderful support. What mattered to them was that I had nearly five years' squadron experience — say three or more times as much as theirs. Experience can keep people alive in wartime which, they felt, was a good idea.

The daily pattern was soon picked up. In the evening the AOC would ring up, telling us how many aircraft should bomb which targets at what time. It was up to the CO — me — to choose crews, the leader, the route, the take-off time and form-up pattern. Next day, it was done as scheduled. And so it went on, day after day. Between raids we amused ourselves as best we could. And each weekend a flight of three Blenheims — nine aircrew, six groundcrew — could be sent to Cairo to savour the fleshpots.

The situation was idyllic. Each squadron was self-contained on its own airfield of flattened, hard sand. Its Squadron Leader CO was monarch of all he surveyed; squadron commander, station commander, god. Not far to the north was the blue crystal-clear Mediterranean, full of fascinating fish. As no women were allowed in the desert, bathing suits were unheard of.

The conditions were horrible. During the day the sweat poured off you, and at night it froze, often. I used six blankets on my camp-bed. We were in tents and, when the wind whipped up the sand, which was much of the time, it was like living in the bag of a working vacuum cleaner. As there was no refrigeration, bully-beef and biscuits were staple diet, to the point of detestation. Water had to be trucked, up to 300 miles. At one time we were rationed down to one gallon, per man, per day. Of that gallon, half went to the cook-tent, for food preparation; a quarter went to the doctor for tending the sick. That left two pint-glasses per day for an individual to drink, shave, clean his teeth — and wash? Everyone was permanently dirty and even swimming in the clean sea left you salty and sticky. You could always tell a desert-hand from a visitor by the yellow line of sand showing at the hair-line round his forehead and temples.

And those flies. Hordes from which you could never escape. They walked over any piece of exposed skin they could get at, rubbing their legs together and sucking whatever moisture — sweat — they could get at. They were so absorbed in their task that they were easy to kill. However, one soon gave up because more fools arrived on your skin to suck at the corpses. As there was no sanctuary one soon learned to let them crawl unharmed and, later, unnoticed. David Potter, after he had been with us for a few weeks, announced at the bar: 'I reckon that I can call myself a desert-hand now. I can let the flies crawl over my eyelids without blinking.' 'No way,' growled Black Metcalfe, 'not until you don't blink when they walk on your eyeballs.' 'Black', one of my pilots, was a short saturnine man — hence his nickname. He was a good match for his macabre sense of humour.

Nevertheless, overall spirits were high and laughter came easily. We had plenty of fuel and plenty of flying. We believed we could nearly always outfly and outfight our current enemies — the Italian Air Force. General Rommel with his Luftwaffe Messerschmitts had not yet arrived to bring us a very different war. Italian desert-pilots were, on the whole, neither very brave nor very determined.

One day 'Fanny' Hunt took an aircraft to Heliopolis, Cairo, on some task or other. There, like everyone else, he luxuriated in several baths followed by everything that a barber's shop could provide — haircut, singe, shave, shampoo, scalp massage and any other cleansing services on offer. He became truly clean, a wonderful feeling. When he got back to Fuka, Black went up and sniffed at him pointedly. 'Fanny, my friend,' he cried, 'you've lost your nice goaty smell!'

We got a free issue of repulsive cigarettes, popularly believed to be made from camel dung, and known as 'Spitfires'. Not even the heavy smokers could stand them; they even preferred to go without smoking anything However, there was a single-track railway line which ran from Alexandria to Mersa Matruh, past the end of our airfield. Its Egyptian driver loved Spitfires, or perhaps he could sell them in Alexandria market. Fanny was the Messing Officer and he found that for those repellent tubes the driver would bring us eggs, fresh meat and vegetables on his daily run past us. More, he would toss out lumps of coal for the fireplace in our wooden Mess hut we had built ourselves from packing-cases. This did much to counter the frigid desert nights and make life more tolerable. Unfortunately the other squadrons soon caught on and embarked on the same trade. The driver was an opportunist, but not exactly bright. It was not long before the train ran out of coal before getting back to Alexandria — and rescuing the train meant he didn't make his next day's run. The AOC was very crotchety about it and forbade further bartering. It didn't stop us, of course, but we were more circumspect; we helped the driver to plan his coal consumption better.

We, in the Air Force, were luckier than the Army. The occasional trips to Cairo were a welcome break, and they gave us a chance to 'repay' the groundcrew for their unremitting labours during the scorching days. Any aircraft going there would take a couple of the ground staff in addition to the crew themselves. And, often, give the odd hitch-flight to someone wanting to get to the other end, or carry odd bits of freight. The entreaties for off-the-cuff airlift were endless. It was no surprise when Fanny asked me would I bring back from Cairo some goodies for the Mess, which he could have delivered to Heliopolis for me? Naturally I agreed — the usual? Surely; eggs, green vegetables and some beer. The flight there was uneventful and the five of us went our separate ways to become blissfully clean before returning to the aircraft at 7.30 in the morning, sharp.

In Tommy's Bar, a favourite hang-out for desert-pilots, an acquaintance importuned me that evening, successfully, for a hitch back the 150 miles to Fuka next day. Indeed, if I would fly him back, he would pay the taxi to Heliopolis for both of us. How could I refuse? I foresaw no weight problem for just one more passenger.

The morning was bright and clear. As the two of us drove up to the aeroplane there were seven people waiting beside it instead of my two aircrew and two groundcrew, as expected. It transpired that my air-gunner and my navigator had each promised a ride to Fuka for 'just one more'. That totalled six. The seventh had merely come out on spec and pleaded eloquently for space. With me and my chum, total nine; seats, three.

Fanny's goodies were there also — two crates of vegetables, two more crates containing a thousand eggs, and a hundred one-litre bottles of beer. I did some swift calculations. With no bombs to carry, we would be, say, about half-a-ton overweight, give or take a bit. The air, at sea level, was still cool and comparatively dense; she ought to make it. OK — let's give it a go. First, we emptied all the vegetables into the space between the main-spars; too bad about Fanny's nice crates but he could worry about that when he found out, later. Next the beer; about the same weight as two people — better have it in the middle of the aircraft; put the vegetables round the bottles standing upright — that way the veg would cushion them and keep them safe from breakage. The eggs? Up in the nose, in front of the navigator's feet; he doesn't need to look out for it's a fine day and I know my way up the coast. Better still, he can have a passenger sitting on his knees. That makes three in front. We can put three other people, lying on their stomachs, on a comfortable bed of vegetables in the middle. And the last three at the back; the gunner on his seat and the other two on the sort of step below his feet — they can't see out, but what the hell? It'd keep the balance about right and they're lucky to get a lift at all. Finally, when everybody and everything was stowed, just before pressing the first starter button I glanced back down the inside of the fuselage; the old girl looked very full indeed — positively pregnant.

We went far, far back down the airfield, almost up against the hangars to get the longest possible run for take-off. There, holding on the brakes, up to full throttle, pull the emergency-only boost lever — and let her go! The acceleration with all that weight on board was deplorably sluggish and when we got almost to the far end of the airfield we were still on the ground. As the boundary ditch approached, this was the moment of truth. Would she lift? She did, but barely so and I held her teetering in the air as I yanked smartly on the undercarriage handle to get the wheels out of the slipstream. Two miles ahead were some low sand-hills and, when we got there, I just had enough speed and height to make a gentle avoiding turn towards Fuka. I took a deep breath and decided I had shown some pretty poor airmanship with a performance like that, and totally inappropriate to my rank and experience.

That same evening I was relishing a glass from one of the transported beer bottles. Hoping to discourage any other pilot, maybe less experienced, trying to duplicate my stupid effort without realising what a narrow squeak it had been, I was holding forth rather audibly to Fanny in the bar that, after all these years, I had made a complete fool of myself and, for a few moments I really thought we were not going to get away with it. Black chipped in brightly: 'You know, Sir, if you *hadn't* made it, and someone had put a match to it — with the vegetables, eggs, beer, and all your meat, it would have produced a damned fine pie.'

In the desert, evenings were monotonous, similar and, mostly dreary. Card games, the same old stories and generally not enough liquor to make one feel as if it was a good time. An almost welcome interruption, occasionally, would be the intervention of an enemy aircraft or two. They used to come over from time to time, usually from Italy, sling a few bombs on to the coastal strip and go home. It caused little concern and no special problems, so long as one was not showing a light for them to aim at. The power operator — the man running the identification beacon from which we filched electricity to light the messes — merely threw the switch to plunge us all into inky blackness as the alarm was blown. This was followed by curses, complaints at losing the only good bridge or poker hand for days, and a few spilled precious drinks as everyone flung themselves into safety trenches. Later after a respectable pause, with or without bombs falling, back to the messes with loud raucous cries for the lights to come on once more.

Naturally, whenever any squadron could collect enough booze to make a good party, one would gather all the neighbours for a break in the nightly routine. This would lead to a late night of pretty solid singing, yakking and drinking. There was, of course, no common transport and everyone had to borrow jeeps, trucks or whatever form of wheels came to hand, unless you were a squadron commander privileged to have your own wheels. After such a party, getting home required a little forethought and a certain well-known technique. Each squadron had its area of hard flat sand, cleared of thorn bushes and rocks, surrounded by dozens of tents in which you ate, slept, planned and worked. You knew precisely where your airfield was but, with no well-defined or posted roads, it was dead easy in the dark to mislay even an airfield. Therefore, upon arrival in daylight, a certain amount of care and skill was needed. You parked your jeep or what-had-you outside your hosts' Mess tent, carefully pointed towards where you knew your own home must be. When, much much later, you finally decided you had had your skinful, you eased into the driver's seat and selected one bright star dead ahead. It was quite likely that you closed one eye — to be sure of only seeing one star. Ignition key in the lock and, vroom-vroom, follow religiously your guiding star, like one of the Magi of the first Christmas, until an airfield rolls under the front wheels. It must be your own. All that remains is to locate your tent and collapse into bed.

This led to a ploy which was reckoned in the desert to have been one of the better jests. Naturally, one always tried to have a 'party', rather than a solid slab of drinking, even though the quantities of alcohol consumed were astronomic. The Mess tent would be tarted up and made as welcoming as possible. Our Mess tents were large and near-oval in shape, with a couple of poles up the middle, semicircular ends and doorways on each side. What better then but to have *two* bars, one at each end? No one need wait for a refill — just go to the twin at the other end. The party started well, and the thoughtfulness of doubling the source of drink was favourably commented upon. In no time the do was showing all the signs of becoming a real wing-ding.

After a couple of hours a willing, carefully briefed and delighted posse of drivers from the Motor Transport section appeared silently and stealthily outside the Mess tent. Carefully, one by one, each visiting vehicle was pushed round to the other side of the tent and left, outwardly in the same position. But, it was facing the wrong way. The noise from inside the tent, at uncounted decibels, ensured that the fiendish act went undetected.

At last, in the small hours, one by one, the visitors said their grateful goodbyes and went out to their vehicles. These they found, apparently as they had left them if they went out through the wrong door or, if they chose the correct door, came to the conclusion after a brief search that they themselves must somehow have got turned round during the evening. Solemnly and with the exaggerated care of men with a lift on, they each climbed in, selected their own stars and sped away into the darkness.

Only two slept that night in their own beds. Most, having done too many miles with no sign of an airfield, suddenly sobered up. It was like ice-cubes down the spine, suddenly being hit by the mortal peril of running out of petrol somewhere, position unknown, far into the desert. The chances of being picked up alive would then be negligible. They spent a bitterly cold and uncomfortable next few hours in the vehicle. After what seemed like an eternity the sun came up; that gave east, and therefore which way for north, the coast, and thence home. The next evening I made a mental note of certain stars — the sword on Orion the Hunter's belt points south, and the Great Bear can show you north. When you could see stars — almost without exception in the desert — one constellation or the other was always visible. The star directly in front of you is not necessarily the best one to choose as a driving guide.

The Desert Air Force voted the joke to be ingenious, successful, diabolical — and an outstandingly good one.

It was a great pity that David Potter was accident-prone. He was an excellent pilot and this was extremely fortunate. If something went wrong with a machine, it was always the one he was flying. We might come back from a raid in apparent good order, and one machine lands 'wheels-up'. Why? A tiny piece of shrapnel damages a single aircraft, cutting the undercarriage hydraulic pipe so the wheels won't come down. Whose? David's. One aircraft out of a formation of twelve has an engine shot out and totters back 125 miles, having produced a masterly piece of glide-stretching with the other. The pilot? Potter.

Once, we ran out of bombs and I sent some aircraft off to bomb-up elsewhere and bring them back. On the way an appalling sandstorm blew up and there was no way of getting down in the desert. Sandstorms put all radio completely on the blink. Three machines, very sensibly, each did much the same thing. They ran before the storm, out over the Mediterranean. There they edged their way down slowly, carefully, and found the surface which they knew would be dead flat. They could be sure that there would be no beige rocky hillocks sticking up, indistinguishable in the thick beige blowing sand outside and waiting to be flown into. Then they turned south for the coast, peering out to catch the sudden slight colour-change of the beach. Then they would be able to turn and fiddle their way delicately along the shoreline, looking for something helpful — like Port Said, or Alexandria, with their coastal airfields. Two were OK but the third met and struck, by the beach, the only clump of palm trees for hundreds of miles either way. With great skill he managed to hold the aircraft in the air long enough for the crew to bale out safely, but the machine was lost. Who was the third man? Potter.

I sent some aircraft to do a few practice landings next door at 33 Squadron's airfield. They had Hurricanes. The CO, my chum Charles Riley, rang me up and our conversation went something like this.

'Before I go any further, your crew are all OK, but one of your Blenheims has been burning in the middle of my airfield. Luckily, we managed to get the fire under control before it was totally destroyed. It came in to land quite normally and, just before touch-down, Air Traffic Control could see the inside of the fuselage burst into a mass of flames. The pilot, with consummate calm, put it down smoothly and braked to a standstill. The cockpit hood was jammed so the two men in front were trapped in the fire. The air-gunner got out of the back and very bravely ran up the wing of the burning aircraft and managed to wrench the hood open from the outside. He got the pilot and crew clear and . . .'

'And the pilot's name is Potter.'

'How did you know?'

'It always is.'

It was a new aeroplane, just received into the squadron and making its first trip. When the remains cooled down we were able to trace the cause to an insecurely fastened petrol pipe in the wing, in which the fuel had collected during the flight. Presumably a pop-back in the exhaust pipe, on landing, had ignited it. Unlucky David who, yet again, had displayed masterly airmanship.

After that episode, I told the unhappy Potter that, good pilot that he was, I simply could not afford to have him around. Where would he like to go and I would do everything I could to help? After much anguishing he asked to go on to Hurricane fighters. So, following his application which I supported, off he went for conversion from Blenheims to Hurricanes which, good pilot that he was, he completed with no difficulty.

The Hurricane squadron that he went to was commanded by an acquaintance of mine called John Ward. Potter duly clocked in and John gave him a Hurry to fly around a bit, to get to know the local topography and do a couple of landings to end up with. To 'run himself in' as it were. Everything went swimmingly and John, watching from the control tent, was delighted that his flying looked clean and competent. Finally, he started his approach for the first landing. The wheels wouldn't come down. Repeated selections with the lever got nowhere. So he tried the old hand's trick of flying upside-down to take the weight off the locks and then selecting the undercarriage to extend upwards — an almost infallible dodge. No joy.

John and David discussed the problem in detail on the radio, but quickly as fuel was beginning to get low. Finally both agreed on the last resort, to try and force the wheels down with the emergency compressed-gas bottle kept for this purpose. This was an unpopular action because the engineers then had to dismantle, drain and clean out the whole hydraulic system which became full of gas bubbles. Still no dice, so Potter put down a beautiful wheels-up landing with minimum damage, considering the cir-cumstances. Ward came racing out in his car and checked the cockpit. Everthing in order. So they got a crane and lifted the machine up while the undercarriage was lowered by hand. It was desert sand in the up-locks and absolutely no fault of David's; his emergency actions had been perfect. John couldn't have been nicer; it really was atrocious luck, on his very first flight with the squadron. 'Look, David,' said Ward, 'I would hate the boys to feel that my confidence in you was suspect, so I'll do something special. My personal Hurricane is over there; take it up and do your familiarisation in that.' David was deeply touched at his new CO's consideration and they went across in John's car.

His take-off was perfect but, as he selected 'wheels-up', there was an almighty bang and the propeller flew off. Oil from the shattered gearbox poured back over the windscreen, completely blotting out the view ahead. David slid back the hood and peered round the edge. In spite of boiling oil in his eyes, and some considerable alarm, he put down another, masterly, wheels-up landing in the desert off the far end of the airfield.

Ward, in his car, was there in about two minutes. David, covered in sand and oil, was standing beside what had been the most cherished Hurricane in the Middle East. Two oily eyebrows were raised and two sad white eyes looked out of a filthy face. He said nothing but the slow shrug of his shoulders said more clearly than words 'I'm very sorry — but what the hell else could I have done that was more than I did?' Ward was very nice about it, but firm. 'That really was unbelievably bad luck. Two aeroplanes in one morning through no possible fault of yours. And two emergencies handled beautifully. However, I am applying at once to Headquarters to move you somewhere else. I can't afford you in my squadron.'

Headquarters made Potter an instructor. One might suppose that no one was better qualified than he to teach the up-and-coming young bloods how to handle flying problems. He must have been good at his job for I never heard of him elsewhere.

# Chapter 20
# The Fox

I stood at the Mess bar, spinning out as long as possible my ration of one glass of lukewarm beer per day. The telephone at the end of the bar rang. 'Milly' Singleton, 21, Old Harrovian and a very gentle person picked it up, listened for a moment and held it out, 'It's for you, Sir.' The AOC 2 Group, Air Commodore Raymond Collishaw was a World War I Canadian fighter ace. Thick-set, bull-necked, grey-haired, he had a unique and disconcerting faith in the ineffectiveness of our Italian opponents. In a period when Hurricanes were at a premium he flew a lone Hurricane which popped up here, there and everywhere to hoodwink the Italians. Holding the telephone in his right hand he would slap his thigh with the left as he said 'We'll fox 'em!' I was never so sanguine. After all, the CR42 biplane fighters were fast, very manoeuvrable and they fired real bullets. Maybe the gun-mountings were not very solid and the guns wavered about. Maybe the pilots were reluctant to press their attacks right up to the hilt. But, with no self-sealing fuel tanks in our Blenheims, one solitary incendiary would be enough. Sometimes we could outwit them, but sometimes we couldn't. I admit now to being endlessly scared, on the ground, not primarily for myself but mainly for my aircrews losing their lives by some fault in my planning or forethought. I hope I didn't show it.

My stomach tightened and prickles went along my spine as I took the telephone. 'Is that you Dudgeon? I want you tomorrow to attack El Adem. Three or four aircraft. 1100 hours on target. OK?'. I thanked him and put down the receiver. The Mess had gone quiet. Everyone looked at me questioningly. I thought fast before speaking. This raid was likely to be very unpleasant. El Adem airfield was a CR42 fighters' nest. It was about 20 miles south of Tobruk harbour, itself a major base which the fighters were to protect. The enemy was in large numbers all along the coast from east to west, and well inland along the Egyptian border to the south. There were only two feasible approach alternatives, if we hoped to achieve any measure at all of surprise. One was to come from far south over the featureless desert, having given no indication of the final target before we turned north. But, having no radio or radar navigation aids — just eyes, a map, and dead-reckoning — an accurate run-in might be difficult . . . The other way was to come over the sea from the north. The harbour with its unmistakable shape would give us a superb navigational fix, but also a superb warning for them. Further, as the CR42s, in the language of the time, 'climbed like a fart in a bath' we would assuredly have a splendid reception committee. I decided to use only three, not four, aircraft so as to retain manoeuvrability with a smaller formation — and I would lead. Everyone was still waiting silently.

'It's three aircraft tomorrow to bomb El Adem, mid-morning.' . . . I could hear the sharp intake of breath and see the eyebrows lift. 'I'll take Nick as No. 2 and Peter as No. 3. Briefing at 0830 tomorrow morning.' I picked up my beer glass and conversation renewed with studied nonchalance. Flight Lieutenant Nicholson was a New Zealander, fair-haired where it wasn't yellow-brown with sand, quiet and 26 years old. He was tough as shoe leather and very competent. Peter Blignaut was a South African with that shadow around his chin which looks unshaven. Tall, slim and 25, he was inexperienced but did not lack guts. The Engineer Officer slipped out to ensure that the aircraft would be readied and bombed-up for next day.

In the morning, planning for the briefing, I faced a horrible decision. There was a 50 mph wind from the south, so sand was picking up. Therefore, if we came in from the sandy desert to the south, navigation would be even more difficult, but we would be coming in from the unpopulated and therefore 'blind' side. Also, we would gain ground speed from the tailwind and this would cut down on our danger time. Probably the safest route, but we could miss the target altogether. On the other hand, coming in from the sea against the headwind, speed would be slower and time at-risk would be longer; seconds could be crucial to our continued existence. Our desert Blenheims with their sand-worn engines and external sand-filters made barely 200 mph on a bombing-run — though you could screw them up to about 240 if you were sufficiently alarmed to thrash the engines by pulling the 'emergency-only' boost lever. Taking an extra two minutes from the coastline, because of the wind, as we came towards El Adem at our ceiling of 15,000 ft (no oxygen), while the CR42s were climbing, was a horrible prospect — even if we came past Tobruk diagonally to one side or the other to avoid their ack-ack. Probably the surer approach, but much more dangerous. Collishaw presumably reckoned the target was important enough for us to be risked, so we had better take the more certain upwind route, from the sea.

I asked for comments from my navigator and rear gunner. The navigator was a small-framed, mousy-haired man who had been a chartered accountant. His eyes were very blue. His alert face was narrow, with a sharp chin and his name was Hornby. Dickie Hornby. No one ever called him that. He was 'Clockwork', from the pre-war Hornby toy trains. My gunner was Sergeant Bennett; he seemed like a grandfather to the crews — an old man of probably almost 30. He was a superb shot. How did they feel about an approach from the north, bucking a headwind like that? They looked at each other, then at me, and shrugged as they passed judgement: 'OK, I suppose.'

We were airborne at about 0930 and turned to go far out over the blue Mediterranean and escape any possible detection from the land. There was no radar in the desert and out of sight was out of mind. Clockwork told me when to turn landwards and by 1050 we were crossing the rocky coast, slanting to leave Tobruk on our right. Even before we were over land, Tobruk was doing its usual nervous act of filling the sky with ack-ack and pom-pom tracer shells as a mark of discouragement. All over the desert below were streaky sand-clouds blown up by the wind; we had been wise not to come in from the south, even though I longed wistfully for the perfect excuse it would have provided for not being there at all. All too soon we could pick out El Adem airfield from the bigger dust trails blown by the slipstreams of the CR42 fighters as they scrambled to intercept us. I hoped like mad that they would go towards Tobruk, being deceived into thinking it was our target because of the anti-aircraft fire over there.

Clockwork was giving me a running commentary as he adjusted his bombsight. Yes — he could see the fighters as they circled upwards. No — they did not seem to be going to Tobruk. He thought there were six — two for each of us. We would be starting the bombing-run in two minutes.

I looked to starboard at Nick. He was sitting rock-steady in formation. Even with his face hidden by leather helmet. goggles and microphone mask, he somehow exuded confidence. I could feel he was calmly and effectively ready to assume the lead if I bought it. I gave him an interrogatory 'thumbs-up'. Gravely he nodded. I might have known. He had his aircraft fully prepared, bombs armed and rear-gunner waiting. I turned to Peter and did the same. Gratifyingly I saw him nod too. Clockwork said 'Steady now. Run starting . . .'

From that moment it was total concentration to hold my aircraft perfectly level and at a constant speed, to make the best possible stable platform for Clockwork's bombsight. Shifts to right and left were only by his instructions for minor corrections. Looking down and to the left I could see the plan-form of the fighters getting uncomfortably close as they strained for every foot of height. Curling and seething black puffs of ack-ack bursts were mushrooming around. Sometimes one would explode near enough to give the aircraft a thump. I could not help but wince if we flew through the dirty smoke of a burst, with its sudden smell of burnt cordite, even though there was then no danger as the shrapnel had already flown away seconds before. Then came what we called the 'flaming ping-pong balls' — CR42 tracer bullets, which seemed to flip past your ears. I could hear Bennett's machine gun spewing out hundreds of bullets per minute, making a sound like tearing gigantic sheets of calico. His shooting paid its dividend for, moments later, I heard his exultant cry of 'Got you, you bastard! He's spinning down . . . ' and then the sound of more firing. I sat immobile, keeping the aircraft a perfect stable base for Clockwork and, incidentally a perfect predictable target for the enemy ack-ack guns. But that is the bomber's trade.

At last came the wonderful words 'Bombs gone!'. In a flash I stopped working for my King and Country and began working for my colleagues and my family. The bombs could look after themselves. My throttle-hand came up in a great sweep across my face to the right, followed by my clenched fist pushing forward from my forehead to the windscreen. As one man the three pilots opened the throttles and pulled the 'emergency-only' super-charger-boost lever for the swing round in a steep turn to the right. Nick had the tough spot, down on the inside of the turn looking up at me, but no complaints. I could still hear Sergeant Bennett firing and, over my shoulders I could see the other rear-guns swinging as they fired too. We were piling on the coal, getting to hell out of there, out to sea and for home. At least, trying to end up on that patch of desert which we thought of as 'home'.

I aimed straight for Tobruk because the fighter pilots could see the ack-ack was very heavy but, for us, ack-ack was far less lethal than a fighter. As I had guessed and hoped, the fighters chose not to continue pressing their attacks close to the shell-bursts. In a moment or two they were gone, except for one only. I turned again, to miss Tobruk itself. He was still with us when we crossed the coast and there seemed no point in giving him a chance to pick us off one by one. It would be better to break up and to use, each of us, the last dregs of throttle which I had kept in hand to let the others hold a tight formation. At the worst, he could only follow one of us.

I waved my hand from side to side above my head and they needed no second bidding. I was alone. Alone, that is, except for the CR42. Hardly surprisingly he stayed with me, for the formation leader is always the juiciest prey. He is the most difficult to replace, and therefore is the crew the enemy can least afford to lose.

I was very lucky. He must have been inexperienced. An old hand would have known that his CR42 could come right in close behind a Blenheim and there he would be completely screened from the rear gunner by the Blenheim's own fin and rudder. My gunner, to his frustration and fury, would see nothing but four wingtips showing, two each side of the fin. Moreover, with his extreme biplane manoeuvrability he could stay right there, firing in peace and comfort however much the Blenheim pilot threw his aircraft about to try and shake him off. Luckily for us he kept too far back for his somewhat inaccurate guns to be effective. He should have come close in and made sure of his kill. I hunched my shoulders together and pulled in my elbows behind the armour-plate at my back, watching his flaming ping-pong balls flip by and metaphorically keeping my fingers crossed. I was not frightened; one never is on these occasions; one is totally preoccupied with trying to stay alive. Fear comes much later, when you are back on the ground — particularly when you get to bed and try to sleep.

Behind me Bennett was cursing bloody murder, telling me what was happening and beseeching me to slow up and mix it so that he could get a clear shot and shoot him down. Clockwork was on all fours, with his bottom sticking up, trying to get a sight on the CR42 with the fatuous under-gun they had fitted below his feet. A device where the belted ammunition came from some distance away, round corners, and nearly always jammed. Even when it worked you had to lie on the floor and sight the gun backwards, under your stomach, through a mirror. Designed doubtless by some office-boy and virtually useless, but it kept Clockwork very happy, and above all occupied, at a trying time.

For my part, I had no intention of mixing it with that superbly agile biplane which was even more sprightly than our Gladiators. I had got my eye on some lumps and rolls of strato-cumulus cloud now barely a couple of miles ahead. Say 40 seconds and if I could just poke my nose into one of them he would never then get a dog's chance of killing us. I shoved the throttles even harder against their stops, hoping for just a few more revs. Then, Bingo! We were there! The grey mist snatched us inside and as it was only a small cloud I flung her into a steep turn to the left. Two things as expected; we came out of its side moments later and, secondly, Bennett told me the fighter was waiting on top of the cloud to see which way we had gone. Already he could report the CR42 swinging round, nose down and black smoke streaming from his exhausts as he thrust his throttle wide open and the fuel mixture richened. I pointed our nose at another small cloud along the roll of them, say 15 seconds away. From there on, Bennett's running commentary was really gratifying and enormously helpful, even if its content was ungrateful. It enabled us to pop into cloud after cloud, just in the nick of time, and just before Bennett, or the fighter pilot, could get the shots they both craved.

I began to get angry with this boy who would not give up. Little horns sprouted from under my leather helmet. A forked tail poked out of my trousers. I would show this whipper-snapper he should not try to kill me. He was playing games with the big boys now. If he wanted to stake his life against mine, I would teach him a lesson he would never forget. It was a perfect day for us. Little lumps of cloud, not too far apart. I let him come as close as I dared, after one cloud and before I popped into another one. Each time he went up to the top and then screamed down the other side with all he had to try and catch us. I teased him and all the time our little darts and turns were generally northwards. Further, and further, and further from the coast. And, behind us, was the 50 mph tailwind. Into which he would be heading when at last he turned for base.

It was well over 35 minutes before he twigged what was happening. Bennett suddenly said, as we popped out of the umpteenth cloud, 'I can't see the bugger. Has he got underneath us Clockwork?' And then, 'I've got him now; he's going for home.' I swung the Blenheim round and followed him, taking up station about a mile behind and 1000 ft above. Now it was my turn to give Bennett a running commentary on what was happening to the machine below and in front of us. He was losing height gently, and flying slowly for maximum endurance. Including his full-throttle climb to height from El Adem, and the chase to the coast, and the pursuit out to sea, he had been squandering fuel for over an hour. With that wind on his nose he was barely making good 75 mph towards the coast which, Clockwork estimated, was over 100 miles distant. Fighters do not have a long endurance. He obviously saw us, for once he turned up for another attack but gave up immediately when we swung away from the land. He got lower and lower to escape the wind until he was only just above the white-caps on the sapphire-blue waves. I sat and waited, feeling rather clever. He was indeed learning his lesson.

The inevitable came 50 miles from the coast and safety. His prop slowed down to windmilling whilst his speed dropped and dropped. Someone, perhaps it was me, said, 'Bloody good show.' His wheels touched, dug into the water and with an enormous splash and shocking suddenness the CR42 flipped upside down. 'That,' I thought, 'will teach you a sharp lesson . . .'

I waited for his helmeted head to appear beside the sinking fuselage as I circled the spot. I told Bennett to get the rubber dinghy pack ready to drop through the rear hatch. We realised that in that southerly wind his only hope would be for the dinghy to be blown the 200 miles north to Crete. His machine sank lower, and lower, and then I realised he was not going to appear. I felt awful. It stopped being, as I sensed earlier, a clean fight with an enemy, and let the best man win. That he would have killed me, if he could, counted for nothing. I had capitalised deliberately on his enthusiasm, inexperience and, probably, youth. I had tricked a youngster, another pilot, into committing suicide. It was a terrible feeling and my flight back to base was a misery.

When I got home and finished my landing run, as usual, I was surprised that on my parking spot there were no groundcrew to see me in. Even more startling, there was no ambulance and no friendly Irish brogue of Flight Lieutenant 'Doc' Read, asking if there had been any casualties. Then the place erupted. My fitter and rigger came running from the tents. The ambulance came screeching round from the sick-bay, trailing clouds of dust and with the Doc hanging out of the door. People started pouring out of the messes and other tents so that in a few moments I was completely surrounded. 'What happened? Where have you been?' In hindsight it was hardly surprising. Nick and Peter had returned and landed an hour and a half earlier. Their story was morbid and sounded true. They said I had waved them away and 'drawn off' the remaining fighter out to sea, to give them a safe run home. Then, as I had not reappeared at base for over an hour, I obviously had not shot him down or evaded him. Consequently he must have got me. A signal reporting me 'missing' had already been sent and my death was confidently assumed.

I seemed to be the only person who suffered distress over the poor fighter pilot's watery grave. When I telephoned the AOC to give him an immediate brief summary of the raid and its consequences, he was simply delighted. On the line I could clearly hear him slapping his thigh as he chuckled, 'You sure foxed him, Dudgeon! You foxed him good!'

At the end of de-briefing the crews I asked, as always, 'Any questions?' 'Yes, Sir,' said Nick's sergeant-navigator, 'I want to make a complaint about my pilot, Flight Lieutenant Nicholson.' My eyes must have bulged out of my head. The hairs on the back of my neck fairly bristled. Nick was my best, most reliable, most efficient Flight Commander and pilot. From the corner of my eye I could see Nick's face. He looked stunned. For any crew member to complain of his Captain was unheard of.

'What,' I asked, trying to keep my voice as flat as I could, 'is the complaint?'

'Well, Sir,' the navigator began, 'you will remember that as we approached El Adem we could see the CR42s taking off. And, with the headwind, they were obviously going to intercept us. And there were ack-ack bursts all around us. Also, our approach took a long time because of our low ground-speed. Then the fighters came in and we had those flaming ping-pong balls everywhere. And we still had to get out and away . . . It was exceptionally unpleasant, as I am sure, Sir, you will agree. Well, I found it particularly nerve-racking because Flight Lieutenant Nicholson was just sitting there in formation, flying with one hand while with the other he slapped the windscreen and the side panels, muttering "these bloody flies get everywhere . . . " It's not fair on his crew, Sir! He ought to pay more attention in a dangerous situation.'

This remark, by a sergeant, was incredible, inexcusable and disloyal, if serious. I looked at him closely. His face was expressionless. He managed to hold it for about ten seconds

before the corners of his mouth began to twitch. Then he started
to shake and in a second the whole Ops Room exploded with
delight to witness (as the AOC might have said) the Sergeant out-
foxing the boss.

Bad news travels fast; good news catches up more slowly. Phyl,
in Karachi, was sad when she heard within days on the grapevine
that I had 'bought it'. News to the contrary took several weeks.

# Chapter 21
# Thirty-nine Men

The Postings Officer looked at me across the desk. 'You,' he said 'are losing your squadron because they say you are to have a rest from ops. Over fifty raids is enough. For the time being you are going to 4 FTS — to run the Oxford flight; chauffeuring pupils round on their exercises, I suppose.' I argued and wriggled, but to no avail. Thus, in early April, 1941, I clocked in to No. 4 Service Flying Training School, Habbaniya, Iraq. '4 FTS' had been in existence for years and years and years. It used to be in Egypt but had been moved to Habbaniya on the outbreak of war. There, it was a thousand miles behind the Western Desert battlefields and, it could be assumed, completely secure from any enemy disturbance. In what follows there are hardly any names. This is deliberate. I can remember some, but not all — 'Butcher' Saville the CO, Larry Ling the Chief Flying Instructor, 'Stooge' Garner, Jimmy Broughton, John Hawtrey, Dicky Cleaver, 'Horse' Evans and maybe a dozen others — but these were only part of a team. To cite only those to whom I was closest would be most unjust to the others.

Habbaniya was a magnificently appointed RAF camp and airfield, built seemingly regardless of expense. Work had started on it in 1934 in accordance with the Anglo-Iraq Treaty of Alliance and Mutual Support, signed in 1930, and it had been occupied since 1937. It had playing fields, golf course, riding stables, polo pitch, hospital, the finest swimming pool in the Service, 56 tennis courts and a magnificent gymnasium. It did its best to be something of a garden, thanks to its situation in an angle of the Euphrates and reliance on the great river for irrigation. Trees lined its 28 miles of roads which, in themselves, reminded one of home, named as they were after such London and Air Force landmarks as Piccadilly and Cranwell. Lawns and flowerbeds were everywhere.

Air Headquarters Iraq was located here and the Training School flew from the large sandy airfield. On its north was the Euphrates. Some distance to its south lay Lake Habbaniya where the Imperial Airways passenger flying-boats alighted. At Shaibah, near Basrah, there was a second RAF base which was also used as a staging post between Egypt and India.

Habbaniya was between Rutbah Wells and Baghdad — 200 miles from the one and 50 miles from the other. The outlook, as far as the eye could see after the scrubby cultivation, was just desert. Over to the east, towards Baghdad on the Tigris, some of the area between the rivers was marshy or semi-cultivated. Except where the ground was made wet it was yellow-brown sand and gravel everywhere.

One of the airmen was besought by his Mum in England to send her some snapshots so that she could 'see what it was like'. He was thoroughly fed up and lonely at the time so he got four copies of a picture of featureless desert. These he sent to her entitled 'Habbaniya looking North — South — East — and West.' Not wholly accurate but, for him, nearly so. The nearest bar was in Baghdad, 50 miles away.

Typically, nearly all the flying instructors were young, enthusiastic and madly frustrated at being divorced from the sharp end. A plaintive little poem was running round the FTS at the time. It was called 'An Instructor's Lament' and the opening verse went:

> 'What did you do in the War, Daddy?
>    How did you help us to win?'
> 'Circuits and Bumps, and turns, Laddie;
>    And how to get out of a Spin.'

There were several more verses, well known to the Air Force, all bewailing an instructor's enforced separation from the fighting. Endless circuits and landings with ham-fisted pupils was no satisfactory substitute. On the other hand the most senior officers were of World War I vintage, properly and contentedly beavering away to have their organisation churn out lots of pilots and observers for the war elsewhere.

Except for the very senior, everybody was also frustrated by the absence of women; when I was censoring letters I noted that an airman had written to his girl-friend, 'Have the ceiling painted a colour you like, because its all you're going to see for weeks after I get home.'

Towards the end of March 1941, shortly before I arrived in Habbaniya, the tranquillity of this 'dream' purpose-built desert station began to be disturbed by some ripples from the unwelcome activities of an Iraqi politician, Raschid Ali el Gailani. The Regent, Abdullah Ilah, had ruled in place of his nephew the boy king, then aged five. On 31 March, learning of a plot to arrest him, the Regent fled from Baghdad to Habbaniya whence he was flown to Basrah and given refuge by the Royal Navy aboard HMS *Cockchafer*.

By early April Raschid Ali had seized power. Together with four senior Iraqi army and air force officers he swiftly established a pro-German regime, officially the National Defence Government but known, more colourfully, as the Golden Square.

Thus Britain was suddenly confronted by a potentially hostile Iraq in place of the acquiescent State it had counted on since the outbreak of war. At that time, while not going to war as an ally against Germany, Iraq had broken off diplomatic relations. Unfortunately however, Iraq had left a backdoor open by retaining relations with Italy, even after Germany's Axis partner had entered the war in June 1940. Thereafter, Germany had used Baghdad as a centre for subversion — much aided by Britain's enemy, the Mufti of Jerusalem, who had made off from Palestine and found asylum there not long before hostilities began.

Encouraged by Germany, Raschid Ali began to present a very serious problem. The main worry was that under the 1930 Treaty, Iraq was pledged to protect the oil pipeline linking its northern oilfield with Haifa in Palestine and Tripoli in Syria. Moreover, Britain regarded the Basrah-Baghdad-Palestine overland route as an emergency corridor to the Red Sea to reinforce Egypt.

At first, Raschid Ali's coup did not seem to upset our people in Baghdad greatly. On 16 April Sir Kinahan Cornwallis, the British Ambassador, informed the rebel leader that Britain intended to move troops through Iraq under the terms of the Treaty and no objections were raised. But later, when the troops arrived at Basrah from Karachi and Sir Kinahan refused to give Raschid Ali an undertaking that the troops would move out of Iraq, Raschid Ali was angered. Also, knowing that yet more troopships were due at Basrah, he decided to pre-empt the arrival of further reinforcements. He would make an example of Habbaniya.

Raschid Ali, to help him in his ambitions, had an army and an air force; both, ironically, largely British-trained. The only counter to that force was what could be found inside Habbaniya.

His Army strength was about 45,000, fully equipped with guns, tanks and armoured cars. Our 'army' was less impressive. In addition to the 1300 RAF officers and men, there were four Assyrian and two Iraqi locally recruited and trained levies, totalling about 1000 men in six companies. We hoped they would be loyal to us in the event of trouble. There were 18 RAF armoured cars. These had armour plate bodies on a standard Rolls-Royce saloon-car chassis, First World War vintage. There were a few trench mortars and plenty of rifles. There was no artillery. Nor were there any tanks and modern fighting vehicles.

The nearest reinforcements, if needed and if they could be spared, were separated from us by more than 500 miles of roadless and waterless desert.

Raschid Ali's air force had about 80 aircraft for warlike operations. American Northrop and Italian Savoia twin-engined bombers, Breda six-gun monoplane and CR42 biplane fighters, British Pegasus-engined Audaxes and Gladiators. On the whole a formidable force. Even a dispassionate look at the FTS as a fighting force was not encouraging. It was only a mixed bag of training airraft.

There were 21 Audaxes. These were, in effect, the ubiquitous Hart biplanes but fitted out for Army co-operation. This meant that they had an exhaust pipe so that when flying at night blue flames from the stub exhausts would not blind the pilot. Also most had 'an 'ook' on the end of a long rod to be lowered in flight for snatching up message bags on strings without having to land. They had lightweight bomb racks for carrying eight little bombs. There was the usual one front gun and the mounting for a rear machine gun.

Next, we had three Gladiators, between-the-wars biplane four-gun fighters which had been retired from the Western Desert as out of date when the Hurricanes arrived. They each had their four machine guns, but we had no ammunition belts for them. They had been used by the communications flight, for making liaison visits.

Then there were 27 Oxfords, originally designed as a small twin-engined civilian-transport aeroplane, to carry five or six passengers. They had been modified to have a rear machine gun for training air-gunners, and they could be fitted with cameras for photography. There was a square hole or recess under the fuselage, fitted with racks for carrying practice smoke-bombs; no type of explosive bomb existed that would go on to the racks in the recess. Oxfords were made largely of plywood and, never having been considered for any kind of warlike operations, were about as battle-resistant as an electric light bulb. But, they could carry one rear gun and we had 27 machines — even though we had nothing like 27 machine guns to go in them, and only two air-gunners.

Lastly there were seven Gordons. This was a somewhat updated WW1-type biplane with, after all its outside bolted-on excrescences, modifications and age, a cruising speed of around 85 mph. Built by Fairey's between 1930 and 1934 it had long since been withdrawn from any sort of warlike role. Their sole job was to tow fabric targets for teaching air-to-air gunnery. But the fact remained that they *could* be fitted with 'Universal' bomb racks — and on each of those we could put two decent-sized high-explosive bombs — 250 lbs. And they were the *only seven machines* in the place allowed to carry bombs of that calibre.

There were another 24 aircraft for which we could find no operational use whatever. They were the dual-control Hart trainers, on which there was no way to attach a gun, bomb rack or even a camera.

In all we could muster 58 machines which, if pressed, could take *some* kind of warlike action and, for most, that was not much; and, we did not have the crews to fly even those, all at once.

While Raschid Ali was setting up trouble, Habbaniya from AHQ Iraq at the top and going down through the FTS, started to take precautions. To have a proper perspective of what this meant, it must be accepted in no derogatory sense that in that period of the war the younger fire-eaters gravitated towards the operational commands whilst the older, more placid and rule-orientated types congregated in Training and Maintenance. Indeed, for maximum overall effectiveness, that is the way it ought to be. In practice, at Habbaniya, whilst the more junior bods at the bottom were sweating their guts out trying to make things work for real, the senior officers at the top were fussing themselves to bits over doing only what was laid down in 'the books' and at the same time keeping up to their training targets. This produced some hectic and at times positively farcical situations.

Our crucial shortage was pilots. Not one single pilot was, on paper, experienced *and* fit for active operations. Most were the instructors, raring to go but who, through no choice of their own, had never fired a bullet or dropped a bomb in anger. Some were pilots who for whatever reason had been put on the shelf as 'unsuitable for operational flying'. Some, although woefully out of flying practice, were culled from the Headquarters Staff. There were three, specifically at the school for a 'rest' after a surfeit of operational sorties: one Warrant Officer, one Flying Officer and one Squadron Leader — me. As in my case, no one foresaw what kind of a 'rest' was ahead.

We gathered together 39 who could and would fly. Plus perhaps, if the task would not be too demanding, some of the students. Most of the students were only beginning their training. We even had some Greeks whom we were training for the Greek government. But we hoped we could use some who, nearing the end of their course, had quite a few solo hours notched up. From the outside, with deep gratitude we got some help. Between 27 and 30 April India flew in about 300 men of the King's Own Royal Regiment.

Naturally, we in Habbaniya were totally unaware of the rarefied discussions and decisions which were going on in Whitehall and Cairo, and which were way above our heads. We had to cope with what we had as best we could. Nevertheless, in hindsight, it is interesting to reflect on what transpired there at that time.

On 1 May, as Colonel O.L. Roberts of 10th Indian Division assumed command of land forces in Habbaniya, we were still the operational responsibility of India Command. But, by 5 May we had been transferred to Middle East and, as Winston Churchill signalled to General Wavell, 'whence alone immediate assistance can be given.' It so happened that it was around the date of Wavell's birthday and he let it be known in Whitehall that the additional worry of Iraq was an unwanted birthday present. He repeated earlier pleas to London that diplomats should attempt to negotiate a settlement. He feared that a campaign in Iraq would imperil his responsibility for the defence of Palestine and Egypt.

Habbaniya was not alone in its frustrations concerning what was or was not being done by the Middle East Command. Winston was losing patience with General Wavell who, he thought, 'showed himself most reluctant to assume more burdens.' On the other hand, General Auchinleck in India was finding favour with the Prime Minister through his positive offers of reinforcements. In his account of this period (*The Second World War*, Volume 3, Cassell, 1950) Churchill has freely acknowledged that Iraq was 'but one small sector of the emergency which lapped General Wavell on all sides simultaneously.' Nevertheless, whatever were the global reasons he relieved Wavell of his command (in June, after the campaign) and appointed Auchinleck to bring 'a fresh mind and a hitherto untapped personal energy.' Wavell took Auchinleck's place in India.

Meanwhile, towards the end of April and totally unknown to us in the FTS, Middle East was feverishly trying to put together an Army relief column to be called 'Habforce' (Habbaniya Force) which could cross the desert from Amman to Habbaniya, even though, inevitably, it would be several weeks before it could arrive. An advance flying column, under Brigadier J.J. Kingstone, managed to reach Habbaniya on 18 May. The story of Kingcol's epic journey is told in *The Golden Carpet* (Faber and Faber, 1944) by Somerset de Chair, a Conservative Member of Parliament who was serving as the column's intelligence officer.

Also, Middle East flew in six more Gladiators, time-expired from the Western Desert, raising our fighting strength to 64 aircraft. They were delivered by six ferry pilots and we in the FTS made loud noises to hijack them and keep them in Habbaniya. We needed pilots desperately and those six would have increased our effective strength by 15 per cent. Air Headquarters went so far as to send a signal asking permission, but when a negative answer came back the pilots were meekly returned.

There being only two observer/bomb-aimers and two air-gunners, we devised and injected a crash course in these two arts for the student-pilots. As none of them had received their 'wings'; we would use them in other ways.

In case of surprise air attack, the polo pitch and the nine-hole golf course in the middle of the camp were flattened and made into a small dispersal airfield. Each night the Harts and Audaxes were flown there — and flown back again the next morning to the main airfield to keep up with the regular training schedule.

Our three Gladiators were given a somewhat sketchy overhaul and added to the six we had received. Having no belted amunition for them, we put teams of pupils on to hand-belting. A thankless task — one cartridge, two clips, one cartridge . . . then feed it through a device which you wind like a mincing-machine and which adjusts the belt properly. Say 25 cartridges a minute, for an adroit student — remembering that the guns on *one* aircraft are going to fire nearly 5000 in that space of time. Heart-breaking for the youngsters, but they responded magnificently.

The Audax bomb racks carried eight 20 lb anti-personnel bombs — 160 lbs. A pitifully small load. However, the wing attachments were the same as for Harts and I suggested hanging on a pair of Universal bomb racks instead, and carrying two 250 lb bombs. The 500 lbs of high-explosive per Audax would vastly increase our attacking capacity. Air Headquarters, having looked into the Audax manual and found nothing there, contended that there must be a difference in the aircraft, or the installing of Universal racks would have been mentioned. We eventually pressed them so hard thay they sent a signal to Air Ministry quoting our proposal and asking for their permission to go ahead. The answer came back next day saying what we already knew: 'The stated bomb-load of an Audax is eight 20 lb bombs.' So AHQ vetoed our proposal and assumed that the matter was closed.

The Chief Flying Instructor, Wing Commander Larry Ling, was made of sterner stuff. He knew I had done hundreds of hours in India flying Harts with this load, and that I was very keen to give it a whirl. So we had an Audax fitted up with two Universals carrying two 250 lb bombs and he said I could be on my way. Our WW1-vintage officers in AHQ and elsewhere were appalled at Larry proposing to let me do it without their permission from above. They actually asked him to sign a piece of paper before my take-off, saying that the flight was being made without proper authority and entirely on the pilot's sole responsibility. Imagine — in a war situation! Larry told them what to do with their piece of paper and within the hour the Audax was airborne.

Of course, an Audax is merely 'an 'art wiv an 'ook', so there was no problem whatever in the flying. AHQ then agreed we could fit the larger racks. Regrettably, there were only 38 Universals at Habbaniya. Fourteen were on the Gordons so we could only equip a dozen Audaxes. Nevertheless, the extra 24 250-pounders nearly trebled our potential strike power in high-explosive.

Next, what could be done about the Oxfords? The rear-gun fittings were OK, even if we could only find about ten machine guns for them. What about some real, instead of smoke-bombs? The Oxford bomb racks would take 20 lb explosive bombs, but the bombs couldn't be put on the racks when they were bolted into their recess under the fuselage. The bombs were too long. So? How about making the racks hang down a bit, underneath the fuselage? Then the bombs could be carried because their tail-fins would stick out and clear the edge of the hole. I drew a sketch of some little metal distance-pieces which would tilt the rack downwards at the back. We asked Station

Workshops to make them for us. Making was no difficulty — but Workshops asked Headquarters to give their blessing. The technical staff at HQ suggested that the tail-fins might disturb the airflow under the fuselage; the machine (already unpleasantly sensitive at low speeds with the wheels down) might become uncontrollable. No one could tell. It might crash. They said that if bombs could be fitted like that, 'they would have done it in the first place'. Moreover, they noted that (true) it was an unauthorised change to the bomb-rack mountings of the aircraft itself. This made it, they said, a design change, and that was the sole prerogative of London, in conjunction with the makers, and no one else. They gave their categorical refusal. The answer was an unequivocal 'No, no, no.'

With Larry's connivance we rustled up some sheet steel, a hacksaw, some drills and a few nuts and bolts. Drawing on my Cranwell training in sheet-metal working I made a prototype set of distance pieces. Then, having bolted on the racks and fitted eight 20-pounders, I made ready to fly the aircraft, with bombs loaded, on a suck-it-and-see basis.

The buzz went round as to what was going on. Larry and I could hardly believe our bosses' reaction. They became almost apoplectic. Their instructions were to be flouted? More, had already been disobeyed in part? I might kill myself and, worse, we would then lose one of our aircraft. There was no regulational permission for it. It went on for quite a while. At last, Larry actually signed a piece of paper saying that they had not been told about it and that the pilot was well aware that they could have forbidden the test if they had. They, therefore, were completely exonerated if anything went wrong.

The Oxford flew quite happily and all was forgiven and forgotten. Station Workshops then made all the necessary distance pieces to double our bombing force, with 27 Oxford 'very light bombers'.

Finally, with all our modifications completed, we agreed that if real ops were called for, the war posture of the FTS would be to divide it into two halves. We conceived five 'squadrons'. Larry would have 21 aircraft in two squadrons; nine and 12 Audaxes with 20 lb and 250 lb bombs. He would have 19 pilots. I would have 43 aircraft in three squadrons; 27 Oxfords with 20 lb bombs, seven Gordons with 250 lb bombs and nine Gladiators with front-guns only. I would get 20 pilots. Of the two trained bomb-aimers and two air-gunners, Larry got one of each and so did I. The

Audaxes and the Gordons could do dive-bombing while the Oxfords would only bomb from level flight.

That lot used up every pilot who could or would fly, and every bomb rack and front-gun in the place. For bomb-aimers and rear-gunners in the Oxfords and Gordons we would use the pupil-pilots, and any odd bod from the camp who was prepared to come up with us to help.

Meanwhile, although every effort was being made by us to prepare for maximum scale air operations, at the same time every effort was being required by AHQ not to let the training programme slip behind schedule. A truly British compromise resulted, although there were some pretty frustrating moments in the FTS and some pretty tart comments during the tea-breaks.

Completely unknown to us, Raschid Ali the rebel leader was also in touch with the German High Command. They were planning to work together and for the Germans to obtain a foothold for their armed forces in Iraq. They would then build up, through Vichy-controlled Syria, and thus establish a real fighting force behind our supply bases in Palestine and round the Nile delta. Worse, they could also cut off the oil supplies upon which our entire Western Desert effort depended. By incredible good fortune Raschid Ali made a monumental error; he moved against us before the Germans were ready.

Towards the end of April things were obviously hotting up in Baghdad. Their radio broadcasts and rebel propaganda were becoming increasingly anti-British and indicated that an attack on Habbaniya could be in the offing. The FTS started daily reconnaissances of the roads to the east and west of the camp to check on any movements, for we had no idea what form the attack — if it came — might take. I in an Oxford, drawing upon my Indian aerial-survey experience, made a photographic mosaic of Baghdad and its airfield. It was, to put it mildly, a bit unnerving to sit in a lightly built aeroplane and to make a series of straight and level runs backwards and forwards, backwards and forwards, over the city. It felt like walking down Piccadilly with no clothes on. However although the Iraqis may have watched me very closely, they did not attack — as Headquarters had feared and half-expected.

Reconnaissance pilots next saw that some troops were gathering in Fallujah and Ramadi, east and west of the camp, so a demonstration was planned. We would use every available pilot including some of the more experienced pupils and even some

Greek instructors for whom we were providing facilities to train the Greek pupils. The dual-control Harts were pressed into service as well as the Audaxes; that only left nine pilots for the Oxfords. Finally, four squadrons of Hart types in diamond formation, with the Oxfords doing 'S' turns above, and the Gladiators on a freelance commission below, sailed majestically back and forth over the two villages and Habbaniya. The British Lion thus demonstrated British Air Might. Little did they know how few teeth were in the lion's gums.

On the 29th a full day's training was demanded, with redoubled efforts urged upon us to try and catch up with time lost on the demonstration and the other non-training diversions. Every pupil possible was put was put into the air, not forgetting the Greeks. An equally intensive effort was planned for the following day.

Next morning, at about 3 am a warning signal was decoded from the British Embassy in Baghdad saying that they had seen military forces moving off in the direction of Habbaniya. Someone promptly blew the General Alarm. At that time no one in the camp had the slightest idea why. Gradually, as dawn came up, we saw that there was indeed cause for alarm. The camp was infested. To the south east of the airfield and overlooking it there is a plateau, about 200 ft high. On it could be seen bodies of troops marching around, digging trenches, installing machine guns and generally settling themselves in. They had guns mounted, covering the airfield at point-blank range. Armoured cars were within 500 yds of the perimeter and there were pom-pom guns on the approach lanes. To us, on the airfield, the plateau as seen through binoculars looked like a great deal of nastiness.

AHQ, in best WW1 style, promptly commandeered every single Senior NCO, airman and pupil-aircrew — and put them to digging trenches and manning machine guns around the camp.

The Iraqi commander sent in a polite note, under a White Flag, saying that the camp was surrounded, all flying was to cease, and that any aircraft taking off would be fired on. The AOC sent back a reply, also under a White Flag, to the effect that on no account would he cease training flying; firing on an aircraft would be an Act of War and would result in immediate reprisals.

Having lost all the ground crew, and the pupils, the only people left to move and arm-up the 64 aircraft, plus moving the 24 Harts, were the 39 pilots. It was tough work in the heat. The Oxfords and the Gladiators were moved, out of sight of the guns as far as possible, behind the hangars at the end of the camp furthest from the plateau. All the Harts and the Audaxes were flown across to the polo pitch in the middle of the camp and tucked in behind the trees. The Gordons got the stickiest wicket behind the hangars nearest to the plateau. Butcher Saville, commanding the FTS, set up an ops room in an office at the back of the hangar furthest from the plateau. To help him he had some clerks.

Around mid-morning they sent me off in an Oxford fitted with a camera to do a discreet recce of the plateau and from it make a photo-map. We could then get some idea of the forces up there. There was no ground fire from the enemy. Later in the day, to most people's horror, Air Vice-Marshal M.G. Smart, the AOC, required Larry to send off an Audax on a provocative flight to see if the Iraqis would give an excuse to start something. By the greatest good fortune they didn't, for, with everybody in the trenches, we had nobody even to start the engines — it took two people to start an Audax for someone had to wind the starting handle. And, as for putting on more bombs after a sortie . . . ? It was a tense night. Winston Churchill signalled: 'If you have to strike, strike hard.'

During 30 April and 1 May the Iraqis continued their build-up on the plateau. Later intelligence and photographic analysis showed that they had 4000–5000 troops, 30 guns including howitzers and 18 pounders, pom-pom guns, 150 machine guns, 200–300 transport vehicles with, worst of all, armoured cars and light tanks. In fact, an overwhelming force with which, if they had chosen, they could have driven straight through the camp to Air Vice-Marshal's Smart's office, for we had nothing effective to stop them. Air Headquarters still woodenly refused to let any of the ground crew and pupils leave their trenches round the airfield, insisting that they were essential to defend the camp against an attack.

Protests and demands for a withdrawal, from the British Ambassador in Baghdad and downwards, produced precisely nothing. So, at 8 pm (darkness) on 1 May a conference of senior officers and squadron commanders was held in the Air Head-quarters building. They decided that if the Iraqis were still on the plateau at earliest dawn next morning, 5 am, a bombing and ground-strafing attack would be started. There was the great news that Wellington bombers of 70 Squadron, recently arrived at Basrah 300 miles to the south-east, would be joining in from there.

Practical problems we raised, such as lack of facilities for prompt resupply of bombs, fuel supplies for the polo pitch which up till then had only been used as a parking area for dispersed aircraft overnight, and so forth, were sidestepped by AHQ with a bland, 'Do the best you can. It won't last long. Have every aircraft in the air before light, and start bombing as soon as you can distinguish targets on the ground — 5 am.' They were convinced that within three hours the Iraqis would be in full flight — by 8 am — so a continuous bombardment was to be kept up with as many aircraft as practicable till they had gone. The Squadron Commanders then went back to the squadrons and briefed the pilots. That was done by about 10 pm and then — not a word to AHQ — we all went round the perimeter filching back all our ground crews and the pupil aircrew, leaving it completely bare. Then we allocated their tasks and named the aircrews for the next day. None of us got to our rooms before midnight, and the last person was back at the aircraft by 0315.

# Chapter 22
# Circuits and Bumps, Laddie

I, like everybody else, took off as soon as the first signs of a grey sheen showed across the eastern horizon — which, as any old Middle Eastern hand can tell you, is 30 minutes before you can distinguish objects on the ground. As the daylight got stronger we could see that the air above the plateau was like the front of a beehive on a sunny morning. You might peer down into the dusk trying to distinguish a gun-emplacement to provide a juicy target — and an Audax would swoop past at some crazy angle. Or a Wellington would sail majestically across your bows, giving you heart-failure and leaving you bucketting about in its slipstream. Luckily, no one hit anybody else.

Dead on 5 o'clock the first bombs went down and within a few minutes we could see the camp being fiercely shelled. However, we could also clearly see the flashes from the guns, so we were able to retaliate. Luckily for us the pom-poms were using a lot of tracer which marked them very clearly and we could keep out of their way. The Wellingtons seemed to be very precise with their front and rear guns and we could see their tracer bullets hitting vehicles and the gun-positions.

My observer/bomb-aimer in the Oxfords was Sergeant Prickett. I guess he was a few years older than I, and he was a tower of strength. His bombing corrections were impeccable, and he had an eye like a hawk when it came to picking out pom-pom guns, machine-gun emplacements or other unpleasant devices. We, the aircrews, were only too well aware that we had nothing — just nothing — which could halt a tank driving up to the front door of AHQ — except a bomb. Hence we believed our very survival depended on, in effect, knocking out every offensive weapon before the Iraqis could pull themselves together, and to keep going till they left, as confidently predicted by Headquarters. This drove us into a routine which was to fly, fly, fly any offensive aircraft that remained flyable. Something had to crack, and it could not be us. We bombed, and gunned, and looked for other targets. Back on the ground, one of the two crew members — taking turns alternately — would report to the Group Captain in the ops room with results. At the same time the crew member would suggest possible new targets that he had seen. The Group Captain would then plot both on the photo-map I had taken, and allot the crewman his next target. Meanwhile the other crewman, often with the engines still running, be he pilot or bomb-aimer would re-arm and check for any additional damage. Surprisingly, no one got clouted by a spinning prop. When the first chap returned with the new targets, off they went again.

Over the plateau the Oxfords were cruising around at about 1000 ft for maximum accuracy, while the dive-bombing and machine-gunning Audaxes were going really low. Ground fire was both intense and accurate. You could watch bullet holes being punched up through the wings from underneath and several aircraft had bullets through the cockpit. One Oxford was shot down in flames, killing the instructor and two pupils, and one Audax came back with 52 bullet holes in it.

After their crash course, the pupils acting as bomb-aimers and rear-gunners quickly became remarkably accurate — even if some of the bombing-run corrections were a bit garbled at first. Not the placid and experienced, 'Left, left — steady . . . Right — steady . . .', ending up with a flat 'Bombs gone' which I was hearing from Sergeant Prickett. More like, to begin with: 'Left, left . . . Right . . . Right . . . RIGHT . . . LEFT, LEFT!!! Oh Christ, bomb gone . . . Sir.' However, they all did a fabulous and courageous job, and soon became highly efficient.

There were quite a lot of casualties but those who got back showed real guts. One pilot was shot through the jaw, with the bullet lodging in his face and causing great pain; even though he could barely see, he managed to land OK. Another was shot through the thigh with the bullet splitting in two; one piece lodged half-way between knee and groin and the other tracked up to his rump, but he got the aircraft back without a crash. An Audax pilot had three bullets through his shoulder and right lung, causing him to collapse over the stick. The crew member although he also had been wounded, realised, to put it mildly, that things were far from well in the driver's seat. He managed to reach over to the front cockpit and, though perilously near the ground, succeeded in pulling the pilot back into an upright position. He, though only half conscious and with only the use of his left hand, managed to right the aircraft, bring it back, land it safely on the polo pitch — and then he passed out cold. The hospital said his injuries would probably be fatal, but he pulled through eventually. Larry Ling, after an extremely painful and uncomfortable flight back to the polo pitch, had been taken off by the doctors to lie on his face because of a bullet through his bottom. No doubt he felt unfortunate, but he escaped the rest of the campaign.

The Wellingtons, being so much larger, took much more damage and all that got back to Basrah were unserviceable. One did not get back. It made a forced landing on our airfield. The Iraqis immediately swung the guns away from the camp as the crew piled out and sprinted for the hangars. Machine-gun bullets were kicking up the sand around them but they made it safely. Meanwhile we tried to save the aircraft. Within minutes a tractor was on its way out, with an RAF armoured-car on each side to screen the unpleasantly exposed driver from machine-gun bullets. By the time they reached the Wellington the firing was intense. With shells falling round him the driver managed to get a rope round the tail-wheel but, before they could get the aircraft rolling, the Iraqis had bracketed the Wellington and scored a direct hit. It promptly burst into flames. The tractor was also put out of action as well, but by some miracle the driver was unharmed. They bundled him into an armoured car and headed for home. When they were about half way across the airfield, the bombs in the Wellington exploded, blowing it and the tractor to bits. A very gallant effort which deserved a better result.

Damage in the air was not the only way we were losing aircraft. We did our best to screen the machines from the sight of the guns on the plateau, tucking them in behind the hangars which therefore caught and exploded the shells on their way over. Nevertheless one Gordon got a direct hit and blew up, killing one man and injuring two more. Two Oxfords were hit and set on fire; we just pulled them out of the way and let them burn.

I, like everyone else, was flying sortie after sortie as fast as the aircraft could be re-armed, and at the same time I was trying to do some kind of briefing and aircraft allocation in between. I was tired and irritable. One pilot had been given the objective of trying to silence a couple of guns we had seen firing regularly into the camp, and I told him which Oxford to use. He trotted off with his pupil bomb-aimer and it seemed only moments before he was back. 'Now what the hell do you want?' I barked. 'Wasn't I clear enough?' With a completely dead-pan face he just said, 'The aircraft you allocated to me, Sir, is on fire. Which other one should I take?'

The other Iraqis, the locally recruited cooks, kitchen staff and barmen, loyally remained on duty throughout. The Mess Sergeant, and the revolver which never left his hand, coupled with his judicious threats, could have had something to do with it. Even so, they very nearly escaped when one of the cooks was hit by a shell splinter. Revolver in one hand and receiver in the other, the Sergeant was telephoning for an ambulance; the doctor asked the fatuous question 'Are you being shelled?' Everyone was being shelled, more or less. The Sergeant, far from giving the type of reply which by then anyone else would have screamed down the line, merely said, 'Listen,' and held the receiver outside the door. Obligingly, a shell landed. 'Good God!' floated down the line, and an ambulance was promptly despatched.

The Iraqi Air Force, fortunately, played only a minor role. They made some spasmodic bombing raids and did some strafing, with nuisance value more than with practical results. We had patrolling Gladiators who made darts at, but could not catch, the Northrops which flew faster. Also, the twin-engined Savoias had oxygen and stayed up higher than the Gladiator pilots could reach. Just one Savoia came over a little lower. The patrolling Gladiator saw him and reckoned he could just make it. Slavering with expectation he climbed like mad, got right on his tail, and took careful aim. Absolutely certain of his kill, he pressed the firing button. All four guns jammed.

Although shells were falling all over the camp, the aircraft on the polo pitch were comparatively fortunate. The casuarina trees round the landing and parking area hid them completely from the plateau. They could actually get their wheels off the ground before the enemy gunners caught sight of them. The Gordons, Gladiators and Oxfords were not so lucky. Their trip started behind the hangars which were the shell-catchers; all pre-take-off checks were completed there. Then, using the airfield in full view of the enemy, they had to look slippy. An airman, standing to one side but still hidden from the plateau, signalled the all-clear if no aircraft was on the way in. OK — judicious use of throttles and brakes to come round the corner of the hangar and then through the gate in the airfield fence, coming out across the taxi-strip already doing about 30 mph. Then, lift her off at the earliest possible second and begin a steep turn away from the plateau, with the wingtip just clearing the ground. Finally, take a deep breath and retract the wheels — if you were in an Oxford that is; Gordon and Gladiator wheels don't retract. For the return you came in very low across the camp, along the roads and grabbing what cover you could from the buildings and trees. Then, turn down between the hangars to avoid the pom-poms nearest the edge of the airfield. Finally, land parallel to the airfield fence along the taxi strip in front of the hangars, swing back in through the gate as fast as you dared — usually about 20 mph — and tuck in behind the hangars again.

Far from being in full flight within three hours, by lunchtime there seemed to have been no change or reduction in the shelling. For man or machine the rule was the same; wounds or damage that were not incapacitating didn't count; we carried straight on with no breaks. A splendid samaritan went up to the Mess around lunchtime and came back with a mountain of sandwiches which we ate gratefully 'on the hoof' as it were. We were all feeling pretty neglected and exposed but he also brought back a story which helped a lot. While he had been there, six Iraqi Gladiators had strafed the camp with success and had burned up some aircraft on the polo pitch. However, several stray bullets had come through the corrugated-asbestos Officers' Mess roof. His graphic description of the dives for any available cover by our senior officers who were not flying, and of their rounded backsides sticking out from under tables and chairs, and the knowledge that we were not alone in misfortune, cheered us up no end.

What with one thing and another going on in Habbaniya, there were only two beings unmoved in the camp. They were two storks, who occupied their nest on the wireless mast on the roof of Headquarters with complete unconcern. Later on, even *they* were to have their troubles. Two fledglings crashed on take off. One was eaten by a jackal. The other broke a wing and died of its wounds in the station hospital.

When darkness fell we had our second, unproductive, and last, evening briefing by Headquarters. We could lick our wounds and take stock. We had flown 193 sorties. Of our 64 irreplaceable air-craft we had lost 22 — over a third — shot down or unflyable. Of our 39 pilots we had ten — over a quarter — dead or in hospital. And all these gone in *one* day. The Iraquis were still on top of the plateau; they showed no signs of attacking, but equally they showed no signs of retiring. So what now? The simple, and only possible answer was 'Same again tomorrow'.

It had been quite a performance. It was a far, far cry from 'Circuits and bumps and turns, Laddie, and how to get out of a spin'.

# Chapter 23
# Again and Again and Again

From this point on a period is entered in which it is nearly impossible to identify what happened when, or precisely during which day or night. It lasted about a hundred hours. None of us wrote things down or kept records unless it was essential. We flew, and flew, and flew. And again the day after . . . A diminishing band of pilots went on like automatons. They had a diminishing complement of aeroplanes which looked as if they had the measles, with doped-cloth patches over the bullet holes. Each day's work began at 8 pm, as soon as it was dark. Using screened torches, the squadron commanders worked out what could be done to get as many aircraft into the air as possible, and counted heads for first sorties on the morrow. I do not know how many medals, citations and awards went to the ground crews and the pupil-pilots at the finish, but it was not enough. It couldn't be. They worked all day, being shelled and sometimes strafed when they were working on the ground, and fired at if they were working in the air. And then they worked virtually all night, showing no light or they got fired at. The pilots, most of them, could get away some time after 10 pm to scrounge the remains of whatever meal they could find in the Mess. Then bed. Everybody back to the hangars about 4 am getting the programme into motion for the start at dawn, around 5 am. Fly, fly, fly, till half an hour after sunset (dark) which was 8 pm, and the merry-go-round began again. From this routine only certain highlights remain, and perhaps they will bear the telling.

I had a dachshund called 'Frankie', for Frankfurter or sausage. No one, other than an idiot can ignore being shelled. But Frankie showed it more than anybody. So much so that, contrary to all regulations and usage, I always took him with me if I was flying an Oxford. Very quickly he picked up his own pattern of behaviour. If I carried a flying helmet he would scuttle along in front of me, looking over his shoulder to divine which aircraft I was going to. Then, standing by the door, he waited to be lifted in. Once in, he scampered up front and stood squarely on his Queen-Anne-style front legs, looking out of the plexiglass bomb-aimer's window in the nose. There he stayed till we were off the ground and hurtling away from the plateau. Having adequately supervised the lift-off, he came back to the plywood floor beside my seat, curled himself up and appeared to go to sleep. No amount of swooping and swirling about disturbed him. When the engines throttled back for the approach, he would promptly get up and scuttle back to his station at the bomb-aimer's window to oversee my landing. Only when we came to a halt would he leave his post and run aft, waiting for the door to be opened so that he could jump down. Unfortunate fellow, he went nearly bonkers when I was flying a Gladiator or a Gordon and there was no space for him; poor Frankie, he never came to terms with the sheer treason of my part leaving him behind.

That first night, something over 200 shells landed in the camp, so my night's sleep — between midnight and three, was not exactly restful. I lay awake on my bed and heard the 'sho-sho-sho' of a spinning howitzer-shell on its way in. Crumph. 'About 200 yards away,' I muttered. Pause. 'Sho-sho-sho' . . . CRUMPH!!! and the window blew in, scattering broken glass all over the bed. 'The next one,' I thought, 'is coming in through the roof.' So I got out and crawled under the bed. There, shivering and whimpering, was Frankie. Out loud, I said to him, 'You bloody cissy! You're scared!' and got back into bed, with the dog. If the truth be told, he was probably less frightened than I was, but I admit he helped me to pull myself together. For the record, the next shell did not come through the roof; it landed on the other side of the bungalow and blew in the opposite window.

There were a few women and children in the camp, so we decided to get them out together with surplus wounded. We had no transport aircraft and the Oxfords had no passenger seats. For this job we got the help of 31 Squadron, from India, with their DC2s. The DC2 was no more warlike than an Oxford and far less manoeuvrable. They were brave chaps. They came up from Basrah and we had a patrol of dive-bombing and machine-gunning Audaxes in the air, waiting for them each day. As they hove into view the Audaxes would do their best to hammer the Iraqis and keep their heads down while the DC2s — as they had to — made their approaches over the plateau. The Audaxes did a superb job for them because only a few DC2s were damaged, and there were no passengers injured. The women and children were all gone in a day or two.

Whilst the guns and the forces on the plateau were our main objectives, we also made attacks on the Iraqi Air Force. Wellingtons came up from Basrah to meet us over Raschid airfield in Baghdad. We sent in dive-bombing Audaxes and Gordons while Sergeant Prickett, as the only bomb-aimer, master-minded the pattern bombing by the Oxfords. The British Embassy, although they could not see the bombs actually land, had a grandstand view of the whole show. We later learned that we put 29 Iraqi aircraft out of action and we lost none.

On the way home from that or another raid, a pilot saw a Pegasus-engined Audax flying from Habbaniya in a certain direction. We grabbed the hint; checking along that bearing we found, forced-landed, a Northrop and a Savoia. Good news! That line pointed at an Iraqi airfield about 70 miles away called Ba'quba. We sent some of the Audaxes and some of my Gladiators to pay it a visit. There were 21 aircraft there. The bombers got 10 and the fighters took three. The Iraqis retaliated with some ground fire and an Audax got a bullet through its engine which then gave up the ghost. He glided as far away as he could and landed successfully on the desert. Although he was some miles distant it was not long before some pretty stroppy Iraqis arrived to take them prisoner. They were stripped, had their hands tied behind their backs and were severely beaten. They were then made to run all the way to the airfield, barefoot. They were not, as they might have been, castrated.

The Gordons were doing yeoman service, attacking individual guns or other pin-point targets. This they did in a highly dangerous but highly successful way. The first move was to put on the two 250 lb bombs, fitted with seven-second delay fuses; the next move was to take off their safety devices. These are the things that ensure that the bomb must drop a safe distance before it becomes 'live'. No safety devices meant that if a bomb fell off on the ground, or if there was any mishap on take-off, the aircraft, crew and anyone else nearby would be blown to bits — after seven seconds, of course. Having made his usual hair-raising take-off, the pilot would climb steadily to about 3000 ft over the airfield from where he would pick out and confirm the target he was after. Then, into a near vertical dive reaching the giddy speed, for a Gordon, of about 200 mph and with the bracing wires screaming like a banshee. Pulling out as late as possible, and using every available gully or fold in the ground as cover, the bomb was laid like an egg from about 10 feet. The Gordon, with its highly unusual speed, got just far enough away before the egg went off, although the thump made the pilot's teeth rattle. Presumably, knowing what was coming after the first time, the Iraqis declined to stand up and fire back with machine guns or rifles, so Gordon-damage from ground fire was negligible.

Naturally, if the Iraqis brought up a machine gun, for example, too close to the airfield the RAF armoured cars could sort it out in no time. However, under cover of darkness, they brought up a pom-pom and put it out of our sight just behind the brick-built markers' hut of the rifle range. A pom-pom would have opened up one of our old armoured cars like a sardine tin. The gun was right on the edge of the airfield and smack on the approach path of any aircraft like a DC2. A plan was swiftly made; protection by a building from enemy fire is a two-way street. I shall never forget seeing the Gordon coming down, virtually standing on its nose, flattening out and then streaking across the airfield at no more than six feet, hidden completely from the pom-pom by the markers' hut. It lifted up slightly to clear the building and laid its egg neatly on the other side. The pilot swore he could see the looks of horror on the gun-crew's faces. He may not have scored a direct hit but the Iraqis promptly viewed that particular pom-pom site with extreme disfavour.

Forty miles or so to the south of Baghdad lies the little village of Al Musaiyib, on the Euphrates. There the enemy had a rifle factory. It was not a major target but half a dozen Audaxes paid it a short and unfriendly visit, setting it on fire. Another important duty was to seek out and attack any transport which might bring encouragement and reinforcements to the plateau. An Oxford pilot making one of these attacks was hit by three bullets — one through his thigh, one through his shoulder and one through his wrist. He calmly handed over to the pupil-pilot acting as his bomb-aimer while he bandaged himself up as best he could. Then he took over again and came home to land the aircraft intact. Another Oxford was damaged by a shell-burst during its take-off and came to rest on the airfield. The crew, sensibly, sprinted flat-out for the hangars. Within moments only it had been hit by a shell and set on fire; the Iraqi reactions seemed to be improving, which we found depressing. Also the wreck, which of course we could not clear away, made an additional hazard on take-off — as if we had not got enough difficulties on our hands already.

Capitalising on my earlier photographic survey experience in India I was being asked to make quite a lot of local photo-recce trips. Some were to identify and photograph suspected gun-positions on the far side of the river Euphrates, which ran along the north side of the camp. Others were to pick out, and interpret later, possible encampments nearby which could be used as bases for rapid there-and-back supply runs to the plateau at night. I also took and laid out a full photo-mosaic map of the plateau; this was for better and updated target identification and allocation. These photographic sorties were, for me, a wonderful relief. The Iraqi Air Force was already pretty nervous and we kept a Gladiator on patrol. Floating around up there for an hour or two at 5000 ft over Habbaniya, above the range of gunfire, in the cooler air and away from the shelling, felt like the most delightful and safest place in all Iraq. Photo-trips *away* from the camp and its protective Gladiator were scary beyond belief.

On the third day we had a new problem to cope with. Shelling by day was decreasing, mainly we believed because the flash of a gun brought prompt retribution. But shelling was definitely increasing at night. How about night flying? First of all, any kind of lighting or flare path which the enemy would see and fire at was out of the question. It was agreed that as the moon was up for the first part of the night we could have Audax night-patrols. They could take off, and fiddle their way back down again, by moonlight alone. After moonset they certainly could not get down again, having no landing lights, and the polo pitch area was very small. Did I think the Oxfords could get up and down, working off the main airfield? They *did* have landing lights . . . ? Two two-hour patrols would cover the total darkness period and we could drop one bomb every 15 minutes on the plateau to keep the Iraqis' nerves on edge, unless we saw something more exciting, like gunfire.

I considered the inescapable facts we would have to face. One would have to approach over the plateau in the dark to get a long enough landing run; the plateau is 200 ft above the airfield so, how could one know when it was safe to come down to airfield level? Come down too early and you fly into the plateau; come down too late and you run into that ten-foot-high dyke at the far end of the airfield which keeps out the marshy waters beyond . . . and, to show any kind of light when approaching a few feet over the Iraqis would be suicidal. Instrument take-off in total darkness, by comparison, would not be too bad. The chap doing the second sortie would be somewhat luckier, because he could land in the dawn. Nobody pushed me, but frankly I didn't like the idea one tiny bit. The procedure I dreamed up sounds simple, but in practice it was downright hair-raising. I judged I had two pilots with enough skill to share the load with me, if they were willing.

From the cockpit of an Oxford, without moonlight, all is inky black on the ground outside but, looking down from above, starlight lets you just distinguish trees and roads from desert, and water from ground; this made a sortie possible. It began with start-up and being guided out through the gates by shielded torches. Cockpit lights were off. The pilot then set the throttles to the slightly fast tick-over which would make him taxi at just on 8–10 mph. Releasing the brakes he let the aircraft run in a given direction by his compass. The observer timed him for exactly four and a quarter minutes. By then the aircraft would (or should) be most of the way to the edge of the airfield nearest the plateau. He then turned to a new compass heading that would miss the hangars to his right. He opened the throttles and took off, using only his instruments. Airborne, he went straight into a fast climb to clear the unseen dyke ahead. Once clear, he could turn on the cockpit-lighting and take a break from flying by luminous paint and the seat of his pants.

The return in the dark was horrible because it placed the lives of the pilot and his observer very firmly and irrevocably on the far end of some exceedingly precise instrument flying — and all of us were already very stressed and tired. It went like this. Half an hour before landing the cockpit lights were turned off, to regain maximum night vision. It was then possible to pick out the river Euphrates clearly in the starlight. At the far end of the camp the river makes two unmistakable right-angled bends. Sergeant Prickett, peering down through the nose-window, would guide me over them. When he said we were correctly placed I throttled back and began a carefully controlled descending turn to the right, coming round to finish up facing the opposite direction at precisely 250 ft on the altimeter. If my flying had been good, that was just 50 ft above the Iraqis staring up into the night trying to see me. Also, at that moment, we ought to be over the lip of the plateau with the airfield straight ahead.

Then came the worst bit. We had to come down still further, seeing nothing. Too early — kill yourself on the plateau; too late — maybe kill yourself on the dyke. Perhaps it was simplified by the fact that there was no choice; we came down. At 50 ft on the altimeter the landing light was snapped on; its beam of light let us see to come down immediately to ground level, and wait. In a few seconds the road round the edge of the airfield, and the ditch on its far side, would pass below. Hooray! Snap the throttles shut, land straight ahead. As the wheels touch, flip off the landing light and keep her straight by the instruments till we have braked to a standstill. I have to admit, now, that there was then a powerful reaction and a long pause till I stopped shaking and my breathing returned to normal. Then we looked towards the hangars where an airman with a hooded torch was waiting to guide us in.

Certainly, the shelling at night decreased significantly, but I should never have agreed to the Oxford night-flying in the first place. I got away with it, maybe with some skill but assuredly with a vast amount of luck. One of the other two pilots, who had been sent to Habbaniya for a break after being over-stressed by too many ops, had his nerve crack completely. He got out of his aircraft shaking like a jelly and saying 'I fly no more no more!' Or words to that effect. And I did not blame him in the slightest. The other man, probably nervous of taxi-ing into the ditch near the plateau as he rolled towards it in the blackness, turned for his take-off too early. He clipped the top of the 10 ft dyke, somersaulted into the marshes on the far side and caught fire. That was the end of him and his pupil-observer. And one of my precious Oxfords.

This night-flying certainly piled on the pressure. After four hours' often-interrupted sleep, the next 40 hours saw Sergeant Prickett and me do two day sorties, two night sorties, two more day sorties, and one night sortie finishing in the dawn. We must have been behaving like zombies. The crews that I was trying to organise and operate must have thought me singularly stupid to talk to.

It was about this time that I justly earned the undying enmity of one of my seniors. I can only plead that I was tired beyond belief and under considerable mental stress. He was an instructor, fully fit for flying duties and categorised A.1. Wickedly I said to him, 'You haven't seen the plateau from the top yet, Sir. Why don't I give you an Oxford and you do a sortie?' He made some reply to the effect that he could not spare the time from doing something important. Unkindly, I pursued him. 'Then, Sir, why do you not come as a passenger with me? My Oxford is over there. The engines are running. The bombs are on. If we go now we shall be back on the ground, here, in 20 minutes. I feel sure your task could look after itself for that short time? I have a helmet and parachute ready for you, Sir.' He began to demur but he looked into my eyes and saw what I meant. We walked out to the aircraft together.

Above the plateau Sergeant Prickett picked out our targets and we began to drop the bombs, one at a time. Suddenly my passenger asked: 'What's that phit-phitting noise?' I answered 'Machine-gun bullets going past, outside.' He looked out of the window at the wing and at that very instant before his bugging eyes a line of bullet holes was punched through its plywood surface, leaving little splinters sticking up into the slipstream. 'My God!' he shouted, 'We've been hit! Go back and land at once.' I rubbed salt into the wound. I was captain of the aircraft. 'No, Sir. We are going to finish the sortie, and we shall land.'

He sat looking straight ahead and never said another word, not even after we had landed and tucked ourselves back in behind the hangars. He just turned on his heel and walked away. I had suspected, and he knew I had shown up, that he was gutless and he sent other people to do the fighting. I should never have done it to him. It was the only occasion during the whole campaign that he left the ground.

On the third day, unexpectedly, four Blenheim fighters of 203 Squadron arrived from Egypt — and no one had given them prior warning of what to expect nor any suitable briefing. Completely unaware of our unpleasant neighbours on the plateau, they came in to land doing normal approaches. The Audaxes which were flying at the time saw them coming and tried to keep the enemy heads down by bombing ahead of them. One pilot later swore he flew through the dust of a 250 lb bomb. True or not, after landing, three of the four had bullet holes in them — luckily only minor damage. The pilots could not get over the sight of officers and airmen rushing out on to the airfield and making frantic hand signals which could only mean 'Come in and get behind the hangars, QUICKLY!'

We repaired the bullet holes and next morning we had a Blenheim with its four machine guns on standing patrol. The Iraqis obligingly sent in two Pegasus-engined Audaxes to bomb us in the camp. They obviously saw the wicked shape of the Blenheim fighter. One turned and went flat out for ground level, hotly pursued by a fast overtaking Blenheim. The killing burst came just above the river and the Audax dived straight in. Muddy water was flung up all over the Blenheim's windscreen. Everybody in the camp who wasn't flying had a grandstand view. When the Blenheim returned to patrol and slowly waggled his wings, I expect the enemy on the plateau heard the cheer that went up. It seemed that the other Audax, which escaped, must have seen the incident and told about it when he got home, because the frequency and strength of the enemy daylight raids fell off dramatically. As they did not night-fly this was very welcome.

What with shelling, bombing, strafing and ground fire, consumption of aircraft was high. Of the 27 Oxfords at the outset, only four could be rated as 'flyable' on the morning of the fourth day — and one of those had more than 50 fabric patches pasted over the bullet holes. The Audax, Gladiator and Gordon squadrons were no better off. In addition to the dead and incapacitated pilots, four others had been grounded for extreme nervous strain.

What more could we do? Outside the Officers Mess were two field-guns of WW1 vintage. They were duly stripped and cleaned; legend has it that 22 coats of paint were removed — one for each year they had been an ornament. The only ammunition for such archaic pieces was in India, but 31 Squadron once more came to our rescue. They flew in shells with their DC2s. Rumour was strong that the gun-team would be solely WW1 Wing Commanders, some Warrant Officers and Flight Sergeants. Their leader would be the Group Captain Saville, CO of 4 FTS, who had started his career as a Gunner in the Army. We were quite disappointed that our local ground forces took over. We later learned that they had had a tremendous moral effect which far outweighed their material value. The enemy, on the plateau, were convinced that guns in quantity were being flown in from Basrah and, just like them with us, we also were shooting back at point-blank range over open sights.

On the fifth morning the reconnaissance Audax reported that considerable enemy reinforcements of guns, men and armoured cars were approaching the plateau from the direction of Baghdad. This was daunting news. Also we received our heaviest raid to date from the Iraqi Air Force at about 10 am. It seemed that they had determined to finish us off, once and for all. Curiously, and we think it must have been in ignorance, the Iraqis on the plateau decided at the same time that they had had enough, and that they were going to go. Maybe their soldiers' pay, then worth about £1 every two and a half months, was inadequate compensation for

Left to Right: LAC Burdett; Flt Sgt Greenwood; LAC Dixon; Flt Sgt Graham. Greenwood and Graham have bought and are wearing 'Chogas' – embroidered cloaks made from hand-woven goats wool to make a blanket-type material. Very warm, and smelling strongly of goat – particularly when wet.

Major David Cropper's back view, cantering back having scored a goal. The Gilgiti on the left is going back to collect the ball before hitting the Tambruk for his side. The author, wearing Mrs Cropper's topee, is in the crowd near the middle of the field.

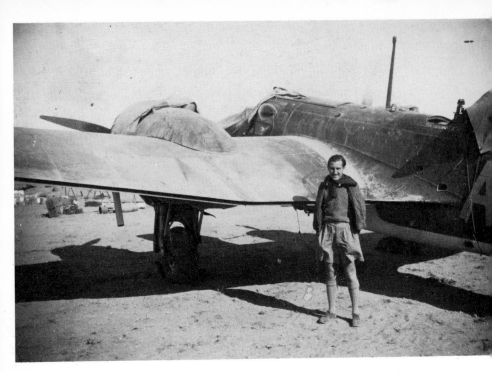

*The author standing in front of 'his' Blenhim IV bomber in the Western desert.*

*The drawing by the author of his modification to the Oxford Trainer bomb-racks and from which (after the successful test-flight) workshops made enough copies to modify the remaining 26 aircraft.*

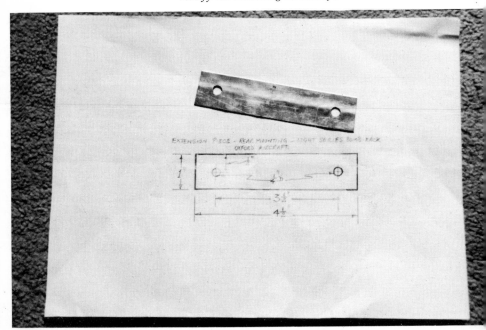

*An airman checks one of the eight 20-lb bombs on an Oxford aircraft for security. It can be seen how the tail-fins of the bombs are tilted down, projecting into the slipstream so that the bombs can be mounted on the racks in the bomb-recess. Frankie the dog sits in the shade, waiting to be lifted into the machine for the next raid.*

*Airborne for a pattern-bombing raid. The No. 3 comes up alongside so that his eight 20-lb bombs can clearly be seen.*

On the first day of the Iraqui attack a damaged Wellington of No. 70 Squadron forced-landed on the airfield towards the plateau in the background on which were the Iraqui guns. A gallant attempt was made by a tractor-driver covered by two armoured cars to tow it in. However, the Iraqui gunners hit it within minutes and it caught fire. The salvage had to be abandoned when its bombs blew up. The armoured cars and the damaged tractor can be seen just by the tail of the exploding Wellington

One of the 'serviceable' Oxfords showing doped fabric patches over bullet holes through non-vital areas. Only about twenty patches can be counted in this view of Oxford 'C' but a total of fifty or sixty patches on a flying aircraft was not uncommon.

Looking across the polo pitch and the camp towards the hangars and the airfield. Some Audaxes and Gladiators can be seen tucked in behind the trees to hide them from the guns on the plateau in the distance. Two of them are burning after a strafing raid by the Iraqui Pegasus-engined Audaxes. The F.T.S. Officers Mess, which also had machine bullets bouncing around inside it, is the large building just behind the burning machines. Some Gladiators and Gordons are tucked in behind the middle of the three hangars on the edge of the airfield. The Oxfords were behind the right-hand hangar and another one outside the picture to the left. The workshops hangar, which was bombed when the Germans joined in, is at the extreme left, too close to the Iraquis on the far side of the airfield to be of use.

raqui tanker lorry found on the from Baghdad. It has been bombed ne of the Oxfords (four small ˙s from 20-lb bombs can be seen on ˙ad) and the fourth bomb, at about ˙ds, has been close enough to set it e. The other four bomb-craters in ˙eld 50 yds beyond, were a less accurate effort.

*My machine was hit by a machine-gun bullet which came through the perspex windscreen and went out through the roof. It did no serious damage.*

*The author, after the Iraquis had been ousted from the plateau, takes a break with Frankie his dachshund.*

*Changing the engine of a Blenheim I, out in the open. The engine is in the packing case under the hoist. It will be changed in shade and shelter under the attap (Malay = leaf-thatched) awning.*

*The virgin forests of Burma and Malaya from the air look like giant parsley gone mad. What you see are, in fact the tops of giant trees, 200 feet high, reaching upward for the sunshine. Below, apart from the incessant snicker and cries of insects and animals, it is almost like being in a vast green-lighted cathedral with great wooden pillars holding up the roof. If you came down in an aircraft, almost for certain the branches would fillet off your wings, leaving the fuselage to plummet down the remaining 200 feet into the bottomless leaf mould.*

*A Blenheim I parked on the airfield. It provides some shade to help the car not to become like the inside of an oven.*

*An Imperial Airways Canopus Class flying boat, named 'Ceres', on the water in Karachi harbour. Egypt ahoy!*

what we had been dishing out. At any rate, the retreating and the advancing forces met on the road about five miles east of Habbaniya at about 4 pm just as every flyable Audax, Gordon, Gladiator and Oxford fell upon them. We threw in every machine that would take off. As the first vehicles met, instead of stopping in dispersed formation they closed up and stopped nose to tail. It was mayhem. Having been regretfully and nervously husbanding our ever-diminishing resources for the previous day or two, we went back to flat-out effort and to hell with the cost — bomb and fire in minimum time, race home, don't stop engines, reload, race back, and so on.

At about 5 pm we had our second heavy raid of the day from the enemy. Together those raids cost us on the ground two Oxfords, one Gladiator and one Audax, seven people killed and eight more wounded. At the moment of the second raid it was my turn to be in the Ops Room, formally reporting to the Group Captain, while it was Sergeant Prickett's turn to put on the new bombs. When I returned, Sergeant Prickett was lying on the ground, under the Oxford. Five out of eight bombs were on and I remember noting the engines still running. I crawled below the fuselage and rolled him over. His eyes were open and his face had a certain yellow-blue tinge. By that stage of the war it told me precisely what I was looking at. One more friend and colleague had gone from my life. To check, I took his wrist. There was no pulse. There was a small wound just over his heart and not much blood. I looked at him and realised that if it had been his turn to report instead of mine, I would have been lying there. Looking up, I muttered a little prayer for him, completely lost in the noise of running engines. 'Please, dear God, take his soul in care and kindness.' Then, looking down I shouted loud and uncouth curses at the bestiality of war; it made me feel a tiny bit better. I pulled the corpse to one side and sent someone with instructions to tell the Group Captain and to get an ambulance to take the body away. A check of the the aircraft showed that there was no significant new damage. I loaded the remaining three bombs and told the nearest pupil-observer that he was my bomb-aimer from now on. His name was Smith. We took off on the next raid.

The attack lasted about two hours. We made 139 aircraft sorties and when the last aircraft left the pilot reported that the road was a strip of flames, several hundred yards long. There were ammunition limbers exploding, with cars and lorries burning by the dozen. We lost one Audax shot down.

The ground forces from our camp also played a satisfying part. They took 408 prisoners including 27 officers; the total Iraqi casualties, including prisoners, on that day alone were later assessed as a thousand. We lost one officer and six British soldiers killed, with two officers and ten British soldiers wounded.

Next morning, after a strangely and blissfully quiet night, a short attack was staged on the plateau at dawn. There was no return fire and the RAF armoured cars went up to report that the enemy had vanished. Later, a few enemy machine guns were located in the little village of Dhibban, just east of the camp, but they too were cleaned up before the evening.

During those five hectic days the Training School had flown 647 sorties. It dropped 3000 20-pounder bombs, 200 250-pounders and fired 116,000 rounds of ammunition. The losses were 13 killed and 21 too badly wounded to work, and four more pilots grounded through nervous strain. But, and a great BUT, the plateau was clear. In bed, we could sleep. Repair work on the aircraft could be done in the shade of the riddled hangars. Our local Army now had, in working order, six howitzers with 2400 shells, an 18-pounder gun, a tank, ten modern armoured cars, three pom-poms with 2500 rounds, 34 Bren guns, 11 Vickers guns, 340 rifles and half a million rounds of ammunition. We felt that if any Iraqi durst show a whisker over the edge of the plateau he would get a very close shave.

The greatest benefit, from the point of view of the FTS, was the free use of the airfield, after we had cleared the two burnt-out aircraft. Above all it meant that we could use pupils, competent pilots in the later stages of their training, as captains of aircraft to take up a bit of the load. Admittedly, many had had no advanced training and others were barely beyond the solo stage, let alone never having dropped even a practice-bomb or fired a front-gun round, but they were mad keen to take a part beyond 'crew member'. Now they had their chance. The pupils flying the Audaxes would only do dive-bombing and armed reconnaissance. We would forbid them air-to-ground front-gunning; judging the late pull-up after firing would have been far too dangerous in their inexperience, and we didn't have a chance of teaching them. In the Oxfords they could make many bombing raids. Some on their own, but most would be pattern-bombing with a leader. The 'leader' for this purpose was to be the young man I took on to replace Sergeant Prickett. Officially, he was LAC Smith, as an Observer-Under-Training. By the end of the campaign he had become so proficient as a bomb-aimer that the rest of his training was waived; he was promoted Sergeant and posted straight on to an operational unit. Shades of AC2 Reed in India! His first squadron found it a bit a odd that Sergeant Smith showed up from school with about 20 live operational sorties under his belt, before he made his first flight with them.

That evening I was with John Hawtrey, in the Mess, swilling down whiskies like there was no tomorrow. He said, slurring his words slightly and earnestly tapping my chest with one finger, 'Do you realise, old friend, it has struck me that during our appalling last five days not one officer from Air Headquarters, nor a Padre, came down to the airfield to give us an encouraging word or to comfort the wounded.' He ordered another couple of whiskies and we sang two more verses of 'John Brown's body lies a-mouldering . . . '

# Chapter 24
# Washing Up

In the days immediately following the evacuation of the plateau a whole series of events occurred and many of them overlapped.

We heard that the Army relieving column — Habforce — was well into its long and arduous journey towards us. AHQ must have moved Middle East because, more than welcome, on 17 May nine Gladiators of 94 Squadron and two flights of 84 Squadron with half a dozen Blenheim bombers arrived from Egypt. Above all, they came with extra pilots and we could now swing from pure survival to the attack. At the same time the Wellingtons were withdrawn from Shaibah; they were needed for raids on Libyan ports and German airfields in Greece.

The FTS turned first to striking at enemy airfields and landing grounds, with some success. In two days we destroyed 13 aircraft and damaged 20 more. These losses virtually eliminated the attacking power of the Iraqi Air Force. Habbaniya, literally, enjoyed a few days of virtual peace.

Not surprisingly, the British Embassy in the middle of Baghdad was cut off from physical contact with the outside world. We wondered if they needed help. So we sent one of the Audaxes over the city at rooftop level. He dropped the necessary equipment with a message bag containing instructions so as to let him hook the bag back off the Embassy roof next day. Unfortunately, when he went back he found that the Iraqis had accurately cottoned-on to our plan. It was quite quiet over the city but there was a mass of machine guns all round the building. The pilot found it prudent to forget the task.

Totally unknown to the FTS, which was basking in its hardly won respite, there was a nasty development on or about 9 May. Two German Heinkel 111 bombers arrived at Mosul, 200 miles north-east, from Syria. Two days later they were followed by 12 more He-111s and 14 Messerschmitt 110 twin-engined fighters.

We might had had some earlier warning of their arrival if I had been cleverer, not that it would have made a scrap of difference in the end. Somerset de Chair, the intelligence officer with Kingcol, tells how they were bombed in the region of Rutbah, 200 miles to the west by German aircraft. He also adds the acid comment that escorting aircraft from the FTS were with the column at the time, but never saw the Germans. I am sure that the escort pilots, who might have missed bombers high up, would have seen clouds of dust from bomb explosions! Nevertheless, I obediently hang my head in shame for I was the pilot of one of the escorting Gladiators. The first news of our new enemy came on May 13 when a reconnoitring Blenheim fighter was attacked by a German-marked Me-110 near Mosul. When he landed, his startling and incredible tale was received with horror and dismay. Meeting up with a 300 mph Me-110 in, say, an unwieldy 85 mph Gordon was a singularly unattractive prospect. But we would have been heartened had we known then that Major Axel von Blomberg, son of the Field Marshal, arriving at Baghdad in a Heinkel 111 to advise Raschid Ali, had been killed by tribesmen potting at his aircraft

Meanwhile, our misgivings were redoubled on the 16th when an Audax, placidly doing a wireless test above Habbaniya itself, was intercepted and badly shot up by one of a flight of six Messerschmitts as they flashed past. The crewman was killed but the pilot, though gravely wounded, managed to survive his crash-landing. Perhaps the Me-110s thought they had disposed of our defensive patrol for, a few minutes later, three Heinkels bombed the camp. They did four runs at 7000 ft, did considerable damage and killed several people. Most of the bombs landed on the hangars nearest the plateau which Station Workshops had been able to reoccupy, so as to get on with badly needed repairs. Our undetected patrolling Gladiator intercepted the He-111s, pressing home his attack to point blank range. He got one Heinkel which broke off streaming fuel or radiator-coolant. He himself was shot down and killed. We later found the bomber, which had had to crash-land, beside the Ramadi–Mosul road.

Our Wing Commander Engineer Officer had been performing miracles on our machines during the plateau affair and immediately afterwards. He was among the finest old-school technicians in the Air Force. If human ingenuity and unremitting effort could make it fly, it was achieved. Then, when he said a pilot could fly it, he would try always to come up in the back seat to prove that he meant what he said.

During our 'peace-time' break after the plateau, and before we heard about the Germans, I had been drinking with him in the Mess one evening. I commented that he seemed far from cheerful. Downright depressed in fact. We had ousted the Iraqis. They were on the run. What was biting him? He was 20 years older than me and he took a long slow look into his tankard before answering. 'I reckon,' he said, still looking far deeper than his beer, 'that I'm unlucky. In the First World War, when I was abroad, some bastard put my wife in the family way. Now, this war, here I am and some bastard has put my daughter in the family way.' He took another swig of beer and shook his head.

I reckon he *was* unlucky. He died in the hangars that the He-111s blasted, a few days later while he was working for us. Our war had taken on a new dimension.

The day before the Heinkel visit, we had received two long-range Hurricanes, with pilots, from Aboukir. So, next day they and the Blenheim fighters paid Mosul a return compliment. They burned one Heinkel, blew up a Messerschmitt and shot up four other aircraft. One Hurricane did not return and it was reported that it had flown into the fragments of his exploding Me-110. The pilot was Flight Lieutenant Sir Roderic MacRobert, the third and last of the three brothers to lose his life flying; two in the war and one in a 1938 accident. Their mother, Lady MacRobert, presented three Hurricanes to the RAF for use in the Middle East, each bearing the family crest and the name of one of her sons. Later she also presented a Stirling bomber to the Air Force, named 'MacRobert's Reply'.

A day or so later, two patrolling Gladiators were having a look at Raschid airfield in Baghdad. What should they see but two Me-110s taxying out to take off! With cries of joy and far too much enthusiasm they dived down to attack. In their excitement they overshot and missed them completely. However, incredible as it seems, the fast, twin-engined monoplane fighters did not just fly away. They turned and accepted a dog-fight with the slower, single-engined, but extremely manoeuvrable Gladiator biplanes. And, apparently, they had no rear-gunners. This, for the Gladiator pilots, was like giving them money for old rusty cans. Both Me-110s were promptly shot down in flames. We in Habbaniya did not know it, but this good fortune, enthusiastically celebrated, went far beyond a victory over two Messerschmitt fighters.

Already in Palmyra, Syria, only a few hundred miles to the south west, many more German troops and aircraft awaited orders. They were to initiate the build-up with the Iraqis and to establish the German military force, behind our troops in the Western Desert, as soon as possible. We now know that, early on, German planners visited their Iraqi counterparts. The absence of rear-gunners in the Me-110s is a powerful indication that the rear seats were occupied by the staff officers who were doing the forward planning. Moreover, the head of the German Mission to Iraq, Major von Blomberg had already been killed. By the time that the Germans had the ensuing confusion sorted out it was too late for those reinforcements to recover the ground they had lost. It was the lynchpin of the entire campaign.

The camp was bombed and strafed by the Mosul based Heinkels and Messerschmitts at frequent and irregular intervals. They burnt an 84 Squadron Blenheim, damaged several other aircraft and knocked down a lot of buildings. They would come in very fast from a shallow dive, make one pass, and away. Without radio or radar we were helpless. It was madly frustrating because we couldn't catch them, except once only. Our one remaining Hurricane was on patrol, facing the right way, at the right time; he got one.

Each day, our damage was checked for them by a photographing Savoia. He came over with oxygen very high indeed, varied his timing, never hung around and he was never intercepted. One morning two Sergeants had got up to the Mess for breakfast and were just about to start when they faintly heard the drone of an aircraft. One looked at the other and asked, 'D'you think that's a bomber?' After cocking his head and listening intently the other replied 'Oh no . . . that's only the old Savoia photographing.' As the noise increased, followed by an uncomfortably high-pitched whistle, both men flung themselves under the table. The Mess got a direct hit. Bricks, plaster and glass flew everywhere. Luckily, neither NCO was seriously hurt. The first Sergeant slowly got to his feet, dusted himself off very deliberately and, fixing his friend with a beady eye said, 'Well . . . I suppose the stupid sod must have dropped his camera.'

On 18 May Habforce's advance party, Kingcol, arrived and was recovering from its epic trans-desert haul, safely ensconced out near Habbaniya lake. Major-General J.G.W. Clark, its commander, flew in from his headquarters at the Haifa–Kirkuk pipeline pumping station, H.4, near the frontier with Iraq of what was then Trans-Jordan. Air Vice-Marshal J.H. D'Albiac also arrived to relieve Air Vice-Marshal Smart, whom the official history states had been injured in a motor accident. After the war, Marshal of the RAF Lord Tedder, writing of his time as air commander in the Middle East (*With Prejudice,* Cassell 1966) disclosed that he had replaced Smart who 'had broken down under the strain of events at Habbaniya.' He recalled that for some time he had doubted Smart's direction of his forces.

Thanks to Habforce we were now really able to go over to the offensive on the ground as well. The first objective had to be the bridge over the Euphrates river at Fallujah. It was the only bridge available for crossing the Euphrates on the way to Baghdad. Intelligence said it was held by about 1000 Iraqi troops, and was in touch with Baghdad by telephone and radio.

The general plan was to put about 1500 of our troops around the village under cover of darkness. Then, at first light, the FTS would produce one of its 'blitz' attacks and go on for about an hour. Pamphlets would then be dropped, inviting the garrison to surrender. If after 30 minutes they had not done so the blitz would begin again and go on all day. If the Army had not been able to capture the bridge by 6 pm they would withdraw back to camp and a new plan would be made.

At dawn next morning the first job for the FTS was to prevent the enemy calling for reinforcements, or air support, from Baghdad. The Audax dive-bombers came in with the first shafts of light, pin-pointed and destroyed the radio station. There remained two telephone lines needing attention; one with a few wires, leading across the cultivation, and another with many wires, running across the desert behind Fallujah village. The first lot were severed by an Audax which flew backwards and forwards between the poles for about a mile. He then returned to have the telephone wires unwound and the minor damage fixed up. For the others, a second Audax landed on the desert and taxied up between two poles. While the gunner stood guard with the machine gun to keep strangers away, the pilot climbed up on to the wing and cut the wires with a large pair of shears. He said the thing he was most scared of was slipping and falling on to the spinning propeller. No strangers had appeared so the pilot manned the gun and gave the gunner his share of the fun. He took the axe they had brought and chopped down two telegraph poles. Then they got back into the aircraft, took off and flew home.

Meanwhile, Valentias from Basrah were landing troops on the

desert behind Fallujah and the FTS had started its attack. It was like a return to the attacks on the plateau (but without the returning ground fire) using every available aircraft and not stopping engines between sorties. The Army reported that the Iraqis were making a spirited and extremely effective ground defence. As there was no surrender, the attacks went on all the morning. By this time the dive-bombers were becoming Dead-Eyed-Dicks with their attacks — one of the Gordons hit the water tower with two successive 250 lb bombs. Such dive-bombing accuracy might have been because they were going *extremely* low! I was pattern-bombing with the Oxfords from only 1000 ft, and photographing the results. One of my prints showed my bombs falling and, far below them, an aircraft pulling out of its dive. By late morning there were hardly any Iraqis to be seen. By 1 pm the defence seemed suddenly to have evaporated. Having made over 100 sorties the FTS called halt. At 2 pm, under cover of a co-ordinated pattern and dive-bombing attack, the Army rushed the bridge in case they might try to blow it up. The whole place appeared to be completely deserted. Finally, a search discovered 26 officers (including a General) and 300 soldiers sheltering in a hospital.

Interrogation revealed the explanation for spirited defence to abject retreat during one hour. It stemmed from the previous year when the Iraqis were being trained by British liaison officers. The annual exercise-manoeuvre for the Iraqi Staff College was the defence of Fallujah Bridge against ground attack. The British had planned the defence magnificently, and played in real life it was superb. The Iraqi problem was that, being an exercise, it stopped for lunch and did not continue in the afternoon. The FTS had made 134 sorties and dropped 9¼ tons of bombs. There were no Army or Air Force casualties. It was very satisfying to find that the Iraqi morale was at rock bottom and that they greatly feared our intensive air attacks.

Next morning, nine Oxfords, 14 Audaxes, five Gordons and four Blenheims of 84 Squadron attacked Raschid airfield in Baghdad. The photographs we took showed excellent results. We had a screen of no less than 13 fighters and, to their disappointment and our relief, no German aircraft turned up. I had been leading the Gordon formation and, on the way home, was really low over the desert — which means at about six to eight feet, lifting up slightly to clear the little camel-thorn trees and bushes. I hoped that the jet-black shadows, showing up vividly on the bright-yellow sand, would be at least partially hidden from any prowling Messerschmitts by the aircraft themselves. We were untroubled but some Audaxes were doing the same when, to their horror and near heart failure, an Me-110 sailed overhead at about 1000 ft. There was nothing they could do, except to try and go even lower. It was not until the Messerschmitt floated serenely into the distance that they breathed again.

After that, and with the Army on the same side of the Euphrates as the city of Baghdad, serious resistance from the Iraqis more or less evaporated. The Germans, lacking Iraqi support and suffering the loss of von Blomberg, also were far less effective. Only isolated incidents followed.

Being forced down, even uninjured, was not the end of the matter as we well knew. A pair of Audaxes on reconnaissance were intercepted by some Me-110s and shot up. Fortunately they could glide down to a safe landing. One pupil-gunner was dead but the two pilots and the other gunner were able to run clear before the Me's strafed and set the Audaxes on fire. One pilot and gunner were befriended by a local sheikh who was giving them a cup of tea. An Iraqi policeman came in, drew his revolver and shot them both. He killed the pilot but the gunner, though seriously wounded, had the presence of mind to feign death. He was later taken off to hospital. The other pilot was surrounded by civilian Iraqis who, after the campaign, said that they were going to take him prisoner; however, they added, some unidentified man threw a club at him, hitting him on the head and killing him.

A forced-landed Me-110 was seen on the desert plain behind Fallujah village. A Tiger Moth went out, found it and guided in two RAF armoured cars. He then landed alongside. It was not booby-trapped, and so a salvage party was sent. They worked for two days, expecting to be attacked at any moment, before towing it 40 miles back into Habbaniya. I, much much later, had the excitement of piloting that same aircraft over Cairo. I was helping test it in the air in mock-battle against our own fighters.

Around the 20th one of my Oxfords on reconnaissance was flying at 3000 ft over Ramadi, to the west of Habbaniya. Although that height was supposed to be safe from small-arms fire, a solitary bullet hit the pilot and went straight through his heart. The Sergeant Gunner (who belonged to the Gordon Squadron) left his gun and came forward. Then, as he admitted later, he embarked on a Walter Mitty day-dream he had nurtured all through the war — to bring the aircraft back safely even though the pilot had been killed. Although he had only held the controls of an aircraft on one previous occasion he flew the Oxford back to Habbaniya and managed to get it down in one piece.

The FTS became positively schizophrenic. On the one hand the Sergeant was brave and astoundingly lucky to get the aircraft down without breaking it or worse. On the other hand the pupil with lower Air Force rank, whom he bluntly ordered out of his way, was a fully competent pilot. Some said the Sergeant should get a medal for his achievement; the others said he ought to be court-martialled for deliberately and unnecessarily hazarding the aircraft, and the pupil. He got the medal.

We were, perhaps unreasonably, angry at this seemingly needless death. Next day we flew all our Oxfords — now up to 15 — on a demonstration over Ramadi, where my pilot had been shot. I then broke off, went down and dropped some leaflets suggesting they might care to surrender before we did to them what we had done to Fallujah. There was no reaction. In truth, any land attack was out of the question because the Iraqis had breached all the dykes containing the river Euphrates and there was extensive flooding. That night, while Oxfords watched the Ramadi ferry to prevent escape, the Army brought up guns. Most were sited on the far side of the river, with some more as close as they could get on the near side. When day broke, the FTS attack was just like that at Fallujah. We set fire to all their lorries which they had put into a courtyard — about 30 — and the smoke drifted 15 miles. By mid-afternoon we and the Army decided that it really wasn't worth the possible casualties to try and take the place. Anyway, it was in the opposite direction to Baghdad, our next objective. Also those particular Iraqis were no longer equipped for, nor were likely to care for any offensive action.

On the evening of the 25th there was a commanders' conference, to plan the advance on Baghdad. A serious problem for the Army soon arose. They had no large-scale maps of the road. It went 40 miles, from Fallujah across desert to Khan-Nuqta, and thence through marshes and cultivation to the city. They needed to know how and where they could spread out either side. Seemingly, attacking armies don't wish to march or drive in a narrow line along a country road. That made great sense to me. I, without much thought, airily suggested that I should fly along their planned route next morning, making a long strip-photo map of the road and a mile each side of it. We could then draw a grid on the map, with numbers and letters. That could then be rephotographed for quantity issue to the Army; it would become their home-made 'map' for the advance. The gunners were quick to point out that it would not be precise enough to shoot from, but it would be perfectly adequate for transport, scouts and minute-to-minute plans. Naturally the details, only 48 hours old, would be far more up to date than any map and any flooding would show up. The idea was received with enthusiasm.

Next morning I waited for the sun to get well up so that the shadows would be short and hide nothing. And the longer I waited the less I liked the project. I wished it had never crossed my mind. And, when it had, giving it a second thought demonstrated my pure lunacy. At last, into the Oxford with LAC Smith and a pupil-gunner and we went to 10,000 ft which, if we were to cover a mile each side of the road, was the height necessary for the only camera lens we had available. Smith and I together picked out Fallujah bridge and, running away to the east, the little dark thread which was the road to Khan-Nuqta and Baghdad 20 miles beyond. The weather was wonderful and the smudge of Baghdad was just visible on the horizon. I nodded to him, and he got down into the nose. I turned towards Fallujah and he began to give corrections to take me slap over the village and then along the road. Soon he said, 'OK — steady — camera running . . . NOW.'

It was horrible, just sitting there and with all the time in the world to work out how foul it was. I was in an Oxford; a light aeroplane, modified only for training and made of plywood and perspex. It had a single-barrelled .303 gun at the back, with no proper rear-turret, and no proper rear-gunner holding it. There was a curved bubble-windscreen whose shape would reflect the rays of the sun, attracting attention in every direction — even if further beams were not already streaming from the circular rear-gun cupola. The whole contraption was painted, as were all training aircraft, a bright shiny yellow to be as noticeable as possible. To be flown dead straight and level for about 25 minutes, at 10,000 ft, on a gin-clear day, to end up over an enemy airfield. And if, as I feared, I was intercepted by a cannon-shell firing Me-110, the end of my little plywood aeroplane would be something like opening a box of wooden matches upside down. I watched Khan-Nuqta, and then Baghdad, getting, oh so slowly, closer in front. The Euphrates was running away to my right; the Tigris and a railway coming in from the left. Below, dark green marshes and fields. Would it never end? It seemed to go on for ever.

When LAC Smith said, 'Last photograph coming . . . NOW!' we had hung around up there long enough. I answered, 'Grip tight!' rolled her on to her back and pulled the nose down into an almost vertical dive. 'OK,' I thought, 'even if one of the bastards sees me now he'll have a hell of a job getting me in this attitude.' I watched the airspeed creeping up and up, feeling better and better with every 10 mph. At about 4000 ft there was a monumental explosion, a terrific blast of wind and debris flying all over the place. 'Oh — dear God,' I thought, 'we've been hit and I'm going straight in.'

It took an age — probably five seconds — to cotton-on to what had happened. I had exceeded the aircraft's design limits and the air pressure had blown in the bomb-aimer's plexiglass nose-window. The fragments flying around had been bits of perspex. Poor LAC Smith was hanging on by his toe-nails, peering vertically down at damn-all. Finally we pulled out quite safely and happily at zero feet and, keeping well clear of any habitations or information posts, wound our somewhat breezy way back to Habbaniya. It was the only time that Frankie the dog did not stand in the nose to watch the landing.

The photographs were excellent and with Smith's help I spent the rest of the day and most of the night creating the original of the photo-strip map we had promised. It was copied and issued on the 27th, ready for the advance which began on the 28th. There was very little opposition — the FTS made only 40 sorties — and the Army reached the outskirts of Baghdad on the evening of the 29th.

On the 30th, the FTS using locally produced 'screaming' bombs, together with 84 Squadron, 203 Squadron and 94 Squadron, made two heavy attacks on Raschid Airfield and Washash Barracks in Baghdad. In the early hours of the 31st our Embassy reported that the Iraqis had requested safe conduct for their flag of truce. Terms were negotiated during the day and on 1 June the signal quoted below went from Habbaniya to Middle East Headquarters and to London.

'June 1st — Baghdad populace extremely friendly and appear relieved and pleased to see British officers and civilians moving about the city again. Villagers on road Fallujah to Baghdad most friendly. Only discordant note were people of Khadimahin. Also those north of that town who show signs of fierce hatred, possibly inspired by propaganda but in keeping with their past record. Reliably reported that Raschid Ali left with 17,000 Dinar [about £17,000] said to be monthly pay of troops. Reported that he was held up at Ba'quba and luggage searched when money was discovered and confiscated. Iraqi troops returning in lorries this afternoon from Khadimahin area were well turned out and showed no loss of morale. Surrender appears due to disinclination to continue fighting after leaders had bolted, plus fear of intensive bombing. List obtained of Germans who stayed in Baghdad hotels. Manager of Sinbad hotel says that of 10 who arrived only 4 left, balance he presumes were casualties. Baghdad airport being used today by RAF.'

Bearing in mind that a flying school is neither staffed nor equipped for warlike operations, its effort was creditable. No. 4 FTS in 30 days flew 1600 sorties in old, slow and unsuitable aircraft. It dropped over 100 tons of bombs, including over 5000 20-pounders. It fired a quarter of a million rounds of ammunition. That was achieved in no small part through the determination and courage of the inexperienced pupils who took on any and every job, not forgetting the ground crews working in the heat of an Iraqi summer when metal parts of an aircraft get hot enough to blister the skin.

In 1942 General Montgomery smashed out along the desert coast of North Africa and was fiercely driving the German Army westwards towards Tunis for the eventual link-up with the American forces coming eastwards from Morocco and Algeria. Behind him his supplies poured forwards from secure bases in Egypt in quantities as never before. They were unhindered by any German forces thanks in large part to our five-day desert Battle-of-Britain. That opinion is not solely a personal one.

The Commander-in-Chief, Middle East, the late Marshal of the RAF Lord Tedder, was an easy man to converse with and he knew all of his squadron commanders personally. One evening, shortly after the guns at Alamein had been heard in Cairo, I took the opportunity to recall the Habbaniya campaign and asked his opinion of its importance to the Western Desert battle then being won. He thought for a few moments and said, 'Well . . . it is a Royal Air Force epic. If the FTS had been overcome the Germans would have got a military foothold in Iraq. If they had then built up a substantial bridgehead behind us, through Vichy-controlled

Syria from Greece, our Middle East base could have been nipped out with German forces both to its east and west — and we might well have lost the war.'

Winston Churchill, too, gave us our little pat on the back when he wrote: 'The spirited defence of Habbaniya by the Flying Training School was a prime factor in our success. The Germans had of course at their disposal an airborne force which would have given them at this time Syria, Iraq, and Persia, with their precious oil fields.'

The Habbaniya campaign never hit the headlines. Maybe those 39 instructors and their pupils really did save us losing the war; maybe not. Who can say? Sometime during our little peace-break in the middle I wrote a new 'Instructor's Lament'. It came from the heart:

'What did you do in the War, Daddy?'
　'I was hustled and ordered about,
Then everything cancelled and changed, laddie,
　I thought I was turned inside-out.'

'Bombed-up and started, then stopped, laddie,
　With never a chance to be lazy;
Stood-by and stood-down — and stood up, laddie.
　Headquarters was certainly crazy.

'Obsolete trainers to fly, laddie,
　With enemy guns on the hill
That covered the whole of the 'drome, laddie,
　And worked like a permanent pill.

'Guns, and no gunners to shoot, laddie,
　Bomb sights with no aimers to fly.
Night-flying without any flares, laddie;
　Not even a moon in the sky.

'I know that you think me a bore, laddie,
　I fear that you think me a fool . . .
If you take on a country at war, laddie,
　Please! Don't take it on with a school!'

# Chapter 25
# Lysander

The reactions after my 'rest from ops' at Habbaniya were both impressive and unpleasant. Insomnia. Nightmares. Weeping. Solace in whisky. Ill manners. Bad temper. In medical jargon, 'Operational Stress'. Correctly, but with poor grace on my part, my sentence was to 'fly a mahogany bomber'. Its seat was in the Training Staff of Air Headquarters Egypt, Cairo. Having complained noisily at the ineptitude and ignorance of staff officers, the biter was now bit. It was soon brought home to me by my colleagues at the sharp end of the war machine that I and my ilk were classified as 'embolisms'. Any doctor will brief you that an embolism is a wandering clot. Reluctantly I had to prove them wrong, and not very joyfully I set about the task.

However, soon after my twenty-sixth birthday, to my delight and to everyone else's astonishment, a signal arrived from London permitting me to have a third stripe sewn on my epaulettes, signifying Wing Commander. This meant that in the future it was likely that, although occasional situations of peril would come my way, my successive days of full-scale war flying were probably past. And I had not been killed. From this moment the bars, night-clubs and floozies of Cairo were all very well but my only real desire was for the girl to whom I had said goodbye in Singapore.

This raised a number of barriers to be surmounted. One was that she was in Karachi, 3000 miles away. Another, and the most difficult, was that wives and fiancees could not travel to a theatre of war to join their real or future husbands. Only wives already there, or those who got married on the spot, were allowed to stay. And there were no passages to be got, for anybody, by boat or air, except for those with military or political authority connected with the war effort. There was probably another barrier for me personally because we had parted on a basis of 'no ties and no commitments until we can again pick up the threads'. To try and play it fairly I had refrained from declaring my lonelines and true feelings by letter for the intervening 22 months. Now, she was working for the Navy, and sailors are reputed to be very attractive. Moreover, she and two other pretty, unattached girls had at their beck and call, and locally at that, the officers and men of an entire armoured division. The chances were that some splendid dream-boat on the spot, rich and with eyes like a bush-baby, was a great deal better placed than some dimmed flame of two years earlier, thousands of miles away and ungetatable to boot. I would not presume less for a girl, free as the wind, who, even then, was only 20.

Somehow I had to break the distance barrier and get to Karachi. There, to test the atmosphere and, if not frosty, to declare myself. If that went well, a way had to be found to get her to Egypt. Finally, after a decent interval, if she still wanted me, we could tie the knot in Cairo. First step: send a letter sounding out my probable reception, if getting to Karachi became possible. The answer came back, 'with pleasure'.

Next day, luck was on my side. My Group Captain at AHQ returned from what had obviously been a Babylonian lunch. I gave him a few minutes to settle down, then knocked on the door and went in. 'Sir; it seems to me that the briefing of inexperienced aircrew flying long distances is inadequate. Like all green crews they think they are appropriately trained. But our maps are inaccurate and misleading. Map-reading is critical and they don't know what to look for. Radio is limited, or non-existent. They get lost. They force-land. If we're lucky we recover the crew but we've lost the aeroplane. I have had an idea.'

The Group Captain looked at me suspiciously. He knew me to have original, unorthodox and sometimes crackpot ideas. 'And what, may I ask, causes this sudden rush of blood to your head?'

Cautiously, keeping my cool I said, 'For many years I have been taking films from the air with a hand-held movie-camera. Next, most of the long-distance flying for inexperienced crews who get as far as Egypt is onwards to India. Third, I have flown the route from here to India twice and I know it well. My suggestion is that I take a 16 mm camera in a suitable aircraft — such as a Lysander — and come back with a comprehensive briefing film of the entire route. The negative stock can be processed here by Kodak. I can edit and title it. Kodak here can make the copies needed. If it saves us just one aircraft we have a handsome return for the effort involved.' I held my breath and waited while he cogitated.

At last he said, 'I disagree. The idea's not bad, but we had better do it with a proper cameraman. Any old pilot can then fly him there and back, and there is no need to waste your time.' My heart sang. He had taken the bait. All that remained was to play and land my fish.

'Yes, Sir,' I told the Group Captain after a suitably deferential pause, 'that is an excellent idea. However, it has some disadvantages. We are working for the aircrews; it would be of tremendous value if the man pointing the camera is aircrew for he will take precisely what needs to be shown, and will not be diverted by "artistic composition". Further, the camera is positioned by the aircraft itself. It will be of great help if the man behind the camera should also be flying the machine — to get both together to the desired and correct spot for the best picture seen through the viewfinder. It so happens I am both cameraman and pilot. No one else around here has both qualifications.'

He did not like abandoning his own ideas and the argument was thrashed back and forth for quite a while. At last, regretfully, he nodded. 'OK. Sounds all right to me. When will you be going and how long do you expect to take on the job?' I replied slowly, as if thinking it through while I spoke. 'I imagine, given good weather for picture-taking it'll be about five days each way. Add a brief rest there between the two slabs of flying. Say two and a half weeks all told. As to when? Well . . . it must depend ultimately on the weather but, apart from that, I'll get on with it shortly. I've got to get the camera and the films first, of course.' He grunted his assent.

A Lysander is a satisfying aeroplane to fly. It has a high-mounted wing so the view downwards in superb. The pilot sits looking over the top of the engine in front of him. The windows on each side go from above his head to below the level of his thighs. Moreover, they can be slid right down into slots in the fuselage so the pilot, when they are open, feels he can survey the countryside from a flying bar-stool. It is beautifully stable and so it makes an excellent camera platform. If the fates were kind it was going to be a wonderful adventure.

Back in my office, I promptly telephoned the Communications Squadron at Heliopolis and booked their Lysander 'to go on a staff visit of several days', starting at eight o'clock next morning. Before tea-time a man could have been seen coming out of Kodak's in Sharia Emad-el-Din, carrying a camera and a great bag of films. The films, unfortunately, were black and white as colour was not available in wartime. Around six o'clock the same chap could have been seen coming out of Poohoomulls, the jewellers opposite Shepheard's Hotel. In his pocket was a simple gold ring, set with a blue-green baguette-cut zircon. Someone was reducing the chances of ill-fortune to a minimum. If next morning, in the less roseate hues of 9 o'clock, the Group Captain had second thoughts I was not going to be there to hear them — and went to bed with a short plea to the Almighty for lovely weather on the morrow.

The Almighty must have been listening for next morning the weather was superb. Amman was to be the first stop, for fuel. I took shots of the green and lush Nile Delta, showing how the dark colour changed abruptly to light desert, as sharply as the colours change in a child's drawing book. I saw, and recorded the unmistakable line of the Suez Canal, and how the Bitter Lakes show no trace of the dredged channel marked so clearly on the maps. Then, across the darker shades of the red hills in the Sinai desert to the graceful bend in the coastline where El-Arish is found. El-Arish; unmistakable at that time for it had the only palm trees anywhere around that corner of the Mediterranean. From El-Arish the course lay over the Holy Land — Bethlehem, Jerusalem, Jericho (where once I forced-landed in a tiny field, out of fuel) and on my right the Dead Sea. Then, over the Jordan river and its valley before touching down at Amman for food and petrol.

Nervously, in the Ops Room I asked 'Anything for Dudgeon?' and breathed a deep sigh of relief when the reply came back, 'No'. The boss might have been astonished at my prompt departure but he hadn't been too cross.

From Amman there are 450 miles of desert. Our maps indicated 'roads', 'rivers' and 'villages'. These usually did not exist except where some vehicles had left tracks in the sand, or there was the dried-up bed of a river which had existed for a few hours after some rainstorm once in every several years, or the village shown might be the spot where some bedouin pitched a few tents, fairly often. Some posers floored me utterly. I could find no way of illustrating vividly on black and white film that a particular spot on a vast expanse of nothingness was where, sometimes, one would see some tents.

Sixty miles after Amman there was, on the map, a long straight pipeline which had to be followed. Even the most debutant of navigators would reckon he knew what a pipeline looked like, but this one could catch him out. It was underground. The only things to be seen were a line of telegraph poles and lorry tracks — and a building holding pumping equipment every so often. After 200 miles the pipeline branched off to the left, towards Mosul, and the 'road' bore off to the right. That is, a hundred different lorry-tracks pointed the general direction of Baghdad, but no real road existed in spite of what the map said. Luckily, after a further 180 miles there was a genuine, pukka, honest-to-goodness landmark for the starving navigator. It was a real river, holding water flowing along the same bed every day of the year. With greenery on its banks. And a road. And a name. It was the Euphrates.

Overnight was spent at Habbaniya, unnaturally peaceful once more and in full training swing again. From there, next morning, the course to Basrah lay between the meandering Tigris and Euphrates rivers. The ground between them had dusty, dirty green vegetation, papyrus marshes and a few hamlets. Map-reading was virtually impossible for the marshes drained and flowed into one another each season; many of the villages were floating and slightly mobile. Only over to the right, on the edge of the desert and nearly out of sight, were a road and a single-track railway which could be relied upon to stay where they were. Legend had it that this was the Garden of Eden. It fell a bit short of my ideas of Eden but, maybe to a desert nomad, the presence of unlimited water might have seemed close to Heaven — serpents notwithstanding.

In the Officers' Mess at Basrah, my next stop, hung a large, gilded picture-frame. It held, on its black velvet background, a unique award for desert rescue. At the bottom was a silver plaque telling the story . . .

In the happy days of peace a Hannibal-class four-engined airliner of Imperial Airways had forced-landed in the desert on its way to Australia. It was many days before a searching aircraft of 84 Squadron from Basrah found it and straight-away landed near the airliner with water and supplies. The passengers and crew, including a woman, had had a terrible time in the scorching heat of the desert days and the freezing cold of the desert nights, but they all survived. Some months later another airliner landed and from it stepped an Australian lady. She found and spoke to a flight commander of 84 Squadron, saying she was the one woman in the forced-landed airliner they had located; she was deeply grateful for having her life saved and she would like to make a presentation to the Squadron. How should she set about it? The flight commander thought only for a moment before asking whether a wild rumour going the rounds of the Squadron was based on fact. It was alleged that, when the rescuing aircraft landed alongside, the woman was wearing only very diaphanous silk French-panties and a brassiere. True or false? 'True,' she replied. 'Then', said the flight-lieutenant, 'how about presenting a pair of your pants and a bra to the Squadron, to be framed and hung in our Mess for evermore as a treasured reminder of how you were saved?' 'I can do better than that;' she said, 'in the suitcase that I have with me are the very ones I was wearing, and you shall have those.' And so it was.

From Basrah I flew onwards to the top of the Persian Gulf and Kuwait. Kuwait, then, was a small town of mud buildings, drab and reportedly a mass of flies and eastern smells. Its little inlet from the Gulf of Kuwait looked muddy and unattractive. After Kuwait I longed more than ever for unattainable colour film. Following the coast, on my right was the beige, yellow and reddish sand, spotted with camel-thorn bushes which looked black from the harsh shadows cast by the blazing sun. Under my nose, mile upon mile of unvisited, untouched, unmarked golden beaches. To the left a clear blue sea; a sea so clear that one could look down 40 or 50 feet into the limpid water; clear so that the sand and corals below gave a mix of colours — light at the shore's edge, through lemon, lime, aquamarine and sapphire far out in the deep. The little yellow islands along the coastline were all surrounded by a halo of bluish-greenish colours, all similar and all different. And so to Bahrain.

Bahrain had no airport. Landings were made on a large salt-flat on Muharrak Island, connected to Bahrain town by a causeway. There was a wooden hut, with a verandah. No restaurant. No food. No water laid on. Someone, kindly, had brought out a cup of tea for me. Camels and cars on the landing-ground seemed, from the mirages in the blazing heat, to be moving across a sheet of water. I stayed as little time as possible. On to Sharjah and a bed.

Sharjah, at the bottom of the Gulf, was comparatively civilised, if isolated. There was a stone-built fort for accommodation, with rooms to sleep in. Food could be had, and beer. The airfield, outside, was more spartan. Hard sand, a ring of barbed-wire to park behind and litte gazelles from the desert tip-toeing gracefully and unconcernedly between my aeroplane and the drums of fuel. There are hardly any gazelles now. They have been reduced to a rarity because of the pleasure sportsmen take in shooting them from a racing Land Rover.

For visitors who had a little money to spare there were pearls for sale. Real pearls collected by the pearl-divers in the Gulf, set on waxed cards to show how they would look if professionally pierced and strung into bracelets or necklaces. Or made into brooches. Reputedly the best pearls in the world; pink pearls, black pearls or ordinary white ones. But, to be practical, who in wartime puts pearl-piercing high on a priority list?

Next morning, last leg. I sent thought-waves to Messrs Bristols to watch over the engine and Messrs Westlands for the aeroplane. Away, over the desert, climbing hard to get over the craggy, 6000 ft mountains of Muscat. Then, down across the Straits of Hormuz towards Jask in Persia, distinctive on its little tongue of yellow land projecting into the blue sea. Prudently, keep well outside the three-mile limit from the Persian coast. Photograph the rugged mountains inland and show how map-reading can only be done by following the shape of the coastline. Past the little landing-ground on the isthmus of Gwadar, for use in emergency only. Another 250 miles and then, over the bathing beach at Sandspit, over the town of Karachi and, six miles further on was my destination — RAF Drigh Road. Barrier number one had been surmounted.

The threads were taken up almost in the manner they had been put down. In the back of a car. Scared to death of a reply like, 'Well . . . I don't really know, now . . . ' I stumbled into my prepared speech. 'I realise we haven't seen each other for a long time; and things are very different to what they were in Singapore; and I'm not asking you to commit yourself now; and I'll try to get you to Egypt before you decide; and if after a while you want . . . Oh hell . . . darling, will you marry me?'

And, to my unspeakable joy, the answer flashed back 'Yes please!' She had moved my second barrier aside.

The ring even fitted, more or less. Feeling practical I asked her at all costs not to wear it on her engagement finger for two reasons; one was that fiancées were not allowed to join their loved ones in another theatre of war so, like it or not, it had to be kept very much under-the-counter; the other reason was that I felt it was tempting providence to assume so much, so soon, after so long. The first reason was acceptable — but my second suggestion, when she had already waited 22 months with no encouragement from me, was an almost suicidal error. I barely redeemed myself, even by promising that I would put a diamond each side of the zircon the moment that our engagement could be made official.

As forecast, after two and a half weeks' absence the mahogany bomber was again in front of me and the films were in the hands of Messrs Kodak. My incredible good luck continued unabated. It so happened that the British Ambassador's wife, Lady Lampson, needed a social secretary. It appeared that there was no one in Cairo who was both suitable and free from war or political ties. However, she had heard by chance of a young lady called Phyllis McFarlane, working as a civilian secretary for the Navy in Karachi. Now, if it were possible for her to present herself for interview, in Cairo . . . ? Which was how authority came to be given for me to buy an Imperial Airways ticket from Karachi to Cairo, in wartime.

For her, Phyl's flight over was spellbinding. At that time the only airliners on the route were flying-boats. She left from Karachi harbour, sitting by the window and watching the sheets of spray as the four engines of the Canopus-class boat lifted her into the air. She retraced almost exactly the same route I had followed on my flying bar-stool, but alighting on water instead of on land for meals and overnight.

First alighting was at Dubai, in its tiny harbour just up the road from Sharjah. Dubai was little more than a village of mud-brick buildings, dirt roads, camel carts and fuel by Shell from a refuelling barge. Next, up the blue Persian Gulf, past those golden beaches and the blue-haloed yellow islands, to the Shatt-el-Arab river at Basrah. From there over the Garden of Eden to alight on the Lake Habbaniya. Then, 500 miles of desert to the Holy Land and the Dead Sea. Lastly, past the red hills of Sinai, over the blue of the Bitter Lakes and the green of the Delta to raise the final walls of spray from the brown, muddy waters of the Nile in the middle of Cairo. The third barrier was broken.

So ended my exciting but sometimes lonely bachelor days. Ended also are the lovely but lonely routes I flew. Now they are bespattered with airports, criss-crossed by radio-lanes and barely recognisable in places under oil rigs, sky-scrapers and the trappings of civilisation.

# Epilogue

Even after I got married, luck followed my footsteps. Also, an apparent reputation grew up something like ' . . . if there's only one of it, or there's no precedent, try it on Tony Dudgeon — he seems to cope.'

I was married and became Senior Air Staff Officer of the first Ferry and Transport Group on the same day. It was a guinea-pig group in Cairo, designed to separate 'Transport' from the old 'Bomber/Transport' role. To provide a mother and father for the people that the bomber boys wanted no part of, but who were the first to holler bloody murder if the Movements task was not completed properly. Its parish stretched from the Gold Coast in West Africa to the Western Desert and beyond. It was brimming with new things to do and I flew no less than 28 different types of aircraft in a year. Overall it seemed to work, and RAF Transport Command followed its pattern. Then, off to Fez in Morocco to a manage a packed-earth landing strip, graded from a farm field. One Sunday dawn the monarch, His Majesty King George VI, was a little surprised to find his aircraft forced-landed there instead of at Gibraltar. His surprise was as nothing compared to mine when they woke me up and told me who was standing on the airfield, wishing to shake me by the hand.

After a spell of shuffling hundreds of aircraft through Fez on their way to Algeria, Tunisia, Sicily and Italy, it was back to England to prepare for the invasion of France, Belgium, Holland and Germany; training and then launching hundreds of para-troop, glider, supply and casualty-evacuation sorties. I was privileged to be one of the first pilots to land in France on a hastily constructed strip in the beach-head, carrying in supplies and bringing out casualties. Later, I felt it a gross breach of contract to be tasked to travel *on the ground* to get in amongst the beleaguered troops at Arnhem, so as to help guide the Dakotas dropping supplies in bad weather. Luckily, I couldn't quite make it — even though at one point I drove through the German lines in an RAF jeep.

All through the war I had assured my wife that when peace was declared, wherever I was, come what may, somehow I would come to her. On V.E.Day I grabbed a chance to go, happily flying a Dakota to Tempelhof airfield, Berlin, listening to Churchill's end-of-war speech on the receiver of the radio compass. She was not pleased. She danced in Piccadilly Circus that night with her brother and said it was not the same thing.

Around 1947 I got embroiled with the Communist uprising in Malaya, commanding two Spitfire squadrons on a small airfield borrowed from the Royal Navy. I returned from that splendid job to a pestilential but fascinating personnel-staff post in London. My brief was to handle the cases for which King's Regulations did not provide. Some pretty odd ones turned up too. A man wrote a legally accurate letter saying: 'One day, in Married Quarters, I shot and killed my wife. I was judged guilty but insane. This is not a conviction in law. Therefore I am fully entitled to the medal for good conduct in the RAF. Please send it to me.'

It found the medal-men, the discipline-drones and the legal-eagles positively poles apart in their views as to what should be done.

In 1953 I had the task of organising 400 modern (then) single-seater Sabre-jet fighters across the Atlantic, landing in Labrador, Greenland, Iceland and then Scotland. One result was that I was able to drive my aircraft through the sound barrier, and becoming (I think) the first RAF Group Captain to do so. Part of my Station's celebrations for the Queen's Coronation was to roast a whole ox, and carve it with a bayonet. When the Powers That Be wanted to make a mass of changes to RAF discipline, mostly taking it from 'bull' towards 'organised good manners', someone asked, 'Who shall we get to try these out?' The answer was: 'Tony Dudgeon has always thrown Queen's Regulations out of the window. Let's open the window for a change.' So the job came my way and many of those changes are now inter-Service practice.

When they made me Director of Flight Safety for the RAF, complete with overtones for British civil airliners, and all the Air Forces of NATO, someone commented, 'That is like setting a poacher to catch a poacher.'

Finally, before the Service decided it had had enough of me, I got an Air Vice-Marshal's appointment in the United States for two and a half years, and topped it off with six months in Belgium.

By then I had flown (at worst from the co-pilot's seat) over a hundred different types of aircraft from an airship to four-engined jets; from landplanes to seaplanes, flying-boats, helicopters and gliders. I served my country in 16 other countries and flew myself to over 20 more. My last flight on a flight-deck, but unfortunately not in the driver's seat, was a Concorde test flight before she ever took a paying passenger.

Indeed I have been, and still am, a very lucky man.

# Index